RELIGION AND CULTURAL MEMORY

Cultural Memory

in

the

Present

Mieke Bal and Hent de Vries, Editors

RELIGION AND CULTURAL MEMORY

Ten Studies

Jan Assmann

Translated by Rodney Livingstone

STANFORD UNIVERSITY PRESS

STANFORD, CALIFORNIA

Stanford University Press
Stanford, California

Religion and Cultural Memory was originally published in German in 2000
under the title *Religion und kulturelles Gedächtnis*, © Verlag C. H. Beck oHG,
München 2000.

Assistance for the translation was provided by Inter Nationes.

Library of Congress Cataloging-in-Publication Data

Assmann, Jan.
[Religion und kulturelles Gedächtnis. English]
   Religion and cultural memory : ten studies / Jan Assmann ; translated
by Rodney Livingstone.
      p.   cm. — (Cultural memory in the present)
   Includes bibliographical references.
   ISBN 0-8047-4522-6 (cloth : alk. paper)
   ISBN 0-8047-4523-4 (pbk. : alk. paper)
      1. Memory—Religious aspects.   2. Memory—Social aspects.   3. Religion
and culture.   I. Livingstone, Rodney.   II. Title.   III. Series.
BL65.M43A8713 2005
306.6—DC22

                                                          2005024771

Original Printing 2006

Last figure below indicates year of this printing:
15   14   13   12   11   10   09

Contents

Preface

"Being that can be understood is language": this succinct statement contains Hans-Georg Gadamer's formula for the "ontological turn in hermeneutics."[1] The theory of cultural memory, which amounts to a kind of "ontological turn in tradition," could be summarized with the words "Being that can be remembered is text." Language is dialogue, exchange of views, communication. Text, on the other hand, is constituted on the basis of prior communication. It always involves the past. Memory bridges the gap between then and now. The messenger memorizes the message that he is supposed to convey to the recipient; the old man remembers what he was taught by his grandfather and passes it on to his own grandson, enriched by his own experience. In this way "texts" come into being. Linguistic communication takes place in the course of conversation; texts, however, arise in the "extended context" of tradition.[2] The need to record events is so great that from a very early stage mankind has had recourse to all sorts of mnemonics and systems of notation with which to facilitate subsequent access. This need has given rise to writing, and writing has extended the fund of memory in leaps and bounds to the point where the gigantic archives of the "fields of memory" can no longer be surveyed.[3] Hermeneutics concentrates on the role of understanding by accessing the text of memorable events; the theory of cultural memory, in contrast, investigates the conditions that enable that text to be established and handed down. It draws our attention to the role of the past in constituting our world through dialogue and intercommunication, and it investigates the forms in which the past presents itself to us as well as the motives that prompt our recourse to it. The theory of cultural memory explores the textuality of the past within the linguistic framework of our experience of the world that hermeneutics has decoded for us. If hermeneutics defines man as a being that understands, the exploration of cultural memory defines this understanding being as one who remembers. Gadamer himself has re-peatedly argued that all understanding is nurtured by a pre-understanding that comes from memory.

The ten studies brought together in this book are based on essays and lectures from the past seven years. They attempt to shed light on the concept of cultural memory and the questions associated with it from a variety of different angles. Religion turns out to be a focal point underly-ing the individual studies, whether in a narrower or broader sense. All the older contributions have been revised, and in places extensively reworked, so as to avoid repetitions, to bring out common themes, and to empha-size new insights. I wish to thank Ernst-Peter Wieckenberg for encourag-ing me to assemble these essays, Ulrich Nolte for his meticulous reading of the whole volume, and Silke Möller for her careful and intelligent pro-duction of the index.

Jan Assmann
Heidelberg, February 2000

RELIGION AND CULTURAL MEMORY

Introduction:
What Is "Cultural Memory"?

1. The Socially Conditioned Nature of Memory: Communicative Memory

Our memory has a twofold basis, neural and social. Without its neural basis memory is not possible; injury to its neural functions can damage the memory and even destroy it. As long as seventy-five years ago, Maurice Halbwachs claimed something of the sort for its social basis.[1] In his books about the social framework of memory and collective memory he proposed the thesis that our memory only develops through our intercourse with other people. I would like to make this social basis my starting point and then take one further step and postulate a cultural basis as well, since only then can we comprehend the vast depths of time, extending to thousands of years, in which man has established himself as a being with memory.

According to Halbwachs, memory is a social phenomenon. It grows into us from outside. Its neural foundation can be thought of as memory's "hardware"; it can be more or less strongly developed and we can perfect it individually through training. But its contents and the use we make of it are determined by our intercourse with others, by language, action, communication, and by our emotional ties to the configurations of our social existence. Like consciousness, language, and personality, memory is a social phenomenon; in the act of remembering we do not just descend into the depths of our own most intimate inner life, but we introduce an order and a structure into that internal life that are socially conditioned and that link us to the social world. Every act of consciousness is socially mediated; only in our dreams do we find that the social world relaxes its structuring grip on our inner life.

Among the aspects of memory that enter us and gradually accumulate, we can distinguish two different modes of remembering: episodic memory and semantic memory, or what might be termed memories derived from experience and learning.[2] Episodic memory refers to our experiences, semantic memory to everything we have learned and memorized. It is called "semantic" because it is connected to meaning and reference. It is difficult to memorize senseless data, such as pages in the telephone directory. It can be done only by people endowed with a "photographic" memory, and this in turn is often accompanied by problems of socialization, such as autism. This fact points to the close links between meaning and society. Semantic memory is preeminently social, "photographic" memory, in contrast, is a special case, uncoupled from its social foundation. At first glance, episodic memory seems no less independent of life in society. We can recollect experiences that do not involve anyone else and that we have not spoken about to anyone. These are experiences with which we are "quite alone." But even episodic memories possess a meaningful structure much of the time. As to their structure, we can perhaps make a further distinction between a visually organized, scenic memory and a narrative memory that is organized linguistically. Scenic memory tends to be incoherent and remote from meaning, while narrative memory tends to have a meaningful and coherent structure. And it is these connecting links that are socially mediated, according to Maurice Halbwachs's theory. These distinctions can be related to the difference between voluntary and involuntary memory introduced by Marcel Proust. Scenic memory is closer to involuntary memory, and it penetrates to layers of personality that are deeper and further removed from consciousness than is the case with narrative memory. Of course, these distinctions are not hard and fast. On the contrary, there is always a lively cross-frontier traffic within the personality. The processes of articulation ensure that stocks of scenic, involuntary memories are transformed into narrative, voluntary ones, and that the acts of forgetting and repression force conscious memories into the depths of the unconscious inner life. Halbwachs undoubtedly exaggerates when he asserts that a human being who grew up in total isolation would have no memories at all. But we can agree that his narrative memory would be underdeveloped and that such a person would find it hard to distinguish between scenes he had experienced and ones he had only dreamed or hallucinated. On the other hand, we can readily agree that our social life with its norms and values, its definitions of meaning and importance, is able to give meaning and structure to our experience in ways that go to the heart of even our most private experiences.

This is why it is difficult, or even impossible, to distinguish between an "individual" and a "social" memory. Individual memory is always social to a high degree, just like language and consciousness in general. A strictly individual memory would be something like a private language that is only understood by one person—in other words, a special case, an exception. For this reason Aleida Assmann and I have proposed the term *communicative memory* to describe the social aspect of individual memory identified by Halbwachs. This memory belongs in the intermediary realm between individuals; it grows out of intercourse between people, and the emotions play the crucial role in its process. Love, interest, sympathy, feelings of attachment, the wish to belong, but also hatred, enmity, mistrust, pain, guilt and shame—all of these help to define our memories and provide them with a horizon. Without such definition they would not imprint themselves on our minds; without a horizon they would lack relevance and meaning within a specific cultural context. For a functioning communicative memory, forgetting is just as vital as remembering. This is why it is not "photographic." Remembering means pushing other things into the background, making distinctions, obliterating many things in order to shed light on others. This is what brings horizon and perspective into individual memory spaces, and these perspectives are emotionally mediated. Emotional emptiness, in contrast, points to arbitrariness of content. Only emotionally cathected forms of communication bring structure, perspective, relevance, definition, and horizon into memory. This holds good for narrative memory, but applies to scenic memory even more strongly. Images and scenes imprint themselves on the mind exclusively through their emotional force, whereas in the case of narrative memory interpretative factors are added to the emotional ones.

Like the neural basis of memory, the communicative side can be subject to disorders and pathologies. The best-known instances of this in recent years have been the cases of false memories; for example, when in the course of psychoanalytical treatment memories of traumatic experiences in early childhood (such as sexual abuse) come to light that on closer inspection turn out to be the "confabulations" of the analyst and his client.[3] The most spectacular case of such a confabulation was recorded in the award-winning memoirs of Binjamin Wilkomirski, alias Bruno Dössekker, that have been translated into many languages. The researches of Daniel Ganzfried have revealed that Dössekker was born outside marriage in 1941 and was subsequently adopted by the Dössekker family. He believes that his early childhood was spent in Majdanek and Auschwitz. His book, which was published with the title *Fragments,* depicted scenes of unimaginable cruelty while largely dispensing with narrative coherence. This means that his reminiscences retained the semblance of authenticity even though they failed to abide by the rules of communicative plausibility. Dössekker's memories have no historical truth, but his book is nevertheless no "forgery" since he evidently regards these "remembered" scenes as the only consistent etiology of the picture he has of himself with all his inconsistencies and contradictions.[4]

It is evident that Wilkomirski's is a particularly grave instance of memory disorder, one that—and this is where its interest lies—explicitly points to the social and affective dimensions of memory. If it is true that memories grow within us via external affective bonds, it follows that much will grow up within us that influences collective life. The Holocaust and the terrors of the past are examples of this. Hence it is possible for someone to believe in all sincerity that he has experienced something which in reality he has only read or heard about and absorbed in the course of collective communicative processes. Wilkomirski remembers a childhood that he never experienced in order to externalize inner problems and to shift the burden of them onto society and history, but undoubtedly also because he wishes to belong to the group of victims and contemporary witnesses who can testify to these atrocities and thus find themselves at the center of public attention and sympathy. Something of this longing for attention and the wish to belong is active in every memory. The socialization process enables us to remember, but the converse is also true: our memories help us to become socialized. Socialization is not just a foundation, but also a function of memory. We can go so far as to speak of a "bonding memory."

2. Memory as a Sociogenetic Force:
Collective or Bonding Memory

The theoretician of bonding memory is Friedrich Nietzsche. Just as Halbwachs has shown that people need bonds in order to develop a memory and to be able to remember, Nietzsche has shown that people need a memory in order to be able to form bonds. What Nietzsche has in mind, however, is not the self-regulating, diffuse, "communicative" memory that Halbwachs described, in which remembering and forgetting interact. Instead, Nietzsche postulated a different, special memory that he called the "will's memory," where in his words, "forgetfulness is suspended in certain cases," namely in those instances where a promise is to be made. Nietzsche takes the example of a promise as paradigmatic, *pars pro toto*, for the entire realm of social bonds. To be able to establish bonds presupposes responsibility, soundness of mind, and reliability. Guided by the "law of obligations," Nietzsche develops his notion of the cultured human being, the "predictable individual" who will still remember tomorrow what he promised yesterday. The "will's memory" is based on the resolve to continue to will over and over again what you have once willed. This memory is not provided for in nature; man has "bred" it into himself so as to be able to live in a society which has been culturally constructed.[5]

Nietzsche is one-sided in his exclusive concentration on the compulsive, even coercive aspect of the acculturation process, the "breeding" of man into a fellow human being. Like Halbwachs, Nietzsche recoils from the transition from the corporeal, neural, and emotional into the purely symbolic. This becomes all too clear in the further development of his discussion, which we shall look at more closely in Chapter 4. The only symbols he can accept are those that are capable of being directly inscribed in the body through the emotions—that is, pain. All the examples he adduces—sacrifices, torments, pledges, cults—are symbols and symbolic actions. But they exercise their power through cruelty and not through any power of conviction inherent in them. Religions are systems of cruelty, for the power they exert over the human soul is not otherwise explicable to Nietzsche. "Only something that continues to hurt remains in the memory."

Nietzsche's assessment of religion reminds us of Freud, who regarded religion as an obsessional neurosis. This obsession arose in his view from repressed truths that had been buried in the unconscious and which re-emerge from the unconscious to plague the conscious mind with all the violence of the return of the repressed. But what Freud had in mind was not Nietzsche's bonding memory. He took the step into the temporal depths of the diachronic, with the intention of explaining transferences across the generations that reach back into the primal history of mankind. But like Halbwachs and Nietzsche, Freud insists on the frontier of the body, refusing to cross it in the direction of culture with its symbolic forms and archives. For him, too, memory is corporeal inscription. What pain, the never-healing wound, is for Nietzsche, trauma is for Freud. Both develop a concept of collective memory, but they anchor it in a very immediate way in the mind and body, and are evidently not minded to extend the concept of memory to the realm of symbolic mediation. The memory function of culture can only be explained, in their view, in terms of mental and physical "inscriptions." Here, too, then, we see a reductionism at work that seeks to limit the dynamics of collective and cultural memory to the physical parameters of the body of the individual.

A further quality that Freud shares with Nietzsche is his pessimistic view of culture, particularly in his essay *Civilization and Its Discontents.* Conceived as a system of values and norms, rules and rituals, culture appears as a kind of straitjacket whose purpose is to train the individual, to knock him into shape, and force him to adjust to its goals and functions. What remained completely obscure in this process was the enabling aspect of culture, which does not just mutilate people and knock them into shape (for which the Jewish ritual of circumcision has always been the most conspicuous symbol—and the Bible itself speaks of the "circumcision of the heart"), but which also (and we would like to say above all) develops forms of life, opens up possibilities in which the individual can invest and fulfill himself. Thus Nietzsche simply ignores the fact that society's interest in subjecting the individual to its purposes is counterbalanced on the side of the individual by the natural (and in Nietzsche's eyes, banal) desire to belong and to develop a social identity. However, the bonding memory has its roots in man's desire to belong, in his nature as a *zoon politikon.* This desire is not necessarily feebler than the corresponding normative and formative acts of coercion that "culture" imposes on the individual.

Alongside the individual bonding memory, there is also a collective memory in an authentic and emphatic sense. The task of this memory, above all, is to transmit a collective identity. Society inscribes itself in this memory with all its norms and values and creates in the individual the authority that Freud called the superego and that has traditionally been called "conscience." In his acceptance speech for the [1998] award of the Peace Prize of the German Book Trade, Martin Walser observed that "everyone is alone with his conscience." He rejected every external interference in how he and others chose to come to terms with the German past. And yet conscience is precisely the authority in which society confronts him with its demands and reminds him about unwelcome memories.

Collective memory is particularly susceptible to politicized forms of remembering. Aleida Assmann pointed this out in the context of the debate triggered by Martin Walser's speech.[6] At issue was the use of history to mobilize support for common political goals with the assistance of catchy formulas, such as "Remember what Amalek did unto thee," "Masada must never fall again," "REM[ember] 1690" (the Battle of the Boyne between Protestants and Catholics in Ulster), "Auschwitz: never again," "Kosovo" (the Battle on Blackbird Plain in 1389). These are the irreconcilable, mutually opposed memories of the winners and losers, the victims and perpetrators. Memorials, days of remembrance with the corresponding ceremonies and rituals (such as wreath-laying), flags, songs, and slogans are the typical media of this form of commemoration.

The political cult of the dead plays a particularly significant role here.[7] Memories can be as short-lived as the collective that makes use of them (who still remembers the memorials of the Nazi period?), but they can also be very tenacious, as we can see from the Battle of Kosovo in 1389, the fall of Masada in A.D. 73 and the villainous attack of the Amalekites during the exodus from Egypt.[8]

Here memories are "made," as Nietzsche puts it. They are not built up gradually as with communicative memory, and they do not disappear again within the cycle of three generations. Sometimes they vanish after twelve years, sometimes they endure for thousands. It is not a matter of a physical wound that never stops hurting, nor is it a memory trace in the "archaic inheritance" of the soul. It is a projection on the part of the collective that wishes to remember and of the individual who remembers in order to belong. Both the collective and the individual turn to the archive of cultural traditions, the arsenal of symbolic forms, the "imaginary" of myths and images, of the "great stories," sagas and legends, scenes and constellations that live or can be reactivated in the treasure stores of a people.

This explains why we must free ourselves from the reductionism that would like to limit the phenomenon of memory entirely to the body, the neural basis of consciousness, and the idea of a deep structure of the soul that can be passed down biologically. Our memory has a cultural basis and not just a social one. This brings me to what Aleida Assmann and I call cultural memory.

With the concept of cultural memory we are taking a major step beyond the individual who alone possesses a memory in the true sense. Neither the group, nor even culture, "has" a memory in that sense. To talk as if they did would be an illegitimate act of mystification. As always, man is the sole possessor of a memory. What is at issue is the extent to which this unique memory is socially and culturally determined. Halbwachs took the step leading from the internal world of the subject into the social and emotional preconditions of memory, but refused to go so far as to accept the need for symbolic and cultural frameworks. For him, that was a frontier that should not be crossed. Memory in his view was always *mémoire vécue*, lived, embodied memory. Everything lying beyond that frontier he called "tradition" and contrasted it with memory. But can that distinction really be sustained? Is not tradition too always embodied in something?

What communication is for communicative memory, tradition is for cultural memory. In her book *Time and Tradition*, Aleida Assmann has contrasted communication and tradition: "Tradition can be understood as a special case of communication in which information is not exchanged reciprocally and horizontally, but is transmitted vertically through the generations."[9] In this way, cultural memory can be considered to be a special case of communicative memory. It has a different temporal structure. If we think of the typical three-generation cycle of communicative memory as a synchronic memory-space, then cultural memory, with its traditions reaching far back into the past, forms the diachronic axis.

The interaction of symbol and memory is a continuous process being played out at every level. That applies in particular to "memory of the will." Whenever we think about something that we do not want to forget under any circumstances, we invent memory aids that range from the famous knot in our handkerchief to our national monuments. Such aides-mémoires are also the *lieux de mémoire*, memory sites in which the memory of entire national or religious communities is concentrated, monuments, rituals, feast days and customs. In short, the entire panoply of things that go to make up what Halbwachs called tradition and which he contrasted with *mémoire vécue* can be understood as a system of memory sites, a system of markers that enables the individual who lives in this tradition to belong, that is, to realize his potential as the member of a society in the sense of a community where it is possible to learn, remember, and to share in a culture. In the last book he published Halbwachs himself crossed the frontier between *mémoire vécue* and *tradition*, communication and tradition. This was the *Topographie légendaire des évangiles en Terre Sainte* of 1941 (*La Mémoire collective* appeared posthumously in 1950). In this book he draws on pilgrim itineraries to describe the Christian *lieux de mémoire* in the Holy Land, and shows the extent to which Byzantine and Western memory politics were influenced by theological assumptions. He applies the concept of memory to monuments and symbols of all kinds and shows that memory and symbolism are inextricably intertwined.

Our expansion of the concept of memory from the realm of the psyche to the realm of the social and of cultural traditions is no mere metaphor. It is precisely the misunderstanding of the concepts of "collective" and "cultural memory" that has impeded comprehension of the dynamics of culture up to now.[10] What is at stake is not the (illegitimate) transfer of a concept derived from individual psychology to social and cultural phenomena, but the interaction between the psyche, consciousness, society, and culture.

3. Rituals of Collective and Connective Remembering

a. The Neo-Assyrian Sarsaru Ritual

The Assyrian state archive in Nineveh contains a text that relates to a collective memory ritual. Entirely in the spirit of Nietzsche, it is concerned to "make a memory," in this case for the subjects and vassals of the Assyrian empire who were forced by King Esarhaddon to swear an oath of allegiance to his successor, King Ashurbanipal. The ritual is based on the experience that was of decisive importance for Halbwachs: the dependence of memory on the general social and above all local context. The subjects and vassals have come to the capital to take their oath; here, where everything reminds them of the power of the great king, there is no danger that they will forget their oath. However, once they have returned to their own cities these larger political bonds and obligations will recede into the background; they will fade and disappear from memory. The task is to prevent this loss of memory by changing the general framework. With this in mind, a memory ritual was introduced that had to be repeated periodically in order to refresh their memories.

They were given water to drink from a *sarsaru* jar by her (Ishtar of Arbela),
She filled a drinking vessel of one *seah* [circa six liters] with water from the *sarsaru* jar, and gave it to them, (saying):
You shall say in your hearts thus: Ishtar, is a narrow "strait"!
Thus: you will enter into your cities (and) you will eat bread in your districts,
And you will forget the oath you have sworn [an expression used in all contracts with vassals].
Thus: you will drink of this water and you will remember
Once more and you shall heed the oath you have sworn and that I have set you on account of Esarhaddon.[11]

Rituals dramatize the interplay of the symbolic with the corporeal. Drinking water is a very potent symbol of the revival of a memory that has been forgotten or is in danger of being forgotten, and so has been incorporated in a symbolic action as a memory aid. What this example shows is the counterfactual character of bonding memory. Bonding memory has a normative, contractual character. It commits the individual to fulfill the obligations he committed himself to the previous day. However, the context may have changed so much from one day to the next that nothing reminds him of the commitment he has made and of the interest that led him to make it. The memory disappears because it ceases to be supported by the new situation. It must therefore be carried through in a hostile environment, where it no longer seems appropriate but instead has receded into the distance and become alien or irksome. Nietzsche was particularly concerned about the oppressive nature of bonding memory. It arises from the clash between the obligations we must remember and the interests of a future present.

We can generalize from the example of Esarhaddon and his water ritual. Major elements of cultural life, more particularly everything that is associated with religion, have the task of keeping alive a memory that has no support in everyday life. Religious rituals are without doubt the oldest and most fundamental medium of bonding memory, and we should note that we are concerned here with bonds and communities that include the universe of spirits and the dead. We shall explain this further with reference to a number of examples.

The simultaneously collective and "connective," bonding nature of memory is expressed with particular clarity in the English-language words *re-membering* and *re-collecting*, which evoke the idea of putting "members" back together (re-membering and dis-membering) and "re-collecting" things that have been dispersed. Thus they interpret memory as the restoration of a lost unity. There is no better illustration of what is at stake with the bonding memory. It refers to cultural efforts that aim to establish connections and consolidate togetherness. Hence just as we can speak of "collective" memory, we can also speak of a "connective" memory. When collectives "remember," they thereby secure a unifying, "connective" semantics that "holds them inwardly together" and reintegrates their individual "members" so that they possess a common point of view. Wherever people join together in larger groups they generate a connective semantics, thereby producing forms of memory that are designed to stabilize a common identity and a point of view that span several generations.

b. The Tribal Festivals of the Osage Indians

Such memories do not necessarily always refer to the past. Typically, tribal cultures obtain their connective semantics not from history but from a timeless cosmic order. The great French structuralist and ethnologist Claude Lévi-Strauss defined the contrast at work here by drawing a distinction between "hot" and "cold" societies. According to Lévi-Strauss, "hot societies have internalized their history (*leur devenir historique*) so as to turn it into the motor of their development." Their relation to their past history provides them with the dynamism that enables them to forge their future history. They remember their history in order to have history and to make history. They dwell in history thanks to the specific nature of their cultural memory.

Cold societies, on the other hand, do not just live outside history; they actually keep history out. They avoid having history by striving "by means of the institutions that they give themselves to erase more or less automatically the effects that historical factors might have on their equilibrium and continuity." They seem "to have acquired or preserved a special wisdom that leads them to offer a desperate resistance to every structural change that would permit history to enter."[12] Thus by *cold* Lévi-Strauss does not mean that something is missing, but something positive that is the product of a special "wisdom" and special "institutions." Coldness is not culture at an all-time low: it must be produced. The elimination of history and the creation of cultural "coldness" is just as much a function of "connective" memory as is the creation of a link to the past. We can understand the particular nature of the historical or "hot" form of memory with its relation to the past only if we juxtapose it to the antihistorical "cold" form. This can be illustrated with reference to the North American tribe of Osage Indians as reported by Werner Müller, the ethnologist specializing in American Indian research.

For the Osage the most visible and tangible sign of the cosmos is the circle of tents. Normally, they do not practice putting up the tepees in this formation during their seasonal migrations. They arrange the camp in this formation only on special sacred occasions, above all for the sun dance, the great tribal festival, in the summer.

For the Osage the tepee circle embodies the entire visible, audible, tangible world, from the stars right down to the insects crawling in the grass: comets, clouds, swarms of pigeons, herds of buffalo, yellow coneflowers, pipes of peace, the spirits of the dead, grains of hail, corn bread, wooden bowls, moccasins, human songs, and so on to infinity. . . . The tepee ring . . . consists of twenty-four small groups, the so-called We-gatche or fireplaces of which 3 x 7 had descended from heaven in primeval times, while three earth-born ones had been added later on. All twenty-four fireplaces are laid out in a circle to make the tent circle. Every group has its own special location, its place in the "world" which has been fixed once and for all. If any group were to put their tepee elsewhere, the camp police would intervene with drastic methods to teach them their true place in the cosmos. Thus the We-gatche serve as the building blocks of the universe.[13]

This invisible membership structure is represented in four different ways: (1) in the arrangement of the twenty-four tents; (2) in the meeting of their twenty-four representatives, the "Little Old Men," or Non-hon-zhin-ga, who form a council of elders, (3) in the symbols they bring with them: every group (We-gatche, "subgroup") brings specific substances (Wa-shoi-gathe) along, such as tortoise shells, reeds, mussels, cedar twigs, corn cobs, and so on, from which it has been made and to which, consequently, it is closely related. The fourth representation of membership is acoustic; it takes the form of the communal recitation of the Wi-gi-es, that is, the ancient legends of the Osage. This is done by enabling every representative (Non-hon-zhin-ga) of a We-gatche to recite the myth of the origin of his specific group:

> Every Non-hon-zhin-ga roars the Wi-gi-e of his own hearth at the top of his voice, without letting himself be distracted by the different text of the We-gatche next to him. This verbal din, which lasts for about a quarter of an hour, sounds from a distance like the buzzing of a swarm of cicadas, a dissonant consonance inaugurating every ritual. At a stroke, the entire content of the world becomes manifest; the simultaneous recitation echoes the simultaneous coexistence of all cosmic creatures.[14]

What we have here is a memory culture that dramatizes the togetherness of the group in a markedly antihistorical form. The Wi-gi-es are creation myths from which the historical past in a stricter sense is barred. The meaning that is articulated in this dramatization is bound not to contingent historical events, but to the cosmos as the epitome of a timeless order and coherence.

Thus in the Osage tribal festival the invisible coherence of the group acquires a fourfold presence: spatial, social, material, and acoustic. Through their arrangement, the tents embody the spatial structure; the "world house," the assembly of the Non-hon-zhin-ga, embodies the tribal identity, the nation of the Osage; the symbolic substances embody material coherence as a network of cosmic relationships; and lastly, the sacral recitations embody the interconnectedness of what has grown up and grown apart in time.

A very similar ritual can similarly be found to have taken place in the context of a society that was highly developed politically and in terms of its literature—premodern China. However, the ritual was not carried out regularly but only at times of extreme danger, such as an eclipse of the sun.

> At once the vassals poured into the midpoint of the fatherland. There they formed into a square so as to contribute to the salvation of the nation and to restore the totality of the disrupted space and disrupted time. They succeed in banishing

the danger if each of them can install himself with the regalia appropriate to his own and his life's particular spatial character. For people from the East who place themselves on the Eastern side, these regalia are a crossbow, green clothing, and a little green flag. Simply by virtue of the proper arrangement of emblems at the site of the assemblies the space is renewed in all its dimensions, up to and including the stars.[15]

This ritual memory culture is concerned with maintaining the course of the world and the survival of the group. "We continue our ancient customs so that the universe can continue to exist," an Eskimo said to Rasmussen.[16] What is at work here is a functioning memory technique [*Mnemotechnik*]. The Non-hon-zhin-ga are above all memory specialists. What they remember, however, has nothing to do with history. Their memory makes present an order of things that is fundamentally timeless.

c. The Canopic Processions of the Osiris Mysteries

Among the ancient Egyptians we come across a ritual very similar to the Osage summer dance festival, one that serves the annual renewal and reaffirmation of the collective, cultural context. It represents not just a dramatization of "connective" memory, but an act of "re-membering" in the most literal sense of the word, that is to say, the rejoining of scattered limbs into a living body. This festival stands midway between the "cold" cosmos-related memory cultures of tribal societies with an oral tradition and the "hot" memory cultures, oriented toward the past, characteristic of literate, state-organized high cultures.

The Osiris mysteries were celebrated at the end of the inundation of the Nile basin, when the farming land once again emerged from the floods and was ready to receive the new seed, at the end of the month of Choiak. In the Late Period these ceremonies were the supreme Egyptian festival. It began with the finding and embalming of the scattered limbs of the murdered Osiris, which were ritually joined together and animated. It ended with the resurrection of Osiris (the feast of "raising the Djed pillar") and the elevation of Horus, his son and avenger, to the throne. The forty-two limbs of Osiris that were collected, joined together, and revived in the course of the ceremonies correspond to the forty-two provinces of the land.[17] It was believed that each region was a home to a particular member of Osiris's body as its central mystery and sacred object. Such a system is known in ethnology as a "symbolic classification." What is meant by this is the "totemistic" procedure of taking a collection of discrete units of the visible world—such as animals, plants, and stones—and mapping them onto the world of society so as to give that world a structure and to enable it to be imagined and represented as an internally differentiated unity. Thus the Egyptians projected the fragmented body of Osiris onto the multiplicity of regions in order to represent and create the unity of the land through the ritual of reuniting the limbs into a single body. What was a cosmic symbolism in the case of the Osage becomes a body symbolism here. The unity that was remembered and renewed in the course of these ceremonies has a political, historical, and cultural meaning, not a cosmic one. It is the land of Egypt that is re-membered in this ceremony and thereby united, regenerated, and celebrated. Osiris's death and Horus's accession to the throne is a political myth. Its ceremonial staging enacts and confirms the political, cultural, and religious identity of Egypt, which is exposed to all sorts of threats and centrifugal tendencies in the course of a year and needs to be reinforced and renewed again.

The collection and regeneration of the *membra disjecta* of the murdered Osiris is celebrated in the "Grain Osiris" ritual. In this ceremony a mummy-shaped wooden container is filled with earth and planted with moistened grains of barley. Watering this garden of Osiris with water from the Nile imitates the flooding of the Nile that inundates the whole country every year, thus renewing its fertility and vitality. The Grain Osiris *is* this country, and the green that sprouts a week later is the Egyptian vegetation. The recitations during the festival evoke the myth and the accompanying knowledge of the forty-two provinces of Egypt, their sacred traditions and their cultic and cultural associations. Of all the Egyptian myths, that of Osiris is the most historical, and the historical actions of the kings are constantly mirrored and interpreted in its various motifs and episodes. By relating to this myth, the rites relate to a past that stands midway between myth and history.

It cannot be a mere accident that this rite only emerges in the Late Period, after the experience of the centuries-long fragmentation of the monarchy of the pharaohs into minor kings and chieftains and after the Assyrian invasion, and that it was celebrated in all the temples of the land during a period of subjugation by Persians, Greeks, and Romans when its semantics of fragmentation and reunification overlaid a variety of other rituals. With this ritual of remembering reunification (where the English terms *re-membering* and *re-collecting* are so remarkably apposite), late Egyptian culture reacts to the threats of disintegration and oblivion which faced all the ancient high cultures in the Hellenistic period.

4. Counterfactual Memory and the Normative Past: Deuteronomy

All these rituals of connective memory contain a counterfactual element. They all involve introducing into the present something distant and alien for which there is no room in everyday life and which therefore has to be ritually imagined at regular intervals in order to maintain a context that is threatened by disintegration and oblivion. After completion of the rites, the Osage Indians disintegrate once more into their individual clans and Egypt fragments into its forty-two provinces, just as the Assyrian vassals lose sight of their membership of the Assyrian empire. We undoubtedly can speak here of a cultural, ritual memory technique that stands in the service of bonding memory and has the purpose of bringing to life and stabilizing a collective identity through a process of symbolic dramatization.

What is by far the most impressive example of such a memory technique in the service of bonding memory is provided by Judaism. In an age of extreme political jeopardy, from the seventh to the fifth centuries B.C., the Jews established bonding memory on the foundation of a highly elaborate memory technique, in full consciousness of its counterfactual nature. Exactly as in the case of Esarhaddon, the task faced in the Bible is not to forget the commitments that one has entered into in completely different circumstances from those in which one is supposed to abide by them. The people entered into these commitments at Mount Sinai when it accepted God's covenant and His commandments. After that, it wandered through the desert for forty years. Now, at the end of those forty years, the children of Israel stand on the banks of the River Jordan, ready to cross the river and enter into the Promised Land. With that their general circumstances will change far more drastically than in the case of the vassals who return to their cities from Nineveh. In a long farewell speech in Deuteronomy, Moses, who cannot accompany them to the Promised Land since he will die in Moab, impresses on them the memory that they must take with them into the Promised Land.

In this scene everything is significant. What we have here is a liminal situation, a threefold transition, moreover. Spatially, the scene marks the crossing of the Jordan, the transition from the desert to a fertile land. Temporally, it marks the end of the forty years' wandering in the desert after the exodus from Egypt. Forty years is the limit of a generation; the passing of the generation of contemporary witnesses and the transition from the lived, embodied memory to a tradition that is to be handed down from generation to generation. Thirdly, it marks a changed way of life, from the nomadic life in the wilderness to a settled existence in the Promised Land. A more drastic change of circumstances can scarcely be imagined. "Only take heed to thyself and keep thy soul diligently, lest thou forget the things which thine eyes saw, and lest they depart from thy heart all the days of thy life; but make them known unto thy children and thy children's children" (Deut. 4:9).[18]

And it shall be, when the Lord thy God shall bring thee into the land which he sware unto thy fathers, to Abraham, to Isaac and to Jacob, to give thee; great and goodly cities which thou buildest not, and houses full of all good things, which thou filledst not, and cisterns hewn out, which thou hewdst not, vineyards and olive trees, which thou plantedst not, and thou shalt eat and be full; then beware lest thou forget the Lord, which brought thee out of the land of Egypt, out of the house of bondage. (Deut. 6:10–12)

Here, if anywhere in world literature, we have a text whose theme is "making memory" in Nietzsche's sense. What the children of Israel must not forget is, on the one hand, the law, and on the other, the story of the exodus from Egypt that has been lived through and that thereby acquires the status of a normative past. These things have been experienced by the generation of contemporary witnesses who now, after forty years in the wilderness, are about to die. To make sure that this memory does not die with them, it has to be transmuted into tradition, into the symbolic forms of cultural memory. Moses solves the problem of how to achieve this by employing an elaborate memory technique that puts Esarhaddon's *sarsaru* ritual in the shade. Twice, in chapters 6 and 11, the framing text of Deuteronomy spells out the forms of this cultural memory technique that salvages memory from oblivion and elevates the experiences of the exodus, revelation, and the wilderness to the status of a normative past for all future generations. Deuteronomy lists no fewer than seven procedures of culturally formed memory:

1. Learning by heart as making conscious, taking to heart: "And these words, which I command thee this day, shall be upon thy heart" (6:6; see also 11:18: "Therefore shall ye lay up these my words in your heart and in your soul").[19]

2. Education and "conversational remembering." Transmission to succeeding generations through communication, circulation: always talk about it, everywhere and on every occasion: "And thou shalt teach them diligently unto thy children, and shalt talk of them when thou sittest in thine house, and when thou walkest by the way, and when thou liest down, and when thou risest up" (6:7; see also 11:20). See also the Lord's reminder to Joshua after Moses' death: "This book of the law shall not depart out of thy mouth, but thou shalt meditate therein day and night" (Josh. 1:8). The law should be not only "in thy heart," but also "in thy mouth."[20]

3. Making visible through body-marking, through signs on the brow: "And thou shalt bind them for a sign upon thine hand, and they shall be for frontlets between thine eyes" (i.e., tephillin, Deut. 6:8; cf. 11:18). Furthermore, a making visible through a "limiting symbolism"—inscriptions on the doorpost (mezuzot—as a way of marking the boundary of what is one's own): "And thou shalt write them upon the door posts of thy house and upon thy gates" (6:9; see also 11:21).

4. Storing up and publication: the law is to be written on plaster and thereby be made permanent and accessible:

And it shall be on the day when ye shall pass over Jordan unto the land which the Lord thy God giveth thee, that thou shalt set thee up great stones, and plaister them with plaister; and thou shalt write upon them all the words of this law, when thou art passed over. . . . And it shall be when ye are passed over Jordan, that ye shall set up these stones, which I command you this day, in Mount Ebal, and thou shalt plaister them with plaister. . . . And thou shalt write upon the stones all the words of this law very plainly. (27:2–8)[21]

5. Festivals of collective remembering—the three great festivals of gathering and pilgrimage on which the entire people, great and small, is to appear before the face of the Lord.[22] Matsah = Passover, the festival to commemorate the exodus from Egypt: "that thou mayest remember the

day when thou camest forth out of the land of Egypt all the days of thy life" (16:3);[23] Shavuot is the Feast of Weeks, on which people are meant to think about the sojourn in Egypt: "and thou shalt remember that thou wast a bondsman in Egypt" (16:12);[24] and Sukkot, the Festival of Booths, in the course of which the entire text of the Torah is to be read aloud every seven years.[25]

6. Oral transmission, that is to say, poetry, as the codification of historical memory:

Now therefore write ye this song for you, and teach thou it the children of Israel: put it in their mouths, that this song may be a witness for me against the children of Israel. For when I shall have brought them into the land which I sware unto their fathers, flowing with milk and honey; and they shall have eaten and filled themselves, and waxen fat; then will they turn unto other gods, and serve them, and despise me, and break my covenant. And it shall come to pass, when many evils and troubles are come upon them, that this song shall testify before them as a witness; for it shall not be forgotten out of the mouths of their seed. (31:19–21)[26]

7. Canonization of the text of the covenant (Torah) as the foundation of "literal" adherence.[27] Canonization means an intervention that subjects the constant flow of traditions that are being handed down to a strict process of selection. This intervention consolidates the selection and sanctifies it, that is to say, it exalts it to the status of an ultimate authority and in this way calls a halt to the stream of tradition once and for all. From now on, nothing can be added or taken away. The contract turns into the canon.[28]

Deuteronomy describes and codifies this transition from a tradition of living to one of learning, as the shift from direct witness and living memory of the generation in the wilderness to the cultural memory of Israel that is built upon an elaborate memory technique. In this transition Israel constructs itself as a community of learning and remembering. This aspect of Jewish identity, one that has been absolutely central to the present day, took shape as early as the Babylonian captivity. Here religion changes from a matter of cultic purity to one of learning and education. The ideal of the literate priests of the *goy kadosh*, the "holy nation," and *mamlechet kohanim*, the "kingdom of priests,"[29] has its counterpart in the deuteronomistic ideal of the "wise and understanding people" (*am hakham ve-navon*) referred to in Deuteronomy 4:6. The wise and understanding people has learnt and learnt by heart the Torah that had now been written down.[30]

In comparison with Esarhaddon's *sarsaru* ritual, Deuteronomy has a threefold lesson for us. First, in both cases the aim is to establish a bonding memory that can withstand changed circumstances and that must be stabilized counterfactually through the use of a memory technique. Second, this shared foundation enables us to see that Deuteronomy emerges as an infinitely more comprehensive and complex memory. It is not concerned just with bonds in the sense of a political allegiance, but also in the sense of establishing a common identity that ties the individual into the learning and remembering community of the people. In other words, what is instilled are the bonds of community, and not just the bonds of rule. History plays a major role alongside the laws, and narrative alongside particular norms. The story that is told in order to frame the laws and explain them has the function of a foundation myth, and what is founded here is the identity of the people of God who have been led by God out of Egypt. By remembering the story (*zakhar*), it is in a position to abide by the commandments (*shamar*). Third, what we learn from Deuteronomy is the historically significant, even epoch-making step into writing which now becomes privileged through the media of bonding memory and within the spectrum of symbolic forms. What writing makes possible is the perpetuation of memory, its liberation from the rhythms of forgetting and remembering. The Assyrian vassals had constantly to perform the *sarsaru* rites in order to remind themselves of their obligations toward Esarhaddon and Ashurbanipal. The Jews, in contrast, are expressly exhorted to study the Torah "day and night" (Josh. 1:8). It is this that has turned them into the "people of the Book" more than every other people, because in their case this concentration on the written word was enormously enhanced by the prohibition of graven images. Writing, however, contains, latently at least, the further emancipation that Hegel called "the free life of the spirit," the possibility of transcending bonding memory, the collective memory par excellence, in favor of a learning memory. Here we see opening up the further "memory spaces" of what might be thought of as an authentic "cultural" memory.

Of course, even societies without a written tradition, tribal cultures and archaic civilizations, possess a cultural memory; these societies, too, live in memory spaces that extend backward to creation and are transmitted in tribal myths, initiation rites, festivals, and heroic lays. But in their case it is difficult to distinguish between bonding memory and cultural memory, collective and cultural memory. Only with the emergence of writing does cultural memory "take off" and allow the horizon of symbolically stored memory to grow far beyond the framework of knowledge functionalized as bonding memory. Only cultural memory enables the individual to dispose freely of his stock of memories and grants him the opportunity to orient himself in the entire expanse of his memory spaces. In certain circumstances cultural memory liberates people from the constraints of bonding memory.

5. The Problematic Nature of Collective Memory

The Israeli writer Amos Oz once said, "If I had any say in the peace negotiations—no matter whether in Wye, Oslo, or wherever—I would instruct the sound technicians to switch off the microphones as soon as any of the negotiating parties began to talk about the past. Because they are being paid to find solutions for the present and the future."[31] This remark sheds light on the dark side of bonding memory. In actual fact conflicts such as those between Israelis and Palestinians, Catholics and Protestants in Northern Ireland, Serbs and ethnic Albanians in Kosovo typically derive their irreconcilable emotional force from the way the past is anchored in the group memory of the warring parties. Political cults of the dead play a particularly disastrous role in such conflicts. In line with the slogan "You shall not have died in vain," obligations toward the dead are used to justify a duty of revenge and intransigence. This too is all part of the phenomenology of the bonding memory. In such situations it really is a good idea to draw a line under the past if a better future is to be achieved. However, helping people to forget is not as easy as switching off microphones. The only solution is to acknowledge other people's memories and to negotiate a common past in which the sufferings of the other side and one's own share of the guilt have their proper place. In other words, it is necessary to blast asunder the all too narrow horizons of one's own collective memory.

In this context we are of course reminded of the problem of the Berlin Holocaust Memorial and the basic question of German memory politics, namely how to come to terms with the crimes of the Nazi past. This, too, is a question not of cultural, but of collective bonding memory, a question of political identity. Why is it not alright to draw a line under the past in this instance? An impassioned debate broke out following the speech that Martin Walser gave on October 11, 1998, on being awarded the Peace Prize of the German Book Trade.[32] Should not the memory of Auschwitz be consigned, as Walser proposed, to the innermost conscience of the individual and be excluded from public discourse, which "instrumentalizes" it for other purposes and misuses it as a "moral club to beat others with"? Or should we not rather, as Ignatz Bubis and others believed, perpetuate this memory in the symbolic forms of cultural, public memory, particularly at the present time, when the generation of direct witnesses is dying out? Curiously enough, Walser was supported by many victims and their descendants, among others. Many Jews, too, are sick of being confronted with images that Walser cannot bear to look at any more. Like him, though for quite different reasons, they feel it diminishes their self-respect or they fear the desire for vengeance that may be kept alive by the memory of such atrocities. As we have seen, one of the central commandments of memory in the Bible is the injunction to remember the archenemy Amalek. In Paris there is a monument to the unknown Jewish martyr with inscriptions in Hebrew and French. The French inscription appeals unctuously for our sympathy and respect: "DEVANT LE MARTYRE JUIF INCONNU INCLINE TON RESPECT TA PIÉTÉ POUR TOUS LES MARTYRS. . . . " The Hebrew text, in contrast, appeals to the collective memory with the relevant quotation: *Zakhor et-asher assa lekha Amalek*—"Remember what Amalek did unto thee" (Deut. 25:17–19).

Are we not taken aback by these words? What good can come from keeping one's hatred alive at any price? There are of course voices in Israel, too, that call for an end to hatred and agree with Walser. The situation in Germany, however, is quite different. Here we are looking at the mass murder of innocent people. There can be no question of negotiating a common history of suffering; the suffering is all on the other side. It is incumbent on us, therefore, to incorporate the suffering we have caused into the collective political bonding memory of Germany, and that can only be done in the form of public pronouncements and recognition.

There are no historical precedents for such an expansion of bonding memory. It is quite true that history is full of one-sided histories of suffering. However, mankind waits in vain for them to be publicly acknowledged by the perpetrators. It is right that the Holocaust Memorial in Berlin should take the first step, since mankind has not yet witnessed a history of suffering on such a scale. If a line is to be drawn anywhere, it should not be drawn under the memory but under violence, and that can only be achieved through memory. This step will be followed by others. The day will come when memorials will be erected by Americans for the Africans who were carried off and enslaved and for the Indians robbed of their land; by Israelis for the Palestinians who were driven out; by the Russians and Chinese for the murdered opponents of the regime; by the Catholic Church for the victims of the Crusades and the Inquisition; by the Turks for the murdered Armenians; by the Japanese for the Chinese and Koreans they invaded; by the Australians for the Aborigines whose land they stole; by the United States for the Japanese who died in Hiroshima and Nagasaki—the list unfortunately could go on forever. Everyone knows and feels how urgently this utopian form of remembering is needed. Such a remembering is a paradoxical intervention in the history of violence, injustice, and oppression that reached its horrific climax in the twentieth century despite all the dreams of progress of the nineteenth century. In such acts of recognition of the suffering caused to others through no fault of theirs we can discern the outlines of a universal form of bonding memory that is committed to certain fundamental norms of human dignity.

Auschwitz, the darkest chapter of German history, has long since assumed the dimensions of a "normative past" that must not and cannot be allowed to fall into oblivion under any circumstances because its importance goes well beyond the memories of victims and perpetrators; it has become an instance of universalized bonding memory and the founding element of a global secular religion that is concerned with democracy and human dignity. Its commandment is "never again, Auschwitz," and this means not just that there should never again be victims of a German fascism, but that we—and this "we" includes humanity—wish never again to be perpetrators, fellow travelers, or electors of a regime that tramples on human dignity. If we wish to procure world-wide recognition for these principles, we would do well not to repress what we mean by "Amalek," that is to say, the essence of all that we must reject if we are to secure a better future. Instead, we must publicly take responsibility for it, in solidarity with those sections of mankind for whom Auschwitz has become the normative memory of a guilt incurred.

This lengthy digression on collective bonding memory should make clear the topicality of the concept. Only by clarifying the function of this form of memory and laying bare its enabling, limiting, positive, and negative aspects will we be able to grasp what is meant by contrasting it with the concept of "cultural memory."

6. Cultural Memory

With cultural memory the depths of time open up. We arrive here, in the first place, at a point far beyond the horizon of communicative memory. The nature of this horizon has been illuminated by research in the field of oral history. This has shown that with the methods of oral interrogation it is not possible to progress further than a horizon of eighty to a maximum of one hundred years. That is the distance in time achieved at best by personal memory relying not just on actual experiences but also on the direct communications of others. This is the past that accompanies us because it belongs to us and because there is a living, communicative need to keep it alive in the present; it sustains us and is sustained by us. We remember it because we need it. Communicative memory is a generational memory that changes as the generations change. Second, we arrive at a point that goes decisively beyond the horizon of collective and connective bonding memory. Its horizon is determined by the memory formulas and configurations that underpin our sense of community and by the memory needs of a clearly defined "we." Within the framework of a bonding memory, the past is always "instrumentalized."

The position with cultural memory is different. Needless to say, here, too, much is remembered, that is to say, handed down, learned, taught, researched, interpreted, and practiced, because it is needed, because it belongs to us and sustains us and for that reason has to be sustained and perpetuated by us. But it is only in "oral" societies, societies without writing, that the stock of what is needed coincides with the totality of cultural memory. In written cultures, handed-down meaning, translated into symbolic form, swells into vast archives of which only more or less limited, albeit central parts are really needed, inhabited, and tended, while all

around hoards of knowledge that are no longer needed languish in a state
that at the margins comes close to disappearance and oblivion. For this
reason Aleida Assmann has proposed that we should distinguish between
functional memory and stored memory.[33] The concept of stored memory
moves toward the cultural forms of the unconscious. Culture is a palimp-
sest and in this respect resembles individual memory, for which one of
Sigmund Freud's favorite metaphors was the city of Rome. For Rome is
not just a vast open-air museum in which the past is preserved and exhib-
ited, but an inextricable tangle of old and new, of obstructed and buried
material, of detritus that has been reused or rejected. In this way tensions
arise, rejections, antagonisms, between what has been censored and uncen-
sored, the canonical and the apocryphal, the orthodox and the heretical,
the central and the marginal, all of which makes for a cultural dynamism.
The frontier between stored and functional memory is constantly shifting. Aleida Assmann regards this as "the precondition of the possibility of
change and renewal."[34] This is why the concept of tradition, as usually understood, is completely inadequate as a description of this phenomenon.
"Tradition" refers to the business of handing down and receiving, as well
as the continued existence of what has been received. The only dynamics
conceivable in terms of this concept are those which are released in cultural
work in a controlled and conscious fashion; every interaction with the dynamics of identity and memory is cut off. The concept of tradition leaves
no space for the unconscious.

Now, it certainly goes too far simply to equate stored memory
with the cultural unconscious. Stored memory is amorphous and without boundaries; the structuring principles that create form and horizon
because they grow out of the group's need for identity, normativity and
orientation are absent. This does not mean that the contents of stored
memory are inaccessible in principle, repressed, banished, or otherwise
unavailable. They may be all or any of these things. This is why we must
look to cultural memory, and specifically the stored memory, for analogies
for what Freud called repression on the level of individual memory. In his
theory of repression in particular, Freud yoked mass psychology and individual psychology together in a way that is still hotly debated. The historian Yosef Hayim Yerushalmi placed at the center of his analysis the problem of the religious tradition that Freud had interpreted as the return of
the repressed, focusing his argument on the distinction between the biological and genetic inheritance on the one hand and the conscious process

of handing down memory on the other. In light of this distinction he then assigned Freud's theses to the side of biological inheritance.[35] This referred not just to the phylogenetic memory traces of the "primal horde," when the father was murdered by his sons whom he had threatened with castration, memory traces that became condensed into the form of "archaic inheritance" and that generated the Oedipal conflict. His classification applied also to Freud's thesis of the murder of Moses that was supposed to have led to a special traumatization of the Jewish soul, but also, via the return of the repressed, to the acceptance and preservation of monotheism. Yerushalmi rejects this as "psycho-Lamarckism." Early in the nineteenth century, Jean-Baptiste de Monet de Lamarck had maintained the inheritance of acquired characteristics and thereby contributed more than a little to the emergence of theories of race.

Jacques Derrida devoted a four-hour-long lecture in London on June 5, 1994, to a discussion of Yerushalmi's reproach of psycho-Lamarckism. It was published in 1995 with the title *Mal d'archive*.[36] Like Derrida, Richard J. Bernstein breaks open the logical alternatives of genetic inheritance and conscious tradition and introduces a third possibility.[37] In Bernstein, what Derrida calls the archive becomes an expanded concept of tradition that includes unconscious aspects of transmission and transfer across the generations. In Freud's eyes the customary concept of tradition fails to do justice to the dynamics of religious traditions (by "tradition" Freud understands oral transmission, which he contrasts with written historiography). These dynamics are characterized by ruptures, discontinuities, submergings, rediscoveries, breakthroughs, and so on, that can never be reduced simply to the conscious process of handing down memories and are comparable only to the phases of an individual neurosis: early trauma—defense and repression; latency; outbreak of neurotic illness; partial return of the repressed. The history of religion exhibits a similar pattern. Adapting Hans-Georg Gadamer's "ontological" concept of tradition, Bernstein develops an expanded conception of tradition that takes up Freud's criticism and makes room for unconscious memory transfer. For Bernstein, Gadamer's position represents the opposite, culturalist, pole to Lamarck's biologistic conception. In *Truth and Method* (1960), Gadamer develops Heidegger's notion of the linguistic embeddedness of human existence and extends it in the direction of "text," that is to say, of substantively determined, linguistically articulated and consolidated traditions that constitute present realities by forming the ground of preunderstanding from which all understanding is nourished. There is no understanding without memory, no existence without tradition. Derrida, whose thinking is likewise influenced by Heidegger, has probed the concept of "archive" in a Heideggerian manner as a form of memory that constitutes the present and makes the future possible through the medium of symbols that are linguistic and extralinguistic, discursive and nondiscursive, and that are permeated by the political structures of power and domination. In this latter respect, guided by the etymological associations of the word *archive* (*arché, archeion, archonten, patri-archive, matri-archive,* etc.), he goes beyond Gadamer.

The concept of cultural memory corresponds to what Derrida calls "archive" and Bernstein "tradition" and, like them, is indebted to Freud's insights into the psychohistorical dimension and the dynamics of cultural transmission. Cultural memory, in contrast to communicative memory, encompasses the age-old, out-of-the-way, and discarded; and in contrast to collective, bonding memory, it includes the noninstrumentalizable, heretical, subversive, and disowned. With the concept of cultural memory we have reached the furthest remove from our starting point: the individual memory in its neural and social conditioning factors. We must ask, therefore, in what sense is it still legitimate to make use of the concept of memory with reference to the cultural phenomena relevant here?

What justifies us, and indeed compels us, to speak of a form of memory is the much more loose and expanded, but nevertheless real, link with the structures of collective and individual identity. This is in marked contrast to bonding memory. From the standpoint of this identity cultural memory acquires a breadth of vision and of force. Goethe alluded to this breadth of vision and its importance for individual memory in verses in his "Book of Anger" that we shall examine more closely in our last chapter:

> Wer nicht von dreitausend Jahren,
> Sich weiss Rechenschaft zu geben,
> Bleib im Dunkeln unerfahren
> Mag von Tag zu Tage leben.

> Those who cannot draw conclusions
> From three thousand years of learning
> Stay naive in dark confusions,
> Day to day live undiscerning.[38]

This is in fact one of the accolades that the West bestows on itself: that it lives not from day to day, but in the light of a memory that goes back for three thousand years.

With cultural memory, the memory spaces of many thousands of years open up, and it is writing that plays the decisive role in this process. This was already evident in antiquity. In the first millennium B.C., following the end of the high cultures of the Bronze Age, memory cultures emerged in various locations in the Old World that took their lead from the heydays of the past. In Egypt of the Twenty-fifth and Twenty-sixth Dynasties, a marked archaism developed toward the end of the eighth century B.C. that encompassed all facets of culture. All the epochs of the past, from the Old Kingdom (third millennium) down to the Eighteenth Dynasty (1400 B.C.), and particularly, however, the period of the Middle Kingdom, are now regarded as the authoritative models. A grave owner of the seventh century B.C. in central Egypt visits a namesake's grave that is fifteen hundred years older to copy a wall for his own grave. In a papyrus from the Roman period there is a copy of the facade of a grave from the end of the third millennium. Culture becomes conscious of the depths of time and develops a sense of cultural simultaneity that makes it possible to identify with the forms of expression of a past going back thousands of years, so that it is often difficult for us to date with precision the texts and works of art of the Late Period.

Another, less eclectic form of relating to the past and the culture of memory developed in the Late Period of Mesopotamia.[39] Whereas the Egyptians sought their models from different periods of the past, the Assyrian and Babylonian kings took their lead from the period of the Agade empire (2334–2154) that in retrospect was elevated to normative status for the people of the Late Period, whose actions it legitimized. Looked at from the vantage point of this past, Mesopotamian culture always succeeded in surviving its crises: the fall of Sumerian culture, the various waves of immigration and periods of foreign domination, the major conflicts between the Assyrians and Babylonians, and the Persian conquest. In the first millennium B.C., by which time the ruins of the Agade empire had more or less completely disappeared, Mesopotamian society was transformed into a "digging society" that organized proper excavations in search of the traces of its normative past. Cultural memory assumed the form of a *topogra-*

phie légendaire, as Maurice Halbwachs has demonstrated in the case of the Church in Palestine in late antiquity and the early medieval period.[40]

As far as Greece is concerned, we need only think of the well-known case of the Homeric epics. Not only do they reach over the abyss of a "dark age" of four to five centuries, back to the Late Bronze Age, and elevate the Trojan War to the status of a normative past; but in the fifth and sixth centuries, they themselves, particularly the *Iliad,* acquire the status of a central, identity-creating, and in this sense "connective" memory. Transcending the individual states, what is mirrored, reinforced, and renewed in every recitation of this story of a pan-Hellenic coalition engaged in a war with an enemy in the East is the identity of a pan-Hellenic group consciousness.[41]

No doubt, these early instances of a writing-based cultural memory that digs deep into the spaces of memory also contain their fair share of memory politics in the service of bonding memory. Nevertheless, the stock of memories stored up in the medium of writing quickly transcends the horizons of a knowledge of the past that can be put to immediate use, and transforms the bonding memory through a cultural memory that operates on a much larger scale. Such normative texts as the Torah in Israel, the *Book of the Dead* in Egypt, the *En ma Eliš* and the Gilgamesh epic in Mesopotamia, and the Homeric epics in Greece constitute a nucleus around which whole libraries have developed. The palace library at Nineveh is the earliest example of a comprehensive cultural collection that aimed to assemble the entire knowledge of past and present, the most famous instance of which is the library of Alexandria five hundred years later. Cultural memory is complex, pluralistic, and labyrinthine; it encompasses a quantity of bonding memories and group identities that differ in time and place and draws its dynamism from these tensions and contradictions.

Cultural memory has its own outer horizon of knowledge beyond which the concept of "memory" no longer applies. By this I mean knowledge that has lost every link to a collective identity, however broadly conceived, and therefore possesses neither horizon nor force. Western man's curiosity about theory is not deterred by exotic knowledge. On the contrary, quite frequently, the more remote it is from our actual concerns, the more interesting it may appear. My own subject, Egyptology, is a good example of this. The very preoccupation with the outer realms of cultural memory sharpens our perception of its limits. One of the most important functions of such exotic disciplines as ethnology, Oriental languages and culture, or old American studies is to investigate the formation of horizons in the social nexus of bonding knowledge and cultural knowledge. Only when we examine culture from the outside can we perceive the extent to which it is informed by memory.

1

Invisible Religion and
Cultural Memory

1. Preliminary Remarks

In recent decades it has become increasingly clear that the concept of "tradition" does not reveal its own meaning in a transparent way.[1] Concepts such as *traditio, paradosis,* and *qabbalah* refer only to the process, the technique of handing down and receiving as such, without reference to the driving forces, interests, and needs that motivate this incessant labor of passing things on and adopting them. Two concepts that have been placed in the foreground in research in the sociology of culture in recent decades appear to me to be especially well suited to shedding new light on the problem of the function of tradition. One is the concept of "invisible religion," introduced by Thomas Luckmann.[2] The other is the concept of memory that has been made so productive for cultural theory in the writings of Freud, Warburg, Halbwachs, and others, particularly in the form of "cultural memory" that we find, for example, in the volume edited by Aleida Assmann and Dietrich Harth with the title *Mnemosyne.*[3] Both concepts refer to the knowledge shared by a group, the question of its extent, elaboration, and transmission. The concept of religion highlights the binding character of this knowledge; the concept of memory emphasizes its ability to establish connections and constitute identity.

Invisible religion relates to individual religions much as "language" relates to particular languages. It designates the general, functionally determined framework that the individual religions fill out in their own particular way. To that extent the analogy with language is valid. But in the case of religion there is a further factor that has no parallel in language. Invisible religion is not merely an abstract function standing above the many specific religious systems. It also exists within a given culture as a higher and ultimately validating framework of meaning for the different fields of cultural practice, communication, and reflection that have emerged as distinct forms within this framework or "world picture" and to which this "visible religion" belongs as one field among others specific to this culture. Thus Luckmann's concept of an invisible religion leads to a distinction within the concept of religion. For simplicity's sake we can label them IR and VR. IR is the higher, invisible religion that determines the relationship of the individual to society and the "world." VR is the religion that has become visible in the specific institutions of the cult and the priesthood and that is responsible for the tasks involved in transactions with the sacred and the administration of the sacred properties associated with them.

What Luckmann makes clear in his essay is twofold: (1) The failure to make this distinction between IR and VR leads to an ethnocentric narrowing of our conception of religion, since we tacitly base our definition of religion on the familiar characteristics of VR and thereby mistakenly "identify religion with one of its particular forms"[4] (2). We can speak of processes of secularization, loss of validity, and marginalization only with regard to VR—that is to say, the religion of the institutionalized churches—but not with regard to IR.

The following contribution is concerned with this intracultural tension that we have described as the tension between IR and VR. With Luckmann we understand by IR "symbolic universes in general," and by VR, a "religious cosmos in particular" (43), and inquire into the forms of its social objectivation. I would like to begin with the example of the ancient Egyptian conceptual world and attempt to show how both Luckmann's distinction and the resulting tension between the comprehensive and the specific can be clearly seen. In the process I shall treat the concepts "invisible religion" and "cultural memory" as largely synonymous. I then wish to take a further step and sketch in the transformations of cultural memory that emerge from specific applications of writing.

2. Invisible and Visible Religion in Ancient Egypt: "The Egyptian Triangle"

Ancient Egyptian culture confronts us with a model that explicitly fleshes out Luckmann's distinction between visible and invisible religion. That is surprising because on the basis of our own religious tradition we would have supposed that visible religion—VR—would claim a competence, indeed a monopoly of interpretation that includes IR too, in other words, the whole "world" as the totality of reality and the norms and values contained in it. We might have supposed therefore that the norms that govern the conduct of the individual and his orientation in the world, and the purely theoretical distinction between IR and VR in the concrete conceptual world of the Egyptians, would have collapsed into a compact religious concept. That is the precise opposite of what happened. What, after reading Luckmann's essay, we might think of as specific to modernity, namely the drifting apart of visible and invisible religion, turns out to characterize an early stage of culture. Looked at from the vantage point of Egypt, the cultural process in fact runs in the opposite direction, toward a progressive unification of religion. The initial differentiation between invisible religion, which is responsible for a view of the world as a whole and is not capable of being institutionalized, and visible religion as one of the institutions responsible for keeping the world going, gives way to a model that makes the institutions of visible religion responsible for the universe.

The Egyptians had a concept that comes close to what Luckmann calls invisible religion: *maat*. *Maat* signifies the principle of a universal harmony that manifests itself in the cosmos as order and in the world of human beings as justice.[5] Such concepts exist also in other cultures to describe the totality of meaningful order on the highest plane of abstraction. Examples are the Greek concept *kosmos*, the Indian *dharma*, and the Chinese *tao*. What distinguishes the ancient Egyptian idea of *maat* is its coupling with political power. The king is responsible for ensuring that *maat* rules on earth. Without the state, the symbolic universe would collapse. However, the state is not the institutionalization of *maat*. This is not capable of being institutionalized or objectified, that is, codified. What we are confronted by is a hidden theme that manifests itself in its success, not a fully articulated norm. What *maat* is can be gleaned from the texts of the wisdom literature where it is presented casuistically, not apodictically; it is not found in a code of religious or juridical rules in the narrower sense.

This framework for a meaningful order that the king is supposed to uphold breaks down into two opposing cultural spheres of "law" and "cult." These are the spheres in which *maat*—which is otherwise a higher, invisible form and as such is not capable of being institutionalized—is made visible. The text that unfolds this conception deals in a very fundamental way with the relationship between Re, the sun god and the god of creation, and the king:

> Re has installed the king
> on the earth of the living
> for ever and ever
> so that he may give justice to mankind,
> and please the gods,
> so that he may create *maat* and drive out *isfet.*
> He (the king) brings divine sacrifices to the gods
> and offerings to the dead.[6]

This text distinguishes between "law" and "cult," the "moral and legal" cosmos and the "religious cosmos" as the two spheres through which the kings uphold the world, and both are brought together in the higher concept of making *maat* a reality. The king—the political order, the "state"— has been placed on earth by the Creator himself with the general task of bringing *maat*—justice, truth, order—into being and expelling its opposite, *isfet*—violence, lies, and chaos—which normally reigns supreme on earth. It is this that I would like to call religion in the broader sense, IR. Here religion is not contrasted with some "secular" order or other, but rather stands for order as opposed to all forms of disorder. That is the first, primordial distinction. In Egyptian terms it is the contrast between *maat* and *isfet. Maat* contains the idea of the all-inclusive divine or religious foundation of all order. On this plane religion can be equated with order as such. Here sacred order is not opposed to profane order, but order is sacred as such, in contrast to disorder. All order is sacred. We can see this from the example of the order of time. For us it is self-evident that both profane everyday time and ecclesiastical time have their order. We may even believe that profane time is more strictly regulated by hours, minutes, and seconds than the religious order of time. Formerly, it was the other way around.

And a lot earlier still, the order of time was exclusively religious in nature. In Egypt the measurement of time was reserved exclusively for priests; clocks were cult instruments. The calendar was a calendar of festivals; the names of the months were based on the chief festivals. It was religious rites and not everyday life that called for the precise measurement of time. Only gradually did a secular temporal order start to emerge. Order as such was originally a religious phenomenon, established, framed and maintained by rituals, festivals, gods, and myths.

Within IR, however, we now see a second distinction introduced: "administering justice and pleasing the gods." Here, men and gods, law and cult are contrasted and this draws a line between the sphere of the social and political order, that is, "justice," and—once again—"religion" (for after all that is what is meant by "pleasing the gods"), but now in a narrower, more specific sense.[7] That is VR, divided once again into cults of the gods and the dead. This "moral and political cosmos" is contrasted with the "religious cosmos" as something else, something that is not religion in the narrower sense. This sphere too has a religious foundation, but it has nothing to do with placating the gods, with cults, theology, and the priesthood. Instead, it forms its own "sub-universe of meaning" to use the terminology of *The Social Construction of Reality*.[8] We encounter here a structure that I would like to call the "Egyptian triangle":

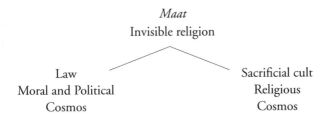

Maat
Invisible religion

Law · Sacrificial cult
Moral and Political · · · · · · · · · · · · · · · · · · · Religious
Cosmos · Cosmos

What we can now observe, in the course of Egyptian and ancient Oriental history in general, is the gradual erosion of this distinction, the increasing porosity of the frontier between the two worlds of submeaning or systems of action, "cult" and "justice." In the framework of the system of "justice," social relations always tend increasingly to be interpreted as religious relations, as relations between God and man. In extreme cases that leads to the dissolution not only of justice as a system of action, but also of the cult as a system of action. In that event a new type of religion arises that no longer has room for the distinction between VR and IR. God can no longer be placated just by the cult; he also and above all demands justice. Justice becomes the foundation of the relation to God. That leads to what Max Weber called the "methodical conduct of life." The whole of life is now placed in the framework of the relation between man and God, that is, of religion in the narrower sense, and subordinated to the requirements of justice. The concept of justice thus ceases to be the foundation of a sphere outside specific dealings with the divine; it is incorporated into a relation with God and in this sense it is theologized. When this stage has been reached we find ourselves confronted with a new form of religion, a "secondary" religion.[9] We mainly think of the course of the history of culture as a path toward ever greater differentiations. In the beginning is an undifferentiated totality of order from which the individual orders of the religions, politics, law and the economy, the arts and sciences emerge as independent or "autonomous" value spheres (Max Weber) via processes that last for centuries. Here, we have the opposite development. Secondary religions arise from a process of de-differentiation. What had previously been divided by the line drawn between cult and justice now collapses into one thing. Concepts that had previously belonged in the sphere of justice are now inscribed theologically in this process of de-differentiation.

Today we mainly live in or with "tertiary" religions that have emerged as a result of the processes of differentiation from secondary religions that we have referred to. In consequence we look back at the secondary religions and tend to regard them as providing the paradigm of religion in general. Many students of religion unthinkingly apply such concepts as faith, confession, parish, church, and others that belong entirely in the realm of secondary religions, to primary definitions of religion and thus arrive at those anachronistic definitions of religion to which Luckmann objected.[10]

Thus, like Luckmann, the Egyptians drew a distinction between visible and invisible religion, and this distinction enabled them to form a relatively secular notion of justice as the totality of norms that regulate the harmonious nature of social existence. I would hazard the guess that most, if not all "primary" religions are based on this distinction and that one of the defining characteristics of "secondary" religions is that they abolish this distinction. In this respect primary religions are differentiated: they are based on a supreme concept of a sacred order within which "a religious cosmos" appears as a VR with limited claims to be a meaningful subworld. Secondary religions, in contrast, elevate this religious cosmos to the rank of an ultimate reality that determines all knowledge and action and thus annuls the distinction between the different planes of IR and VR. At bottom, Luckmann's theory of an invisible religion is a plea for the reintroduction of the distinction. Or alternatively, it is an acknowledgment of the fact that in the course of modernization the old distinction has made its reappearance, only this time with changed significance.

3. Transformations of Cultural Memory

In what follows we shall inquire into the driving forces that underlie the abolition of the primary distinction between visible and invisible religion and the origins of "unified" or de-differentiated religion. I would like to describe this process as the "theologizing of cultural memory." Knowledge of the world in the comprehensive sense of an ultimate framework of meaning can be described very accurately as an invisible religion, since there can be no doubt that what is at issue here is carefulness, attentiveness, obligation, reverence, "stopping and thinking,"[11] "prudence"—in other words, everything that is implied by the Latin concept of *religio*. But no less important are continuity, identity, and the imagined presence of the nonsimultaneous, that is, whatever can be described by the concept of memory. Cultural memory can be understood as the "institutionalization" of the invisible religion (in the sense in which it occurs in Berger and Luckmann), that is to say, the totality of the forms in which a comprehensive symbolic world of meaning can be communicated and handed down.[12] If we speak of cultural memory in what follows this is not to abandon the object of what Luckmann calls invisible religion, but only to shed light on it from a different angle. We are concerned in the first instance with the question of "the maintenance of symbolic universes over the generations,"[13] that is, of tradition in the sense of the continuity of meaning, "world," and identity.

Luckmann closely linked his concept of the invisible religion with the process of individuation, the formation of a personal self. According to Luckmann, a biological organism "becomes a Self, by embarking with others upon the construction of an 'objective' and moral universe of meaning" (48–49). In the absence of such a universe, immediate, individual experiences "cannot be integrated into a socially defined, morally relevant biography" (48). Collective and individual identity, society and self, cultural and individual memory, the social origin and individuation of consciousness and conscience mutually condition each other and form two sides of the same culturally objective and socially mediated knowledge. The possibility of developing a personal self and a meaningful biography is predicated on a stable worldview (that is, what the Egyptians call *maat*). This stability in turn is a function of cultural memory, the symbolic and institutional, in short, the cultural forms in which this worldview is objectivized, continued, and practiced.

Along with a particular worldview, cultural memory disseminates and reproduces a consciousness of unity, particularity, and a sense of belonging among the members of a group. To create this consciousness it does not confine itself to linguistic objectivations and symbols. As the ethnologists have shown, in the production of mutual dependence and social interconnections, the exchange of goods and of women are among the most effective media.[14] But to the extent that rites and texts play a role here, they do so mainly in two contexts; we call them "formative" and "normative," and subsume both (including the rites) beneath the concept of "cultural texts."[15]

Normative texts—for example, proverbs, rules of games, laws—answer the question "What shall we do?" They help us to make judgments, arrive at legal findings, and make decisions. They transmit practical knowledge and point the way to right action. "The path of life" in Egyptian is a common metaphor for didactic literature; the Chinese *tao*, "the way," points in the same direction; and the Jewish concept *halakhah*, the principle of the normative interpretation of texts and right action, is cognate with *halakh*, the verb "to go."

Formative texts—for example, tribal myths, heroic lays, genealogies—answer the question "Who are we?" They help us to define ourselves and establish our identity. They transmit identity-confirming knowledge by narrating stories that are shared.[16]

Since cultural memory is not biologically inherited, it has to be preserved across the generations by means of cultural activities. That is a question of the objectification, storing, reactivation, and circulation of meaning. It is obvious that in the history of these functions the invention of writing as an extraordinarily efficient means of symbolic objectification is the decisive turning point. With writing this history divides into two phases: the phase of rite-based repetition and the phase of text-based repetition. *Repetition and interpretation are functionally equivalent procedures in the production of cultural coherence.*

The watershed between these two phases is self-evident and has often been described. The best-known attempt is Jaspers's concept of the "axial age," which refers precisely to this transformation (even though, oddly enough, he was unaware of the role of writing in this change, an omission that has since been made good by others).[17] From the viewpoint of the early high cultures, however, this transition from ritual to textual coherence was by no means achieved simply by the use of writing as such. What was crucial was the adoption of a different principle, that of "canonization." Not the introduction of writing, but the process of canonization was what triggered a fundamental change in cultural continuity.

a. Symbolization and Ceremonial Circulation:
Societies Without Writing

Without the possibility of preservation in writing, human memory is the only means available to a group that wishes to store the knowledge that secures its identity. Three functions are required if the normative and formative impulses that establish identity and provide a guide to action are to be guaranteed: preservation, retrieval, and communication, or: poetic form, ritual performance, and collective participation. We may take it as proved that poetic form chiefly has the mnemonic function of ensuring that the knowledge that establishes identity can be put into durable form.[18] We have also become just as familiar with the fact that this knowledge is customarily presented in the form of a multimedia production that firmly embeds the linguistic text in voice, body, mime, gesture, dance, rhythm, and ritual action.[19] What I am concerned with above all is the third point: the form of participation. How can the group acquire a share in the cultural memory which even at this stage is in the hands of individual experts (bards, shamans, griots)? The answer runs: through coming together and personal presence. In societies without writing, participation in the cultural memory is only possible through being there. For such assemblies it is necessary to create pretexts: festivals.[20] Because they recur regularly, festivals and rites provide for the imparting of the knowledge that establishes identity and hence for the reproduction of cultural identity. Ritual repetition secures the coherence of the group in place and time. By organizing cultural memory primarily through festivals, the time of oral societies is structured into everyday time and holiday time. In the holiday time or "dreamtime" of the great assemblies people's horizons expand to embrace the universal, the time of creation, of the origins and great transformations that brought forth the world in primordial times. The rites and myths paraphrase the meaning of reality. Observing, preserving, and passing them on with care makes the world go round and maintains the identity of the group.

b. Codification: the "Stream of Tradition" in Early Written Cultures

Writing developed in Mesopotamia from preexisting forms in the realm of everyday, not of ceremonial communication.[21] It was not incorporated into the realms of cultural memory until later. If only because of its multimedia complexity, which makes it impossible to write it all down, ceremonial communication remains a domain of ritual repetition, as always the basic principle and the backbone of cultural cohesiveness.

Gradually, however, alongside the practical texts for everyday communication, we see the emergence of a stock of texts with normative and formative claims that arise not through putting oral traditions into textual form, but directly from the spirit of writing. This literature constitutes what Leo Oppenheim aptly termed the "stream of tradition" that absorbed the texts that were destined for further use.[22] This stream of tradition is a living river: it shifts its bed and the water it contains ebbs and flows. Some texts fall into oblivion, others are added; they are expanded, shortened, rewritten, and anthologized in a constant flux. Gradually, the center and the periphery become identifiable structures. Because of their importance, certain texts acquire central status; they are copied and cited more frequently than others, and finally come to be seen as classics, embodying normative and formative values. In this development the school of scribes plays a central role.

With the emergence of classics the temporal form of culture undergoes a change. The "festive" distinction between primordial time and the present is now joined by another: the distinction between past and present, antiquity and modernity. The past is the time of the classics, "classicism." It is no longer primordial time that remains at a constant distance from the advancing present, a distance that is not temporal, but ontic; it is the historical past and people are aware of its growing distance from the present. In Mesopotamia, in the first millennium, we find early forms of historiography relating to the past.[23] In Egypt, we discover an interest in the preservation of historical monuments and an archivarian interest in old monuments and texts, the cultivation of the archaic and the consciousness of age-old traditions.[24] Libraries and book culture grow up around the temple scriptoria and schools. As before, however, it is the festivals and rites that embody the principle of cultural coherence.

c. Canonization and Interpretation

It is not writing, but the damming up of the stream of tradition by the act of canonization that produces the decisive shift from ritual to textual coherence. It is not the sacred text, but the canonical one that calls for interpretation and thus forms the starting point for interpretative cultures. As Carsten Colpe has shown, there are only two mutually independent canon formations in the history of mankind: the Hebrew Bible and the Buddhist Tripitaka.[25] All other canon formations depend upon those initial inspirations: in the West, the Alexandrian canonization of the Greek "classics," the Christian Bible, and the Koran, and, in the East, the Jain canon and the canonizations of Confucian and Taoist writings. A rich literature of interpretation grows up almost immediately around these canonical texts and this secondary literature at once becomes canonized in its turn. Thus cultural memory is organized, on the one hand, in first-, second-, and in certain circumstances even third-order canons, and on the other hand, in primary and secondary literature, texts, and commentaries. The most important step in the formation of canons is the act of *closure*. It draws the two crucial lines between the canon and the apocrypha, and between the primary and the secondary. Canonical writings cannot just be continued. That is the crucial distinction between them and the "stream of tradition." Canonical texts are sacrosanct: they call for literal transmission.

Not a jot may be altered. "Ye shall not add unto the word which I command you, neither shall ye diminish from it, that ye may keep the commandments of the Lord your God," it says in Deuteronomy (4:2). This quotation also makes it clear that the Hebrew canon was born of the spirit of the contract, the "covenant" that the Lord made with His people.

4. Canonization as De-differentiation

The canonical text combines the binding force of a legal contract with the sacred authority of a ritual utterance. It contains the spheres of "justice" and the sacrificial cult, the realms of politics and morality as well as the religious cosmos, all in one. But in order not to restrict the concept of canon too narrowly to the specific conditions of the Hebrew canon, I define the canonical text as the combination of the qualities of cultural and sacred texts. Sacred texts exist at every stage of cultural symbolization. They belong in the sphere that the Egyptian text described as "appeasing the gods," that is to say, creating a proximity to the gods. They may exist in oral form (the most impressive example is that of the Vedas) or in written form (e.g., the Egyptian *Book of the Dead*). Sacred texts require verbatim transmission. This explains why the Vedas, for example, were not written down. The Brahmans trust script less than their memory. A sacred text is a kind of linguistic temple, a recalling of the sacred through the medium of the voice. The sacred text calls for no interpretation, but for ritually protected recitation while scrupulously observing the rules about place, time, cleanliness, and so on. A "cultural" text, on the other hand, embodies the normative and formative values of a community, its "truth." These texts ask to be taken to heart, obeyed, and translated into a lived reality. This calls less for recitation than interpretation. It depends on the "heart," not the "mouth" or "ear." But the text does not address the heart directly. The path to the understanding heart from the listening ear or the reading eye is as long as the path from the graphic or phonetic surface to the normative and formative meaning. We speak of "canonization" when the normative and formative authority of cultural texts coincides with the literal sanctity of sacred texts. Our dealings with canonic texts call for a third party, the interpreter who intervenes between the text and its addressee, thus liberating the normative and formative impulses that are imprisoned in the sacrosanct surface of the text. Canonic texts can only disclose their meaning in the triangular relationship between text, interpreter, and listener.

In this way, wherever there is a canonical tradition this gives rise to interpretative institutions surrounding it, and therewith a new class of intellectual elites: the Israelite *sofer*, the Jewish *rabbi*, the Hellenistic *philologos*, the Islamic *sheikh* and *mullah*, the Indian *Brahman*, the Buddhist, Confucian, and Taoist sages and scholars. The crucial feature of these new agents of cultural memory is their spiritual leadership, their (relative) independence of the institutions of political and economic power.[26] Only from such an independent position can they defend the normative and formative claims made by the canon. They share and embody the canon's authority and the truth revealed in it. In early literate cultures the agents and guardians of the "stream of tradition" were also administrators and dependent officials who received (and also issued) the orders of the political organization. There was no room here within the tradition, there was no Archimedean point from which it was possible to oppose the organization and to confront it with demands for normative and formative change. Thus the process of canonization is also a process of social differentiation: the separating out of a position that is independent of the political, administrative, economic, juridical, and even religious authority. The business of this position is, to use the words of Hölderlin, the cultivation of the "solid letter" (*der feste Buchstab*).[27] To care for the solid letter is to interpret or care for the meaning of the text. Because the letter is "solid" and cannot be altered by a single iota, but because, on the other hand, the world of men is subject to continuous change, there is a gulf between the established text and the changing reality that can only be bridged by interpretation. In this way interpretation becomes the central principle of cultural coherence and identity. The normative and formative impulses of cultural memory can only be gleaned through the incessant, constantly renewed textual interpretation of the tradition through which identity is established. Interpretation becomes the gesture of remembering, the interpreter becomes a person who remembers and reminds us of a forgotten truth.

5. Concluding Remarks: The Decanonization and Differentiation of Cultural Memory—Return of the "Egyptian Triangle"?

"Secondary religions" do not permit the distinction between "justice" and "sacrificial cult" of the kind made by the Egyptian triangle. The canonical text refers to both spheres of social action, and both determine man's religious attitude to the world. Not merely the act of sacrifice, but also, and above all, right conduct keep the relationship of man and the individual to God in order. The "religious universe" extends its sway to the individual's conduct of his life and the political order of the community. This process of de-differentiation of the religious is partly determined by the evolution of the media that we have described, with its stages of "ceremonial circulation," "codification," and lastly, the "canonization" of symbolic universes. In later chapters (especially Chapters 2 and 7) I would like to show that this obliterating of the distinction between "sacrifice" and "justice" that is characteristic of the secondary religions is linked to another distinction that they introduce: the one between true and untrue in the sphere of religion. The idea of "false" gods and of religions based on such untruth is a feature of the secondary religions and invests them with a truth value that had been alien to the primary religions. In the latter, distinctions were drawn between sacred and profane, pure and impure, but not between true and false. In light of this new concept of truth, the sacred texts obtain their canonical status within the horizon of the secondary religions, and this leads to the "theologization of cultural memory."

This is the condition which forms the starting point for Enlightenment. In the modern age, religion's authority and monopoly of interpretation (VR) is losing its grip on our view of the world and our ultimate guide to meaning (IR). With the emergence of competing cultural disciplines like metaphysics and ethics, art and literature, the natural sciences and the humanities, politics and law, and finally, economics, the original separation of visible and invisible religion has surfaced once again. Secular texts acquire the status not just of literary classics that influence the literary activities of subsequent epochs, but even of *cultural texts* that shape the self-image and worldview of the group and the conduct of the individual, a task once performed by myths and the works of wisdom literature. With this, we have arrived at a structure that resembles that of the "Egyptian triangle," albeit in completely different circumstances.

As Enlightenment progresses, what encroaches on religion (in the sense of VR), differentiating itself from it and delimiting it, is no longer simply "justice" in the ancient Oriental sense of the knowledge of the foundations of harmonious living. What we find nowadays is philosophy, art, science, and all the other distinct spheres of value (in Max Weber's sense). In contrast to visible religion, these spheres constitute, on the one hand, the realm of the profane, and on the other hand, they are still able to rise to the rank of substitute and civil religions since they can still be enveloped by invisible religion. In other words, they can remain within the compass of our striving for a meaningful universe, even though such a universe today will inevitably be more problematic, less accessible, and more unstable than ever before. In short, they can be reshaped into something like what the Egyptians called *maat*.

Monotheism, Memory, and Trauma:
Reflections on Freud's Book on Moses

1. The Archaeological Gaze and the Hermeneutics
of Distrust

In his last work, *Moses and Monotheism*, which appeared in 1939, the year of his death, Sigmund Freud uncovered a surprising relationship between monotheism and trauma.[1] This trauma, he writes, is what gives monotheistic religion its peculiar power over the masses and procures it the privilege of suspending the laws of reason. For Freud, the history of religion is a psychodynamic process of repressing and remembering. On the surface we have the codification, canonization, tradition, and interpretation of sacred writings, a vast archive of the more modern, writing-based, chiefly Western, history of religion and of the spirit, although in the meantime it has expanded throughout the globe, thanks to the efforts of Islam and Christian missionary work. However, to the archaeological gaze of the analyst who digs rather deeper, religion appears more like a psychodrama whose origins reach much further back, long before the invention of writing, and indeed into the earliest phylogenetic roots of the human race. It is from these roots that the dynamics of religion are fed, which Freud represents as a complex of traumatization and guilt feelings, repression and remembering.

In this chapter I would like to show that Freud is right and in what way he is right. He is right to place the concepts "trauma" and "guilt" at the heart of the history of religion, especially of monotheistic religion, and to interpret this history in terms of remembering and forgetting. However, I would like to question his methodology. By this I mean that the themes of "trauma," "guilt," and "memory" that Freud has brought to the surface and placed at the center of attention have nothing at all to do with that phylogenetic dimension of depth that Freud believes he must explore. Instead, they form an explicit part of the surface reality of the history of religion and its documents.

It is well known that one of Freud's leading topological metaphors is the concept of depth. This is closely connected with his topology of the soul which consists of the different layers of the id, the ego, and the superego. The id is the deep layer of the unconscious. It lies beyond consciousness and announces its presence only in traces and symptoms. Analysis is the art of plumbing these depths. Freud frequently liked to compare it with the work of the archaeologist. His own archaeological collection is further evidence of his fascination with the subject. In his study of hysteria of 1896, Freud made explicit use of the comparison with archaeology to explain his method:

Imagine that an explorer arrives in a little-known region where his interest is aroused by an expanse of ruins, with remains of walls, fragments of columns, and tablets with half-effaced and unreadable inscriptions. He may content himself with inspecting what lies exposed to view, with questioning the inhabitants—perhaps semi-barbaric people—who live in the vicinity, about what tradition tells them of the history and meaning of these archaeological remains, and with noting down what they tell him—and he may then proceed on his journey. But he may act differently. He may have brought picks, shovels and spades with him, and he may set the inhabitants to work with these implements. Together with them he may start upon the ruins, clear away the rubbish, and beginning from the visible remains, uncover what is buried. If his work is crowned with success, the discoveries are self-explanatory: the ruined walls are part of the ramparts of a palace or a treasure-house; the fragments of columns can be filled out into a temple; the numerous inscriptions, which, by good luck, may be bilingual, reveal an alphabet and a language, and, when they have been deciphered and translated, yield undreamed-of information about the events of the remote past, to commemorate which the monuments were built. *Saxa loquuntur!*[2]

Saxa loquuntur, the stones speak, and they tell a very different story from the one the tradition of semibarbaric inhabitants or surface discoveries could have yielded. The truth of the depths is fundamentally different

from the message, or from superficial appearances. It is from this difference that the principle of Freud's hermeneutics arises. It is a hermeneutics
of distrust that sees in the explicit communications from the surface nothing more than the distorted and falsified traces of a buried truth. This is
Freud's approach to the texts of the Bible.[3] By peering through these texts,
Freud believes that he can discern the outlines of a narrative that has left
profound marks in the souls of those affected by it, the Jews, and that this
is what has made them into what they are in the course of the centuries. I
shall only sketch the story here. Freud's book about Moses has recently (we
should perhaps say: at long last) triggered a very lively, world-wide debate
so that I may assume that the main lines of his arguments are familiar ter-
ritory.[4] For Freud, Moses was an Egyptian, a follower of the heretical King
Akhenaten who around 1350 B.C. had eliminated the traditional religion in
Egypt and replaced it with the monotheistic cult of Aten, the god of light
and sun. Freud ascribes Akhenaten's monotheism to the idea of the world
dominion of the pharaohs, which Akhenaten had transformed into the
religion of Aten, the one god of light and the sun and ruler of the world.
Freud's own summary of his argument can scarcely be bettered:

If we provisionally accept the world-empire of the Pharaohs as the determining
cause of the emergence of the monotheist idea, we see that that idea, released from
its native soil and transferred to another people was, after a long period of latency,
taken hold of by them, preserved by them as a precious possession and, in turn,
itself kept them alive by giving them pride in being a chosen people: it was the religion of their primal father to which were attached their hope of reward, of distinction and finally of world-dominion.[5]

This process of a "transfer to another people" is pictured by Freud as taking place after the death of the king, when the new religion was once
again abolished in Egypt, and Moses, refusing to acquiesce in the return
to the old faith, emigrated to Palestine with the "Jews" who lived in the
Nile Delta and to whom he now passed on the new monotheistic religion.
The Jews, however, proved in the long run to be inadequate to the harsh
demands of an abstract monotheism; they murdered Moses and then repressed their deed.

   This murder was a traumatic experience since it involved the acting
out of a repressed memory, a memory that goes back to the beginnings of
phylogenesis, when human beings still lived in hordes. At that time, the fa-

ther ruled over the horde tyrannically, with unlimited powers, and threatened his sons with death or castration if they ventured to compete with him for the attentions of women. Ultimately, however, when his strength waned, he was killed by his sons and communally eaten, whereupon another took his place. Through repetition this experience of the human psyche inscribed itself in a (biologically) hereditary manner and formed what Freud called its "archaic legacy." Culture and the primeval form of religion ("totemism") arose when an end was put to this murdering and the father was elevated to the rank of a god. The father was then replaced by a totemic animal that was worshipped as the tribal god and was devoured in communal sacrificial meals. The role of father of the horde remained unfilled on a human plane; the group organized itself without a head. Killing was now felt to be a sin because it reminded people of the original sin, the murder of the primal father. The memory of this murder was repressed and transformed into a powerful feeling of guilt that marked totemist religion with all sorts of precautionary measures and anxieties, such as taboos, restrictions, abstinences, self-castigations, cruel sacrifices, and the like. As the most important of these taboos, the taboo on incest prevented sexually motivated conflicts within the group. At a further stage of historical development, the godhead incarnate in the totem animal was also made human and was multiplied; totemism was replaced by polytheism and the original structure of a religion dominated by a primordial father was rendered unrecognizable.

This etiological history seems even more outlandish than the murder of Moses. At this point Freud becomes a creator of myth. However, he needs this myth because it is only through myth that the traumatic violence that characterizes monotheism becomes explicable. "When Moses brought the people the idea of a single god, it was not a novelty but signified the revival of an experience in the primeval ages of the human family which had long vanished from men's conscious memory."[6] Moses' monotheism was the return of the father. Moses' murder was an even more potent repetition which reanimated memories that had been even more deeply buried or encrypted. A natural death would not have sufficed to produce such powerful effects on the collective psyche. The experience had to be traumatic if it was to endure. In Freud's own words, "It must have undergone the fate of being repressed, the condition of lingering in the unconscious, before it is able to display such powerful effects on its return as to bring the masses under its spell."[7] The murder of Moses repeated the death of the primordial father. The paradoxical kernel of Freud's argument is that only through his murder and the subsequent repression of this deed could Moses become what he is: "the creator of the Jewish people," a figure of enduring, indelible memory. Following the death of Moses the monotheism he taught entered into a latency phase that lasted for centuries in order finally to reappear as the return of the repressed and bring the masses under its spell.

In this context there are some very important reflections on the concept of trauma in Bernstein's book on Freud that I would like to discuss briefly here.[8] For Freud the trauma of parricide is a "historical truth" from which monotheistic religion derives its overwhelming persuasiveness. It is a "religion of the father" and as such appeals to the basic Oedipal structure or "archaic inheritance" of the human soul in the depths of which people have always known that "they once possessed a primal father whom they have murdered." Bernstein shows that the historical truth cannot simply be equated with the external factual nature of the act in the legal sense. Neither the "primal father" nor Moses need have been murdered in actual fact for a traumatization of the collective psyche to have taken place. The historical truth lies in the psychic resonance, not the external facts of the case. It only shows itself in the recurrence, when something new turns out to be something long since familiar. Referring to Cathy Caruth,[9] Bernstein makes use of the concept of "retroactive, delayed [*nachträglich*] experience." "Since the traumatic event is not experienced as it occurs, it is fully evident only in connection with another place, and in another time."[10]

If we distinguish between the traumas of the perpetrator and the victim it becomes evident that Freud's examples refer to the traumatization of the perpetrator. The murders of the primal father and of Moses leave traces in the psyche of the perpetrators. It is particularly true in their case that their experience is delayed, since at the time of the deed "they knew not what they did." Freud's concept of a delayed reaction is of importance for his claim that Moses was murdered, since it is thanks to this concept that it can be said that there is no need for an actual deed in a legal sense. The intention to kill is quite enough to produce a trauma in the perpetrator and thus to establish the murder as a "historical truth." This makes it possible to salvage Freud's belief in a traumatic experience at the heart of monotheism.

I regard this as a very profound and thought-provoking analysis of monotheism, that is, of the religion of the Bible. As an Egyptologist, I am also fascinated by the idea of a link between the monotheistic Aten-worship and biblical monotheism. Needless to say, the monotheism of Akhenaten's cosmic sun worship and the biblical belief in a transcendent God are worlds apart. But Freud's conception of a father religion undoubtedly identifies a common denominator, and the idea of the exclusive unity of everything divine was such an unprecedented novelty that it may have weighed more heavily than all the differences of substance.

2. Contrafactual Memory

The idea of a possible link between these two events comes up against the difficulty of the time lag between them. Akhenaten lived in the fourteenth century B.C., and the emergence of biblical monotheism is the product of the prophetic age that began in the eighth century and only developed into a pure, radical monotheism in the post-Exile period [after 530 B.C.]. It is precisely this gap that Freud is able to explain with his thesis of a latency phase. The theory of repression maintains that there is a forgetting that preserves. Under the protection of such a preserving forgetting, the idea of an exclusive monotheism was able to perpetuate itself among the "Jews" (as Freud calls them; it would have been more correct to speak of the Israelites or Hebrews) from the fourteenth century to the eighth.

In my view, however, and in this respect I disagree with Freud, this interpretation reflects the explicit semantics of the texts pretty accurately. The fact is that the texts speak of little else but the forgetfulness of the people who constantly have to be reminded by the prophets of a truth that has been forgotten. Thus there turns out to be no difference between the truth that has been excavated and the traces on the surface. We might also say that the patient says exactly the same thing as the analyst. The archaeologist's love of discovery has nothing to bite on. What Freud unearths and dramatizes as a revelation is not the historical truth, but merely some theoretical constructs that turn out to be superfluous. The truth can be found in the texts themselves. They speak of memory, remembrance, forgetting, and the repressed, of trauma and guilt. In order to uncover this network of meanings we have no need to practice the hermeneutics of distrust; nor need we read these texts against the grain. We need only listen to them attentively.

Here, I would like to take up a few of Freud's central themes and demonstrate their presence in the biblical and non-biblical texts in the history of religion. I shall begin with the topic of memory.

To repeat, Freud reconstructs the history of religion as a dynamic process of remembering and forgetting. The murder of the primal father, traces of the memory of which are engraved in the human psyche as an archaic inheritance, was transformed into a totemist religion of sacrifice. Moses' monotheistic worship of the father may be said to have reintroduced the primal father, and the murder of Moses was a repetition of the murder of the primal father. The repression of both the act and the doctrine led to a centuries-long gap between the appearance of Moses and the gradual triumph of monotheism in Israel. Freud interprets this gap as the latency phase. When, with the later prophets, the memory gradually returned, the worship of the one father prevailed with the irresistible force that is typical of the return of the repressed.

What Freud did not see, or at any rate did not mention, is the central role played by memory in the biblical texts. To see this we need only refer to the excellent book written by Yosef Hayim Yerushalmi, *Zakhor: Erinnere Dich! Jüdisches Gedächtnis und jüdische Geschichte* [Zakhor. Remember! Jewish Memory and Jewish History]. But even Yerushalmi's approach tends to be too general. The dominance of the theme of memory can be shown much more concretely. The Book of Deuteronomy contains a theory of individual, collective, and cultural memory. The text is staged as a valedictory speech, given to the people by Moses on the eve of the crossing of the River Jordan and the entry into the Promised Land. Moses, of course, has to remain behind in Moab where he will die. All his thoughts are concentrated on his fears that in the Promised Land the people will forget everything they have undergone since the flight from Egypt and the obligations they have taken upon themselves as the result of the Covenant with Yahweh. The entire book is based on the deep fear of forgetting that will inevitably occur once the people have entered the cities they have not built, the wells they have not dug, and once they have eaten and drunk the bread and wine they have not produced. And if the people eat and drink and enjoy themselves, they will forget the Lord who has rescued them from Egypt. We have already quoted the relevant Bible passages in the Introduction. The people are expected to master the trick of remembering privation in the midst of abundance, and to recollect their nomadic lifestyle while living a settled existence in towns or in the fields. In short, they must recollect a way of life that is not confirmed by any "framework" of their present reality. That is the exceptional situation of a counterfactual memory. It keeps present to the mind a yesterday that conflicts with every today.

What is at issue in Deuteronomy is the consolidation of memory, which now, after forty years wandering in the wilderness, has to be remolded into a defined shape that can be conveyed to future generations. For this purpose Moses devises a mnemonic technique that combines no fewer than seven different procedures (on this point, see the Introduction, Section 4).

What we have here, then, in the first instance is the most extreme case of what Nietzsche in his *Genealogy of Morals* called "making a memory." For Nietzsche, all civilized human existence is based on the fact that the human animal, as he puts it, has been given a memory so that it is capable of keeping a promise and undertaking responsibilities. Man needs a memory in order to live in a community. Thus Deuteronomy can be interpreted as a highly explicit example of giving people a memory in this sense. The case is far too explicit and too extreme, however, to be explained in terms of universal anthropological structures. Something else must be at work here as well.

The crucial point, it seems to me, is the extraterritorial nature of the memory that Moses wishes to establish. It is constantly emphasized that this memory has no place in the land flowing with milk and honey, and that there is a great risk that it will be forgotten once the Israelites have settled in and filled their bellies. The extraterritorial nature of memory appears to me to be closely linked with the positioning of revelation outside the worldly reality. It is not by chance that the Bible situates in the wilderness the revelation of the Covenant and the Law. The people had to leave Egypt in order to be able to enter into the new world of the Law and of monotheism, and now, everything depends on their being able to remain in this new world, even under the conditions implicit in what was to be the Promised Land. This means that the laws that they are to remember and abide by are not the laws of the land, but the extraterritorial laws from Mount Sinai. By obeying these laws the people live as strangers on earth. Thus it says in Psalm 119:19, "I am a stranger on earth: Hide not thy commandments from me." To abide by the laws means living as a stranger on earth. Here we are concerned with a memory that finds no confirmation in the existing framework of the present, and indeed, that even contradicts it. We are confronted with a counterfactual memory that ensures that people live in this world without feeling at home in it, a memory that far from making you feel at home, denies you a home. This explains why, because of this extraterritoriality, this memory is so greatly at risk, so threatened by forgetfulness, so much in need of every memory technique to help it survive. "Thou shalt not forget" means "thou shalt not become assimilated," not even in the Promised Land. Monotheism forms the basis of an existential estrangement from the world. This estrangement can also be given a positive turn. To use Freud's words, it can mean "spiritual progress."

A counterfactual memory of this kind is not to be found in other societies; it exists neither in Egypt and Mesopotamia, nor in Greece, to say nothing of the primitive societies Nietzsche may have had in mind in *The Genealogy of Morals*. However, there are comparable phenomena in all established religions based on revelation. They are all founded on a corpus of canonical writings and thus on a highly authoritative codification of memory. To belong to such a religion calls for this codified memory to be accepted and taken to heart. Evidently, the importance of the codification and canonization of memory is linked to the structure of the revelation. All revealed knowledge is by definition knowledge of something outside the world. It was what Stefan George called "air from other planets." It does not arise from natural evidence or experience in this world. The senses can neither confirm nor increase this knowledge. God is invisible—that is the central message. No one has ever seen God, it is claimed by St. John, and Paul says, "For we walk by faith, not by sight" (2 Cor. 5:7). Faith, *pistis* in Greek and *emunah* in Hebrew, is just another word for memory, for everything depends on not forgetting what was said to their forefathers and to trust in their testimony. As early as Deuteronomy it is impressed upon the Israelites that "you heard the sound of words, but saw no form" (Deut. 4:12). Revelation is the opposite of natural evidence. The absence of natural evidence to the senses is replaced by memory as an inner, spiritual representation. Freud, too, perceives in this the decisive advance in "spiritual progress."

3. Repression and Trauma

Memory is much concerned with learning, taking to heart, and the conscious process of passing knowledge on to others, but it has little to do with trauma and repression. Nevertheless, repression is referred to in the Bible. I have already pointed out that the prophets depict Yahweh's uniqueness as a truth that has been forgotten. The people have adopted the customs of Canaan and forgotten their extraterritorial obligations. The peculiar delay between the revelation of monotheism and its implementation that Freud interpreted as a latency phase is explained in the Bible as a guilt-laden forgetting that arises from adapting to the customs of the country. There is, however, one story that can be interpreted as an allegory of cultural repression. In 2 Kings 22–23, we learn how during building work in the temple a Book of the Covenant is discovered that turns out to be a work of Moses, in which all the laws are set out that the people should observe in their lives in the land. This discovery plunges the king and the people into the deepest despair. For it is evident that all these laws have been violated and forgotten, and that the most terrible punishments have now become inevitable as the expression of God's anger. In this book we can generally recognize Deuteronomy, that is, the only one of the Five Books of Moses that is dedicated to the themes of remembering and forgetting. We can see that this book not only develops an elaborate set of cultural memory techniques to ensure that the Law and the historical events associated with the revelation of the Law are handed down to future generations and are not forgotten, but also that such forgetting would entail the most terrible punishments. The extremely sadistic account of these punishments fills chapter 28 of Deuteronomy, a chapter which revels in the depiction of the most frightful disasters. This chapter is one long "Death Fugue," an anticipation of Auschwitz. We might call it a traumatized text. Underlying it is the annihilation of the Northern Kingdom by the Assyrians, the destruction of Jerusalem by the Babylonians, and the Babylonian captivity. The entire "deuteronomistic historiography" is the attempt to digest this catastrophe and to come to terms with the guilt that had been incurred. The guilt consists in having forgotten the extraterritorial law and in assimilation to the customs of the country, above all, in the worship of its gods. The biblical texts, then, are concerned not just with remembering and forgetting, but also with guilt and trauma, in other words, with all the themes of the Freudian analysis.

Here the Second Commandment is revealed as the Commandment of Commandments: Thou shalt not make unto thee a graven image (Deut. 5:5). For whoever makes a graven image offends against the First Commandment: Thou shalt have none other gods before me. Every image is a different god. For God is invisible and incapable of being depicted. But a different god is a false god, a god who may not be worshipped under any circumstances. The First and Second Commandments introduce a new distinction into religion, one that was entirely alien to all traditional religions: the distinction between "true" and "false." With this distinction a new concept of guilt comes into being and hence too of trauma. Traditional religions are based on a distinction between sacred and profane, or clean and unclean. Guilt here is a form of uncleanliness that can be washed away by rites of atonement. The distinction between true and false leads to the conception of a guilt that cannot be atoned for. This applies above all to idolatry, the sin against the Second Commandment. This is the subject of the story of the Golden Calf. The people had no intention of turning to other gods when they demanded an image from Aaron. They wanted an image of God they could follow, as a substitute for Moses who had remained on Sinai and whom they believed dead. They wanted to replace God's representative with a representation. That was their sin. The true God, however, cannot be represented. Every attempt at a representation necessarily becomes a lie, a false god.

Following this, God wished to destroy the entire nation, but Moses was able to dissuade Him, and to appease Him with the execution of three thousand people. Even so, the Golden Calf encodes a deeply traumatic experience connected with the prohibition on graven images. We encounter here a trauma that does not indeed find a direct expression in the Bible, but only an oblique one. However, it emerges very clearly in non-biblical texts, the texts of the opposing side. The prohibition encodes an iconoclastic impulse which we might even call a theoclastic thrust. That is the mark of all religions founded upon revelation. They all seek to replace older traditions which they reject as lies, paganism, superstition, and ignorance. That is the meaning of the distinction they introduce between true and false. By the light of the revealed truth everything that already existed and was different is repudiated as darkness and falsehood. The distinction between true and false implies the violent destruction of all traditional conceptions of the divine.

Nothing could have been further from the thoughts of a traditional religion than the fear of worshipping false gods. Quite the reverse, its entire concern was with the danger of ignoring an important deity. The new religions based on revelation are in many respects the exact opposite of traditional, primal, totemistic religions. Their elaborate techniques for remembering, with the help of which the counterfactual truth was to be established in the memory of the faithful, imply at the same time that the ancient traditions which are now dismissed as paganism are to be forgotten. The memory of the monotheistic truth requires that the polytheistic untruth must be forgotten. The imperative "Remember!" implies the opposite imperative "Forget!" However, it is not possible to forget as easily as it is to remember. The imperative "Forget!" is paradoxical. This paradox contains the seeds of anxiety, guilt, and the trauma of monotheism.

The assumption that gods can be false encounters serious resistance in the human psyche. It is not so easy for human beings to renounce gods who have been demoted to false idols. For such gods have the advantage and the seductive attractions that they seem to be based on the evidence of our senses, something that is absent from a revealed truth. We are concerned here with the gods of this world, or the divinity of the world, which is radically stripped of its magical nature by monotheistic religion. The texts of the Bible are full of this resistance to monotheism. Freud attributes this resistance to the ambivalence of the relation to the father.

Ambivalence is an essential part of the relation to the father: in the course of time the hostility which had once driven the sons into killing their admired and dreaded father could not fail to make itself felt. There was no place in the framework of the religion of Moses for a direct expression of the murderous hatred of the father. All that could come to light was a mighty reaction against it—a sense of guilt on account of that hostility, a bad conscience for having sinned against God and for not ceasing to sin.[11]

"A sense of guilt on account of that hostility, a bad conscience for having sinned against God and for not ceasing to sin"—it would be difficult to find a more apposite description of the spirit of the biblical texts, and of Deuteronomy and the history it contains, in particular. And the "murderous hatred of the father" also finds direct expression in the texts. This hatred is aimed not at the invisible god himself, but at his prophets. The Bible is indeed silent on the question of the murder of Moses. But Moses comes close to being stoned on several occasions. "And Moses cried unto the Lord, saying, What shall I do unto this people? They are almost ready to stone me" (Exod. 17:4). "But all the congregation bade stone them [Moses and Aaron] with stones." (Num. 14:10). What happens to Moses and Aaron also happens to many other prophets in Israel, right down to John the Baptist and Jesus, who really are killed. The "violent fate of the prophets" is a recurrent motif of the biblical texts.[12] The crucial text is Isaiah 53, which depicts the sufferings of the servant of God. Freud's theory that Moses was murdered is superfluous. It is all there in plain language.

The revealed truth is not only so hard to *remember* because it is opposed to the evidence and finds no confirmation in the context of the present. It is also hard to *bear* because it renders human beings homeless in the disenchanted world. John the Evangelist has found the most succinct formula for the resistance of the world to revelation: "The light shineth in the darkness; and the darkness apprehended it not" (John 1:5).

The crucial point here seems to me to lie in the completely new emphasis that the texts place on the inner understanding of revelation, on human inwardness. This turns religion into a psychodrama. The distinction between true and false separates not just Jews and pagans, or Christians and pagans, or Muslims and unbelievers, but cuts straight through the human heart that only now becomes the theater of an authentic religious dynamic. Revealed religion becomes a "matter of the heart" in a quite new and emphatic sense. It is enough to refer to the "Shema," for it is no accident that this prayer establishes a very close link between the uniqueness of God and the intensity of an inner understanding: "Hear, O Israel, the Lord our God, the Lord is One. And thou shalt love the Lord thy God, with all thy heart and with all thy soul and with all thy might. And these words, which I command thee this day, shall be upon thy heart" (Deut. 6:4–6). At the same time as revelation appears, "sin" emerges too, as the consciousness of the failure to achieve this inner comprehension and of having succumbed to the temptation of worshipping false gods.

The trauma of monotheism is twofold. On the one hand, it is grounded in the duty, which is never quite fulfilled, to forget one's pagan faith, which keeps surfacing (since, after all, this involves the temptation to feel at home in the world as it is). On the other hand, it is based on the destruction of the gods, who are excoriated as idols, on the deicidal power of the Mosaic distinction. I would like to return here to Freud's idea of a causal link between the monotheism of Akhenaten and Moses. It was undoubtedly Akhenaten, and not Moses, who was the first to introduce the distinction between true and false in religion, and to declare that all the gods of traditional religion were false. In this respect, Akhenaten's and Moses' distinctions are identical. What could be more obvious than to declare Moses the disciple of Akhenaten? We might almost imagine that the two are identical. For Akhenaten is a historical figure who was forgotten and disappeared from the tradition. Moses, in contrast, is a figure who belongs in the tradition, even though there are no historical traces that he existed. The two neatly complement each other. Moreover, Akhenaten was subject to the very fate that Freud attributed to Moses: he was repressed and forgotten, and this repression has an undeniably traumatic aspect. This trauma has nothing to do with parricide or the violent fate of the prophets, but with the trauma of deicide. Akhenaten's persecution of the old gods was felt to be an unthinkably terrible crime, leading to the obliteration of his memory and the destruction of all the visible traces of his heresy. In fact it was not until the nineteenth century that Akhenaten was rediscovered by scholars.

But what is the real connection between Akhenaten and Moses? Here, too, we must attempt to free ourselves from the archaeological perspective that admits only causal connections and is always on the lookout for the discovery of factual causes. There is no causal link between Akhenaten and Moses, any more than there is between the religion of Amarna and biblical monotheism. However, if we substitute the concept of emerging for that of causality, a link can be discerned. This link appears in the course of the process of remembering and its dynamic. The forgotten Akhenaten and the gigantic figure of the arch-prophet Moses, the founder of the norms of monotheism, who is either semifictitious or at best a figure who appeared only in the course of tradition, had become merged into one single being even in antiquity.

For in Egypt Akhenaten was not forgotten, he was repressed. Here, we do in fact find the Freudian model of latency and repression. The magnitude of his deicidal offense had a traumatic impact, and continued to preoccupy the imagination of the people long after the king's name and the historical circumstances of his deeds had been forgotten. The trauma of deicide was combined retrospectively with every conceivable historical experience and had a crucial impact on people's perception of the present. The repressed, traumatic experience of the Amarna religion and the heretical king Akhenaten lived on in the terrifying vision of the offender against God, and survived right down to the Hellenistic period. This hostile image was combined with that of the Hyksos, the Assyrians, the Persians, and finally the Jews. In this way, in the course of the history of the memory, or repression, of monotheistic trauma in Egypt, the figures of Akhenaten and Moses gradually merged.

The earliest author to establish this connection was Manetho, an Egyptian priest of the early third century B.C., whose work on Egyptian culture and history has been lost, two lengthy excerpts from it having survived in Josephus Flavius. Manetho tells us about an Egyptian priest called Osarsiph who made himself the leader of a group of lepers at the time of Amenhotep III (that is, the father of Akhenaten, who had been deleted from the lists of kings). The king had interned these lepers in concentration camps and engaged them in forced labor. He had learned from an oracle that the lepers would pollute the land and so prevent King Amenhotep from seeing the gods. Osarsiph entered into negotiations with the king and obtained his permission for the lepers to leave and move to the old Hyksos city of Avaris in the Eastern Delta. There he organized his lepers into a colony and gave them laws. The first commandment was: the gods should not be worshipped. According to the second, it was forbidden to eat sacred animals and to ignore other eating taboos. In the third, it was forbidden to mix with outsiders. Finally, it is stated, Osarsiph assumed the name of Moses. In this way, the repressed heretical king and Jewish archprophet come together in Manetho's narrative.

Manetho sheds light on the distinction between true and false as seen from the other side, from the side of the pagans. The commandment not to worship other gods becomes in his account the commandment not to worship any gods at all. The prohibition on graven images becomes the commandment to destroy the images and slaughter the sacred animals. The extraterritorial nature of the Law is turned into a prohibition on mixing with outsiders. Above all, what we find here, for the first time, is the language of disease. From the standpoint of traditional religion, with its foundations in the dichotomy of clean and unclean, the new religion, with its destruction of the gods and of images, appears to be the worst form of uncleanness, of leprosy. The fathers of the Church take over this language later and apply it to pagans and idolators. Eusebius speaks of the "Egyptian disease," Theodoret of the "Greek disease." In their eyes, idolatry is a disease, an addiction even, for which the Law should act as withdrawal treatment. In Freud's day it was Jewish diseases that preoccupied the medical imagination. It was believed that certain illnesses, particularly syphilis and insanity, were endemic among Jews.[13] Freud's psychoanalysis of religion must be seen not least as an attempt to rationalize such fixed ideas and to provide them with a universal, anthropological foundation, for example in the Oedipus complex. What is articulated in the language of disease, in particular the metaphor of addiction, is the conscious knowledge of the traumatic aspects of monotheistic religion with its distinction between true and false. Above all, however, it appears that Egyptian hostility to Jews is in fact based on a repression, that is, a collective psychic disturbance. In the encounter with Jewish monotheism the Egyptians experienced a return of the repressed that they reacted to with violent defense mechanisms. In his *Contra Apionem*, Josephus Flavius documented all the manifestations of this Egyptian hostility to Judaism. In this way, as well as through other sources, such as Tacitus and Orosius, who also depict the legend of the lepers as the founding story of Israel, this hostility to Judaism was handed down to the West. Freud was quite right to make anti-Semitism the object of a psychohistorical analysis. All that is needed is to turn his work around and point it in the opposite direction. The path to knowledge leads not from the archives back into the preliterate, and even prelinguistic prehistory of mankind, but instead, the dynamics of memory and repression can be discovered in the archives themselves.

Freud's theory of religion has the indisputable merit of having drawn attention to the psychohistorical dimension of the history of religion, to the central role played by forgetting, remembering, and repression, as well as by both trauma and guilt. By interpreting monotheism as a religion of the fathers, its history could be portrayed as the enactment of an Oedipal conflict. If we return to the biblical texts and view them in the light of these arguments, we are surprised to discover that they say more or less the same thing. No hermeneutics of distrust is called for to shed light on these themes by reading "against the grain" in order to penetrate the hidden depths of what has been repressed. We can just as well read them "with the grain." More important and more productive than a depth analysis, is, so it appears to me, an analysis of the archives of our cultural memory, at any rate as far as the history of religion and culture is concerned. How did mankind live with these texts, how have they influenced and shaped mankind's soul, what conflicts have they encoded and even generated? The antagonistic energy, the polemical potential, the psychometric force of monotheistic religion and its texts are far from having been exhaustively studied. Freud's diagnosis went to the heart of the matter, but his method missed the mark because he failed to take the texts seriously enough, and in this instance he failed to listen to his patients attentively enough. His passion for archaeology blinded him to what lay on the surface. The trauma of monotheism is grounded not in the Oedipal deep structure of the human psyche, but in the Mosaic distinction between true and false. Perhaps Freud's mistake lay simply in his insistence on approaching the biblical text as if it were a heap of ruins, whereas in reality it was an inhabited city, and in tackling it with "picks, shovels, and spades," when he would have been better advised to take a careful look around in the crypts and book stacks.

Five Stages on the Road to the Canon:
Tradition and Written Culture in
Ancient Isreal and Early Judaism

1. Two Preliminary Remarks

a. The Introduction of Writing

The concept of tradition has two meanings. If, like Maurice Halb-wachs, we look at it from the standpoint of memory, it appears to us as the antithesis of what is lived, embodied, and communicated, and as the summation of the knowledge laid out in symbolic forms and administered by institutions.[1] If, however, we consider it from the standpoint of writing, as in the Jewish and Catholic traditions, it appears as the antithesis of what has been fixed in writing and as the quintessence of knowledge bound to and incarnate in living agents. The concept of tradition fluctuates between these two extremes of memory and writing. In contrast to memory, it appears as social, normative knowledge, if not necessarily fully articulated in language; in contrast to writing, it appears as knowledge that is to a great extent implicit, extralinguistic, nonwritten, and transmitted through a mimetic process of showing and imitating. Admittedly, written material forms part of tradition, but tradition goes far beyond its written component. To exaggerate only slightly, we might say that living, embodied memory and communication find their death in tradition, and living, embodied tradition finds its death in the normative written word.

Reflections on memory and tradition must foreground the boundary between knowledge that is lived and knowledge that is formulated, between the individual and the cultural, the implicit and the explicit. In this chapter on tradition and written culture, on the other hand, I am concerned with the other boundary: the one between tradition in its implicit, oral aspects, on the one hand, and the explicit, normative, written word, on the other. Looked at in this way, tradition and writing appear as antitheses, or as complementarities. Traditions are normally not written. Where they are, it points to a break in tradition, or at the very least, a crisis. The tendency toward the use of writing is not necessarily the result of an internal logical development. The natural path of tradition leads not to writing, but to habit, not to explication, but to a process of becoming implicit, to habitualization and a making unconscious.[2] The impetus to introduce writing must come from outside, and when it comes it alters the tradition. It is sensible, therefore, to inquire into the nature of such external stimuli. I shall try to make such an inquiry in the case of Israel and propose five different stimuli that have led not just to writing, but beyond writing to the canonization of the tradition.

b. Canonization

Canonization is a special form of writing. Texts are not merely written down: their authority is increased. This increase in authority refers both to their shape (their wording) and their status, which is closely bound up with it. Authority means that everything the text says possesses absolutely normative validity, and whatever lays claim to normative validity must be able to prove itself to be the meaning of that text. This implies that the text can be neither continued nor supplemented by further texts. This closure conditions its shape, the literal wording of which must now be fixed. We are dealing here with a genuinely final version. The normative character of the text, its authority and binding status, are functions exclusively of this final version, and not of any earlier or primal versions. Within this canonic final version, there are no degrees of authority, no sentences that are of greater or lesser importance, no primary and secondary components. Once it has reached its final state, the historical development of the text is forgotten.

The process of canonization inverts the normal fate of written and copied texts. For the normal path is downhill: the history of texts is the history of decadence. This is why all philologists are at pains to arrive at the oldest and most fundamental version, the archetype. The source of meaning is the author's intention, and the closer a version comes to that intention, the more meaningful it is. Textual criticism works from the latest form to the primeval form. The critique of a canon works in the opposite direction: it uncovers the forces that motivate the development, growth, coming together, and sanctification of the texts. Here we are interested not in the original authors and their intentions, but the editors and especially the last editors who bring the whole corpus together into a canon.[3] Theologically, we can think of canonization as an inspired process, a revelation that unfolds and perfects itself over time, and that, according to the rabbis, continues in the shape of the oral Torah to modify the interpretation of the text.[4] In what follows, however, I wish to speak not as a theologian, but as a historian, and to throw light on the process of canonization from that angle. Taking Israel as an example, I wish to single out five tendencies or stimuli to canonization that occur partly in other cultures as well, but are in some ways specific to the ancient Israelite or early Jewish situation.

2. Five Stimuli of Canonization

a. The Excarnation of Laws and the Invention of a Normative Past

The first step from tradition to writing, and beyond that to the canon, takes place in the context of the codification of laws. I link it tentatively to the end of the seventh century, the age of King Josiah. This codification is generally regarded as nothing much more than the adoption of Mesopotamian forms of written law that go back to the third millennium.[5] This analysis seems mistaken to me. In Mesopotamia, we are concerned with law books [*Rechtsbücher*]; the Torah, in contrast, is a book of statutes [*Gesetzbuch*]. I would describe this distinction, which is fundamental, as follows.[6]

A book of laws is a genre of the literature of bureaucratic knowledge that was uniquely developed in Mesopotamia. A book of laws, however, is not a legal code, a statute book: it has no prescriptive, absolutely binding character. We are concerned here with two quite different types of writing.[7] The first type involves storage, in the sense of an extension and exteriorization of memory;[8] the second is the authoritative publication in the sense of an extension and "excarnation"—I have borrowed this term from Aleida Assmann—of a decree by a supreme authority (legislative or juridical).[9] In the one case writing supports memory, in the other it supports the voice. In the first case a law is written down because it is valid (and, as a written text, it outlasts the period of its validity, whereas otherwise the memory of it would vanish when its period of validity expires); in the second, a law is valid because it is written down. The first function could be called "informative"; it serves to stabilize and communicate relevant juridical knowledge. The other function, in contrast, could be called "performative"; here, through the medium of writing, a linguistic act is performed.[10] A legal code, as the collection of currently valid laws, belongs in the category of performative writing; it produces the substance of a legal system which it describes. A book of laws, in contrast, contains the tradition of knowledge that is necessary for the formulation of laws and legal judgments, but does not reproduce those laws and judgments in a way that is binding. It provides assistance, but no prescriptive rules for arriving at a judgment. The legitimacy of the laws does not arise from a codified tradition, but from the authority of the king who is in power at a particular time. The laws must always be reaffirmed or modified by the king. Writing alone endows them with neither legitimacy nor authority. The laws are conditioned absolutely by their context; they have no need of timeless codification; what they need is a living personification so that they can be constantly renewed and adjusted to changing historical circumstances. That living personification of the law is the king, the *nomos empsychos*, as it was termed in Hellenistic political theory. That theory had already reacted to written codes, and in this confrontation it was the first to identify and conceptualize a far more ancient principle.[11]

Where there is a king, one of whose main duties is to issue laws and put them into effect, no legal code is required: that would improperly restrict the king's own legislative competence. In a sense, then, a legal code may be said to replace the king. And that, precisely, is the point. The Torah replaces the ancient Oriental law-making king. What is put into writing is not juridical knowledge, but the royal decree which on the basis of the king's claim to authority is codified as the word of God. This ensures independence from a king. For very good reasons this step has no parallel in the ancient Oriental written cultures, although there is something similar in the city-states of archaic Greece, particularly in Crete, as well as in the southern Italian colonies.[12]

The Torah is able to replace the king because it incorporates two authorities that in the Oriental law-making monarchies are embodied in the king: the legislative authority and time or history. It must be remembered that in the ancient Orient and also in Egypt time is primarily the time of kings. It is counted by the years of a king's reign, and the counting starts over with every king. The list of kings is the only way to orient oneself in time. From the creation of the world to the present day, time is filled with the sequence of kings and their deeds. Periods of interregnum are noted in the Egyptian list of kings as "empty years," in which time is said to be idle. Time works or passes only when there is a king to fill it with his actions, and that means above all law and justice. This explains why the Torah must, if it is to replace the monarchy, take over the authority to create laws (and it achieves this, as is well known, by causing God to appear as law giver) and history. It achieves the latter by starting with the Creation, and instead of a list of kings, it provides a genealogy, the sequence of generations from Adam to Moses. History frames, or rather "determines," the law. What determines the law is what I call the "normative past." Without that past the law would lose all plausibility. However, God does not demand blind obedience, any more than the Oriental legal culture had done. The law wishes to be understood and to be complied with on the basis of insight. This explains why the question "Why?" is answered with the words: "Because you were a slave in Egypt." The exodus from Egypt constitutes the normative past and founding history that frames and determines the law, so that it may unfold its authority once and for all, out of time and history, simply by virtue of its written character, *sola scriptura*. In this respect the Torah goes further not just than the Mesopotamian law books, but also than all subsequent legal codes. In this sense it is more than a legal code. In the Torah the law is not just excarnated; it is also recontextualized since it is inserted into the determining framework of a history, in other words, a framework that gives it meaning. Its embodiment in a king is replaced by its anchoring in a history. The obedience the Torah requires is, as I have said, no blind obedience, but one that is illumined by the memory of this history. To observe the laws and remember the history are one and the same thing—*zakhor ve shamor be dibbur echad*, as it is put in the Jewish Sabbath song *Lekha dodi* ["Come, My Beloved"].

If we wish to establish a connection between this beginning and a historical situation, then we can find a somewhat conservative entrée in 2 Kings 22 ff., the age of King Josiah. Here we are told how in the course of restoration works a "Book of the Law" of Moses was found that had been completely forgotten, but that was now turned into the foundation of a revolution in cult and culture—the "Josiah reform." In this book emerging from oblivion we can recognize Deuteronomy. Of course, the writing down of the texts of the law was spread over a much lengthier period of Israelite history.[13] Josiah's reign signifies here merely a breakthrough and a climax. Here the laws and normative traditions are not simply collected, but comprehensively codified and put into effect, and that was done, moreover, with considerable revolutionary force.[14] Josiah's reform was political as well as cultic: it was a revolutionary, national liberation movement whose semantics were typical of such movements in the sense that it combined the memory of a forgotten tradition of one's own with an exclusion of outsiders that was justified by reference to that memory. Under Josiah the Kingdom of Judah was able to throw off the Assyrian yoke before succumbing subsequently to a far harsher Babylonian overlordship. The turning point of Josiah's reign occurred in this brief moment of respite, autonomy, and memory. We could, of course, put the entire argument in a much bolder way and interpret the episode as a reconstruction inspired by the exile situation, in which there was no longer any king to personify the law and put it into effect. Today, this interpretation seems to be gaining the upper hand among Old Testament scholars.

The monarchy is not abolished in Deuteronomy, but it is domesticated and reined in by religiously based norms that have always been associated with the name of Moses and which now—around 622 or after 587—were codified, perhaps for the first time, in a comprehensive book. This was the first step toward forming a canon.

b. The Excarnation of Tradition

The second step followed the first directly, but has no logical connection with it. It is not part of any developmental trend in the sense that

if you make a start with something you have to go through with it. It arises simply from the contingent nature of historical events. I place it in the
sixth century B.C., the period of the Babylonian captivity.

If we make use here of the concept of "excarnation" that Aleida Assmann introduced,[15] and apply it to "tradition," we shall understand tradition as the lived knowledge that is embodied in living subjects and that is
passed on in active association with others, through teaching and, above all,
through a nonverbal process of showing and imitating, a form of knowledge that is largely self-evident and that has become unconscious and implicit. The typical situation in which such knowledge is dredged up out of
its implicit, nonverbal status and oral instruction and then articulated in
writing is the break with tradition that occurs when the chain of showing
and imitating is broken and oral communication is interrupted. In such
situations we find not only that new texts emerge, but also that already
existing texts are given an enhanced normative value. Where the contact
with living models is broken, people turn to the texts in their search for
guidance. That is the situation during the Babylonian exile and the Diaspora. Many variants of what is regarded today as fundamentalism arose
from the ruptures in the tradition caused by the Second World War, the
Holocaust, and colonialism.

The written tradition cannot simply be experienced, it has to be
studied. The deportation into Babylonian exile led to the disappearance of
the models provided by older generations that had previously been taken
for granted. The normative tradition has to be put into writing because it
can no longer be followed intuitively. The normative status of the texts has
to be scrutinized and established so that people can have something they
can rely upon. Writing about the situation between the two world wars,
Helmut Lethen has observed:

In such disorganized times, when the fabric of tradition disintegrates, and morality loses its persuasive force, codes of conduct are required that enable people
to distinguish between what belongs to them and to others, between inside and
outside. They make it possible to distinguish zones in which people can feel confidence from those where they feel distrust, and help them to establish their identity.[16]

Breaks in a tradition bring shifts in the pattern of writing in their train.
Things were no different in the Egypt of the waning third millennium, af-

ter the collapse of the Old Kingdom [ca. 2180 B.C.]. The First Intermediate period brought with it not just a break with tradition, but also a shift in the pattern of writing that impinged on the norms of social life in the first instance. Now that the horizon of confidence had collapsed it had to be explicitly colonized and delimited by the written word.[17] That implied an "excarnation" of the tradition, in the sense that a previously implicit body of knowledge was now codified and made explicit. On the other hand, everything depends on being able to re-incarnate this exteriorized and written knowledge once again by learning it by heart and internalizing it. Deuteronomy, in particular, and related bodies of text place great emphasis on reconverting writing into lived knowledge. The words of the Torah shall "not depart out of thy mouth, but thou shalt meditate therein day and night," they shall "be upon thy heart," "thou shalt teach them diligently to thy children," and "talk of them when thou sittest in thine house, and when thou walkest by the way."[18]

c. A Canon from Above: The "Imperial Authorization" of Laws in Persia

The third step falls in the Persian period [from 525 to 404 B.C.]. The Persian empire consolidated its rule in the provinces by assuming the role of advocate and guardian of the local tradition, the *patrioi nomoi*.[19] In Egypt a commission was set up to give an account of the *former system of law that had prevailed right down to when Akhmose II (Amasis) was forty-four years of age*.[20] A certain Udjahorresnet was commissioned to restore the *houses of life*, that is to say, the scriptoria attached to the temples, the most important institutions entrusted with guarding the tradition.[21] However, the impulse to collect and codify went far beyond the legal sphere. The temple that Darius I built at Khargah Oasis can be regarded as the first representative of a new type of temple, one whose decoration is connected not just with cult worship, but also with important bodies of knowledge. We can think of it as the symbolic expression of a fencing-in and consolidation of tradition and identity in Egypt.[22] What the period of Persian domination meant for Egypt was a return to the roots and a codification of tradition.

The Jewish counterpart to the Egyptian Udjahorresnet is Ezra the scribe, a member of the Israelite priestly aristocracy who had been left behind in Babylon and who was sent into the satrapy of Transeuphratene around 400 B.C. with a similar commission: "Forasmuch as thou art sent of the king and his seven counsellors, to inquire concerning Judah and Jerusalem according to the law of thy God which is in thine hand."[23] In contrast to the first two steps, which really involve a process of canonization from below—in the first place, against the monarchy, in the second, against the hegemony of Babylonian culture—what we have here is a process of canonization from above. Ezra and his statute book, using writing to preserve the normative traditions of Israel, marked a further stage along the road of the canonization of the Hebrew Bible.[24] We now see the introduction of a further factor over and above the canonized text, something that can be identified as the necessary corollary to every canon formation: a culture of interpretation. At the water gate of Jerusalem, as Nehemiah reports in chapter 8, Ezra not only reads out the entire Torah to the people, he also interprets it section by section. With this, as the Jewish historian Yosef Hayim Yerushalmi expresses it, we witness the birth not only of the scripture, but also of exegesis.[25] "And Ezra opened the book in the sight of all the people . . . and when he opened it, all the people stood up. . . . And they read in the book, in the law of God, distinctly; and they gave the sense, so that they understood the reading" (Neh. 8:5, 8). The commentary returns the timeless text to the current time. We see a repetition here, on another plane, of what we found in connection with the relation between law and history. The law, excarnated from its living personification in whoever happened to be king, stands in need of an explanatory recontextualization. This is brought about by the narrative of the flight from Egypt, together with its prehistory, going right back to the Creation. Only within this determining framework, that is to say, a framework which endows it with meaning, can the law stand on its own and serve as a timeless, transhistorical guide. But now that this link between law and history becomes part of the canon itself, in other words, now that it is elevated into an absolutely authoritative text, there arises the further need for yet another framework, one that relates to the overall text as history relates to the law within the text. This new framework recontextualizes the overall text for the changing face of the present; it translates the text into historical values and orientations. This framework is the commentary.

Under Ezra's guidance the statute book is expanded into a canon.

The prerequisite of the canon is the end of prophecy.[26] There is no longer any room for prophecy in the depoliticized space of the Province of Judah, which had become part of the satrapy of Transeuphratene. The prophets speak to king and people in the name of Yahweh; now that even the satrap is far away, how much further is the king. The prophet's place is now taken by the scholar who codifies, canonizes, and interprets the tradition. Before the Exile, monotheistic religion, together with its political theology of the People of God in a Covenant with God, had established itself as a counterculture, or what Norbert Lohfink terms a "contrasting society"; now it becomes an "internal culture" within the larger framework of the Persian empire.[27] It is concerned with purity of life, teaching, and interpretation, while delegating the management of worldly affairs to the Persian occupying power.

The process of depoliticizing public life begins to spread generally during the Persian period. In Egypt and Babylon we can witness the "clericalization" of culture, the transition from the scribe who is an official to the priestly scribe as the representative of culture, and in Israel, the transition from prophet to scholar. But only in Israel was religion able to crystallize into a definite and distinctive alternative method of establishing a collective identity. Only here had a "nation" emerged that was able to separate itself from the outside world and create an internal community entirely independently of political and territorial ties, namely, simply through its adherence to "the Law and the prophets."[28]

And yet, even this form of text-related community has parallels in the ancient world. But with this comment we leave the framework of normative texts in the narrower sense and enter a realm of far more comprehensive codifications, whereby it is no longer the statute book that forms the foundation of a community, but a library. This development constitutes the fourth step on the road to the canon. It is connected with the origin of communities that see themselves as the guardians of specific written traditions and their interpretations.

d. Text Communities and Core Libraries

The historian Brian Stock has shown that the heretical movements of the Middle Ages are based on highly authoritative texts whose survival and/or interpretation was peculiar to them. They could only justify their breach with official tradition if they could point to a text whose authority and normative claims could be shown to be superior to all other traditional and institutional claims. Dissidence presupposes literalness. For this reason Brian Stock has coined the term *textual communities* to describe movements of this kind.[29] Many of the features of these movements in the eleventh and twelfth centuries can be found in the community of Qumran and in many similar groups, such as Orphists, Pythagoreans, Gnostics, early Christians, Hermeticists, and so on, who typically formed associations in the Hellenistic period and late antiquity on the basis of a core stock of normative literature.[30] The characteristics of a textual community are, on the one hand, the use of a basic text to define identity, and, on the other hand, the structure of authority and leadership that arises from the ability to handle texts. Philological and political competence come together here. Leadership falls to the person who possesses the most comprehensive knowledge and the most illuminating interpretation of the texts.

The discoveries at Qumran and Nag Hammadi give us an insight into the vestiges of the libraries that were used as a foundation by such textual communities. Despite their fragmentary condition they enable us to infer that, unlike modern libraries, they did not aim at the greatest possible variety and completeness. Instead, they confined themselves to the literature that the community deemed authoritative. This idea of a working library is something they shared with what we know of late-Egyptian temple libraries, in contrast, for instance to the neo-Assyrian palace libraries. The latter were in fact designed with variety, abundance, and comprehensiveness in mind. It was the idea of a treasure house transferred to the world of books. This type of library tradition could be found in the library of Alexandria and survives in the modern institution of national, state, regional, and university libraries. The Egyptian temple libraries, in contrast, contained only what was important and necessary.[31] Clement of Alexandria has left us a description of such a library. He speaks of forty-two indispensable (*pany anankaiai*) books that formed the basic stock of a temple library and that were all supposed to have been written by Thoth-Hermes. The procession that Clement describes belongs to the typical "intellectual rituals" (Bernhard Lang).[32] The arrangement of these forty-two canons in different sections emerges from the order in which the various priests leave the temple in solemn procession, each bearing the insignia of his rank and his specific competence.[33]

For the Egyptians pursue a philosophy of their own. This is principally shown by their sacred ceremonial. For, first advances the Singer, bearing some one of the symbols of music. For they say that he must learn two of the books of Hermes, the one of which contains the hymns of the gods, the second the regulations for the king's life.

And after the Singer advances the Astrologer, with a horologe in his hand, and a palm, the symbols of astrology. He must have the astrological books of Hermes, which are four in number, always in his mouth. Of these, one is about the order of the fixed stars that are visible, the second about the planets, the third about the conjunction and luminous appearances of the sun and the moon; and the rest respecting their risings.

Next in order advances the sacred Scribe, with wings on his head, and in his hand a book and rule, in which were writing ink and the reed, with which they write. And he must be acquainted with what are called hieroglyphics, and know about cosmography and geography, the position of the sun and the moon, and about the five planets; also the description of Egypt, and the chart of the Nile; and the description of the equipment of the priests and of the places consecrated to them, and about the measures and the things in use in the sacred rites.

Then the Stole-keeper follows those previously mentioned, with the cubit of justice and the cup for libations. He is acquainted with all books pertaining to education and those concerned with the slaughter of sacrificial animals. There are also ten books which relate to the honor paid by them to their gods, and containing the Egyptian worship; as that relating to sacrifices, first-fruits, hymns, prayers, processions, festivals, and the like.

And behind all walks the Prophet, with the water-vase carried openly in his arms; who is followed by those who carry the issue of loaves. He, as being governor of the temple, learns the ten so-called "hieratic" books; and they contain all about the laws, and the gods, and the whole of the training of the priests. For the Prophet is, among the Egyptians, also in charge of the distribution of the revenues.

There are then forty-two books of Hermes indispensably necessary; of which the six-and-thirty containing the whole philosophy of the Egyptians are learned by the forementioned personages; and the other six, which are medical, by the Pastophoroi (image-bearers)—treating of the structure of the body, and of diseases, and instruments, and medicines, and about the eyes, and the last about the diseases of women.[34]

We are concerned here with a connection between written culture and memory culture that is both peculiar to and typical of the world of the Orient. The books are not there to be read, but to be learned by heart and mastered. That applies with equal force in rabbinical Judaism down to the present day. The Egyptian priests introduced a division of labor for this that reflects the division of the forty-two books of the canon. The list is arranged in ascending order, so that we need to invert it. This means that the first and highest rung contains, as the Egyptian Torah, the ten "hieratic books" of the *Prophet*: they are concerned with laws, gods, and the entire panoply of priestly education.[35] In the second rank come the ten books mastered by the *Stole-keeper*, dealing with education and ritual sacrifice; they treat of wisdom and piety, sacrifices, first-fruits, hymns, prayers, processions, and festivals. The third rank is occupied by ten books of hieroglyphs that are mastered by the *Sacred Scribe* (the *Hierogrammateus*): about cosmography and geography, the description of Egypt and the Nile; the land owned by the temples, the building of temples, the provisioning and equipping of the temples. They are followed on the fourth rung by the four books on astrology that have been mastered by the *Astrologer* (*Horoskopos*). These are concerned with the order of the fixed stars, the positions of the sun, the moon, and the five planets, the conjunctions and phases of the sun and the moon, and the times of the sunrises. The lowest rung, the fifth, is occupied by the books that the *Singer* has mastered: one book with hymns to the gods and a second book with an account of the life of the king. The six medical books constitute an appendix outside the hierarchy.

This hierarchy is confirmed by the book catalogues of the temple libraries of Edfu and Tod that have been handed down, as well as by other finds.[36] The tendency to establish boundaries and an authoritative structure is evident in this arrangement, as well as in the sacred number of forty-two, which corresponds to the number of provinces in Egypt, just as in Judaea the number twenty-two or twenty-four corresponds to the number of letters in Hebrew or Aramaic. The forty-two provinces correspond also to the number of the limbs of Osiris, whom Seth murdered and whose limbs he scattered throughout Egypt. Every year, the parts of the body are brought together from all regions of the land in solemn processions and joined together in one body. In this way, the number forty-two is associated with the idea of Egypt as a sacred entity that is constantly being salvaged from the fragmentation of history and has to be joined together again. Everything arbitrary is excluded from the form and structure of the canon. The forty-two provinces or parts of the body, and the twenty-two or twenty-four letters, are symbols of totality; they might be thought of as universal formulas. By making a reality of a universal formula, the canon becomes the world in book form.[37]

The Hebrew Bible has all the characteristics of such a "highly necessary" working library. It is far closer to a library than to a book. In its final, canonical form it restricts itself to three sections: the Torah, the Prophets, and the Writings (in an anticlimactic sequence). We gain the impression that with the Hebrew Bible the library of one textual community has prevailed over the libraries of other textual communities. These textual communities can be pictured according to the traditional groupings, such as Sadducees, Pharisees, Essenes, and so on.[38] Admittedly, the original size of the library in Qumran and the one in Tebtunis is estimated to amount to something of the order of one thousand scrolls,[39] which seems huge, but from the point of view of its contents it is pretty clear that this too is a working library as opposed to a general collection.

What the situation in the Middle Ages has in common with that of Hellenistic and Roman civilization is something we can perhaps sum up as the combination of text-ownership and dissidence. I would like to venture the assertion that without normative writings the development of such collective paths and alternative forms of life in a process of confrontation with the universal, public culture would not have been conceivable. Even the Egyptian temple becomes the husk for an alternative form of life in the Late Period, one characterized by asceticism and contemplation. The priests segregate themselves from the Hellenized culture, but also from other temples. Each temple develops its own doctrine, and even its own writing system. However, the contrasts and conflicts are much sharper still in Judaea. In ancient Judaism we have to distinguish between internal and external contrasts or conflicts. On the one side, we have the internal conflicts between such groups as the Sadducees, Pharisees, Essenes, and others. On the other side, there is the external conflict between Jews and Greeks (2 Macc. 2:21),[40] or between Israel and the nations, Jews and gentiles.[41] If Judaism as a whole constitutes itself as a textual community vis-à-vis the entire world, such a mobilization both of writing and identity has a prehistory in the centuries-long history of internal confrontations in which Israelite and early-Jewish textual communities stood opposed to each other.

A sharp distinction is drawn between ethnic identity and religious identity, between "Israel" and the *true* Israel. In this way the traditions of the exodus were inserted into a memory matrix that contained the record of all the historical confrontations, both with the ever-changing foreign cultures of the Assyrians, Babylonians, Greeks, Romans, and so on, and with the internal majority that was willing to become assimilated. And this record has remained legible down to this day.

e. The Anathematizing of Idolatry and the Process of Linguistic Narrowing

The fifth step, finally, has no parallel in the rest of the ancient world, but represents instead a polemical act of self-definition by means of which early Judaism separates itself from everything that is now constructed and excluded as "paganism," for the first time in the history of religion. I refer to the anathematization of idolatry. Admittedly, the Second Commandment and the story of the Golden Calf belong, if not to the most ancient part of the Bible linguistically, at least to its theological core, and it may be thought surprising that I bring this fifth step in at such a late stage. In my view, the Second Commandment has undergone a change of meaning. It was concerned originally less with the prohibition on images of God, than with the prohibition on images in general. What is criticized is not the inability of the images to convey the nature of the invisible, all-encompassing, and transcendent God, but the dangerous, seductive potency of the images themselves. No beings in this world, in the air, on the earth, or in the water should be portrayed because every association with images inevitably ends up in worship. This worship is no less inexorably extended to other gods and represents a betrayal, since Yahweh cannot be portrayed. In the course of the development from "mono-Yahwism," the exclusive worship of Yahweh, while simultaneously acknowledging the existence of other gods (since otherwise the commandment of fidelity to God would make no sense), to a pure monotheism that disputes the existence of other gods,[42] the term *idolatry* acquires a different meaning. The problem is no longer the difference between one's own god and other gods, or one's own religion and an alien religion, but the difference between truth and falsehood. The images become "idols," they are not the images "of" anything, but are simply the expression of deluded ideas. In the light of the distinction between truth and falsehood, which is now introduced into religion for the first time,[43] writing acquires the character of a codification of truth as opposed to which all other representations of the godly are dismissed as the expressions of lies, errors, or ignorance.

With this new concept of writing as a foundation, the link between the prohibition on images and the formation of the canon becomes clear. The argument is that the rejection of idolatry, that is, the expulsion of the divine from all iconic and other forms of incarnation in the world, with the exception of writing, was a decisive step in the formation of the canon. In order to understand this, we need to understand what idolatry does *not* mean. The ban on making images does not at all apply to the proliferating anthropomorphisms of the biblical texts that refer to God as bridegroom, as father and judge, shepherd and gardener. As long as the images are couched in language there is no objection to them.[44] Language is kosher. However, that means putting into language everything which among other peoples is spread across an entire spectrum of forms of expression. As fixed in writing, language replaces not just the king, but also the temple. The canon transforms the temple into writing. In the synagogues, as is obvious to everyone down to the present day, the scrolls of the Torah replace the cultic image that in ancient Egypt remains in a shrine until it is brought out to the public gaze. In the same way, the meditative, mystical act of "contemplation" is transferred from the cult image to the scripture. Meditative or contemplative reading removes the boundaries to the stock of meanings contained in the text and leads to an inexhaustible wealth of possible interpretations. Parallel to this "linguistic narrowing," there is a corresponding hermeneutic expansion that goes hand in hand with the "contemplative" immobilization of the reading gaze.[45]

Ultimately, writing, having been canonized, comes to replace art, public life, and tendentially, the world. The world as such is declared to be the object of idolatry and is thus discredited. The worship of the Creator must not be deflected toward his creation. The radically written nature of God's revelation corresponds to his radical existence outside the world. This step was reversed by Christianity with its theology of incarnation, thus clearing the way for a return to images, to the world, the book of nature, and ultimately—despite Augustine, whose ideas are still rather Jewish in this respect—to natural science. Looked at in this light, the prohibition on idolatry turns out to be the most radical of all excarnations.

Not until Hellenism and in late antiquity did idolatry develop into the central, defining, religious abomination in the eyes of Judaism. What had originally been a political category of apostasy, of whoring after strange gods, turned into the denigration of being at home in the world as such. The world deserves no interest, let alone worship. All worship belongs to God alone and all interest should be reserved for the scripture that codifies His will. Iconoclasm and acosmicism, that is, the rejection of the ancient cosmotheism, go together. Image worship is cosmos worship. Judaism replaces the pagan worship of the cosmos with scriptures that have been elevated into a canon.

Idolatry as a form of cultural loathing may perhaps best explain why Egypt, despite a number of parallels to Judaism in antiquity, went in a different direction, and finally perished. Egypt failed to take the step into writing because it clung to the symbolic presence of the divine in the world. Within the horizon of the manifold forms of cosmic and cultic representation, language is just one among many media representations of the nearness to God. In Egypt the divine did not retreat from the world, its images and rites and did not take refuge in writing. This is why it could not survive in writing, and why it perished along with its images and rites.

In the process of iconoclastic narrowing, in which everything was concentrated on writing, we see the continuation of a monopolistic feature that had earlier characterized Josiah's reforms. One god, one people, one book, one temple, one medium ("you heard the sound of words, but saw no form"). This path is presumably the most specifically Jewish path. But it has a parallel in the linguistic iconoclasm of early scholarship in the seventeenth century, in the attempts to expel all imagery from language and to turn language into an unambiguous medium of scientific communication. In modern art, too, an iconoclastic impulse is unmistakable. Like the Mosaic law, the path of modernism is marked by prohibitions, by the exclusion of imagery, tonality, mimesis, repetition, and other manifestations of "pagan" backwardness. Only by excluding other media and concentrating on writing does the canon become the vessel of revelation and thereby the foundation of our sense of belonging in another world; and only with this final step, which condemns as idolatry our being at home in the world, does the canon become the instrument of radical change in the world.

There may perhaps be a sixth step or path to the canon, which I shall just briefly point to. I am referring to the desire for permanence, the longing for eternity amid ephemeral phenomena and the transitory world. The canon creates an enduring space beyond time and history, a space from which history has been eliminated. It was the same longing that led the Egyptians to build the pyramids. However, Horace rightly placed his book of odes above the pyramids when he referred to it as a "monument," longer lasting than bronze and higher than Pharaoh's pyramids. The canon generates simultaneity. It creates the illusion of a timeless conversation in which we can communicate with Homer and Aristotle. The canon is anachronistic; it is a place with its own time, a "chronotope," to use Mikhail Bakhtin's term.[46] In the canonical chronotope we are all the contemporaries of Homer and Plato, Moses and Isaiah. I would like to illustrate this with an anecdote from the Talmud:

When Moses ascended on high he found the Holy One, blessed be He, engaged in affixing coronets (*taggin*—crownlike curlicues) to the letters. Said Moses, "Lord of the Universe, Who stays Thy hand?" (I.e., is there anything wanting in the Torah to make these additions necessary?) He answered, "There will arise a man, at the end of many generations, Akiba ben Joseph by name, who will expound upon each tittle heaps and heaps of laws." "Lord of the Universe," said Moses, "permit me to see him." He replied, "Turn thee round." Moses went and sat down behind eight rows (of Rabbi Akiba's disciples and listened to the discourses upon the law). Not being able to follow their arguments he was ill at ease, but when they came to a certain subject and the disciples said to the master, "Whence do you know it?" and the latter replied, "It is a law given to Moses at Sinai," he was comforted.[47]

Moses in the Bet Midrash of Rabbi Akiba: that is the Talmudic version of Nietzsche's dialogue of minds, in which time stands still and becomes spatial in a canonized tradition.

Remembering in Order to Belong:
Writing, Memory, and Identity

1. Writing as the Principle of Preservation and Change

In an interview, Thomas Macho, the sociologist of culture, once described cultures as islands in the ocean of oblivion. All culture is a struggle with oblivion. This idea is both fascinating and illuminating. Can we not regard this entire unceasing labor on forms of culture, this constant process of making visible and articulating, of presentation and preservation, as one long mnemotechnical project in which memory creates markers in the struggle against the furies of disappearance and forgetting, and builds stopping places in the river of change and disintegration?[1]

In the same context, the Austrian writer Robert Menasse, the author of two philosophical novels set in the recent past, has denied that memory and recollection are innate human characteristics, declaring them to be relatively late, secondary inventions. Were this not the case, he claims, we would be unable to explain the long duration of early history and prehistory. Fire had to be rediscovered hundreds of thousands of times, the wheel had to be reinvented hundreds of thousands of times, because those discoveries took place in a world without memory. Inventions could only be passed on to future generations with the invention of inventions, namely the invention of memory. And by this he means writing, initially in the general sense of a system of notation of the contents of memory, and then in the special sense of the notation of language itself.

Of course, in this dramatically overstated form, this is not quite true. And it is precisely early history and prehistory as an academic discipline, with its dating methods and periodizations, that can give us a better idea of the situation. The precondition for dating artifacts is that innovations must not be constantly forgotten and so become lost to us. As is well known, the opposite is the case. The development of artifacts follows the rules governing the formation of tradition. We are not confronted here with a diffuse mishmash, but by a distribution of events that enable us to perceive a clear temporal order, a "shape of time."[2] There are systems with common formal characteristics, "styles," that unfold in time and are distributed in space. There are also sequences of such styles that enable us to establish a periodization of cultural developments. All these things are the expressions of memory. Even the world of primitive tools can be understood as a culture of memory that is concerned to preserve improvements once they have been discovered, as well as the solutions to problems and other changes. In their formal consistency and the way they develop, such changes enable us to discern the foundations of a stock of knowledge that is passed down from one generation to the next, and gradually expanded.

Nevertheless, we cannot fail to see that the invention of writing and the establishment of states—the two normally go together—represent a dramatic turning point in the shape of time, that is to say, in the molding of chronological structure in cultural products. The world of symbolic forms that mankind produces from within himself and with which he creates a symbolically organized environment for himself appears from this moment onward to be subject to a particular process of change. The periods of prehistory and early history are counted in thousands and tens of thousands of years. But this notion of time is now changing fundamentally. We may think of the concept of style as the memory of the forms, the quintessence of all the characteristics by which an object signals its membership of a particular age, a group, or a function. If that is so, then as culture develops there seems to be a change from long-term memory to short-term memory. In prehistory and early history, styles were long-lasting, while now they become subject to an ever more hectic process of change. Between the premieres of *Così fan tutte* and *Die Walküre* there are precisely eighty years. What does memory mean in such a case? What kind of forgetting is being combated here? Should we not rather say that forgetting is being promoted and change accelerated?

The fact is that culture appears to create the very thing it opposes. To make things visible is very different from ensuring that they endure, and articulation is very different from conservation. We might assert the opposite: visibility suspends the cultural meaning of change. The ethnologists know all about this. They base their study of oral cultures on the assumption that archaic cultural traditions have been able to survive under the mantle of invisibility. Musical ethnologists study oral musical cultures, for example, in the Orient and in Ireland, in order to discover the secrets of musical performance in medieval music. They do so in the belief— and they are surely right about this—that relatively little has changed in a thousand years. We can infer from this that the more actively the project of objectification, articulation, and notation is advanced, the more change there will be and the more forgetting. In the world of nonwritten memory transmission the heir to tradition is measured by the amount of this invisible tradition that he is able to embody and present in visible and oral form. In the world of written traditions, on the other hand, he is measured by what he has to add that is new and individual to a tradition that has been made visible. This is no modern problem; it can be said to belong to the oldest and most universal experiences of writing. This can be seen impressively in the lament of Khakheperre-sonb, an Egyptian writer from the beginning of the second millennium:

> Had I unknown phrases,
> Sayings that are strange,
> Novel, untried words,
> Free of repetition;
> Not transmitted sayings,
> Spoken by the ancestors!
> I wring out my body of what it holds,
> In releasing all my words;
> For what was said is repetition,
> When [only] what was said is said.
> Ancestor's words are nothing to boast of,
> They are found by those who come after.
>
> Not speaks one who spoke,
> There speaks one who will speak,

May another find what he will speak!
Not a teller of tales after they happen,
This has been done before;
Nor a teller of what might be said,
This is vain endeavour, it is lies,
And none will recall his name to others.
I say this in accord with what I have seen:
From the first generation to those who come after,
They imitate that which is past.
Would that I knew what others ignore,
Such as has not been repeated.[3]

These sentences encapsulate the basic problem of writing and style. The oral bard functions according to the laws of repetition and cyclical renewal. His song is constantly being made new; it "renews" itself in every new performance, even if it is traditional and possibly age-old. From the author who writes, in contrast, we expect novelty: *unfamiliar songs, exotic sayings, new discourse never before heard and free from repetition.* Corresponding to this pressure, we find a change in the form in which time is expressed in written culture; shorter periods, quicker sequences, a more precise, more finely meshed datability. This problem does not exist as long as culture reproduces itself in the invisible space of memory, and this involvement in the more sedate pace of the overall cultural process is even shared by the visible products of culture, such as ceramics, tools, and textiles, and such. But wherever writing penetrates the central spheres of cultural memory, the rhythm changes and we find a pressure to change which forces culture to adopt countermeasures and new strategies in its efforts at pacification. Thus culture is not simply a matter of memory, and certainly not long-term memory. It is long-term memory only in the sense that it does not just objectify meanings and knowledge and make them visible; it also generates techniques of preservation and principles for avoiding change that can effectively counter the tendency to vary, innovate, and make accommodations. These strategies can be subsumed under the concept of "canonization." It is only through the interplay between these processes of making visible and canonization that culture can become an island in the ocean of forgetting that can ensure continuity for centuries and even millennia.

2. Writing as Storehouse and Monument

Why does the invention of writing commonly go hand in hand with the emergence of states? We might answer intuitively by saying that writing makes possible the large-scale communication that is indispensable for the establishment and maintenance of a state.[4] I find it highly questionable, however, whether communication is the proper context within which to understand the emergence of the first writing systems. Writing has two basic functions, which must be carefully distinguished: storage and communication. In the case of storage, writing acts as the exteriorization of our memory, enabling us to recall data which would soon escape us without its aid. In the case of communication, it amounts to an exteriorization of our voice, enabling us to address people who are distant in time or place. All the evidence suggests that writing was invented as a means of storage, not as a method of communication. Where we can trace it back to its origins, it grew out of systems of notation, all of which stood in the service of memory (and not of the voice). Its task was to safeguard and store data that are too complex or haphazard for human memory. Such data occur in the more complex economic and administrative systems that are to be found in early forms of the state. Writing here is part of a "bookkeeping" process at state level, a level at which memory alone is insufficient. The earliest written documents in Egypt are the names of kings or chieftains, taxation entries and information about the origins of products. They are plainly the instruments of a palace administration that uses them to organize, control, and plan a large, complex economy. Writing supports the memory and the purview of early rulers who use it to achieve a hitherto unprecedented degree of insight and control.

In Egypt, however, writing has a further function which might be described as that of a "public memory." This was concerned not with storing data, but with making it visible, creating a symbolic order in which the new, common, all-embracing project of the state could be displayed. In a manner that was typical of Egyptian culture, this symbolic order was linked with the striving for eternity in the sense of an existence that lasted beyond death. This meant the establishment of a prospective memory directed toward the future. All the earliest monuments are concerned with the immortalization of state actions such as victories, foundations, consecrations, rites, and so on.[5] Very soon, however, high state officials begin to take part in this "monumental discourse" and have graves erected for themselves with inscriptions in which they can make their names and titles a matter of enduring public record.[6]

However, writing soon emancipated itself from its origins in the storage of data and public, prospective memorialization. As early as the third millennium, we find both letters and literary documents in Mesopotamia and Egypt that transmit meaning to a reader or the person who reads aloud and do not just set out to remind him of something he knew already. Above all, we see the emergence of texts that aim to convey basic knowledge. On the other hand, it is enough to remind ourselves of Plato's critique of writing, in the *Phaedrus* or the Seventh Letter, to realize that even two thousand years later such a project could be unmasked as an illusion. For Plato writing was nothing more than a system of notation, a memory aid, that used outward signs to remind a knowledgeable person of something he already knew, not to convey this knowledge to an ignorant person. Meaning cannot be encoded. It is always "inside" and can be communicated only directly, through living with others. Writing is an ensemble of signs that always runs the risk of lapsing into a realm lying beyond lived and communicated meaning. This internal space is what we call the communication situation. With the aid of writing communication can be extended over space and time, but it can never be inserted into writing. Writing constitutes an outer horizon. Uncoupled from actual communication, it represents a more or less disorganized, unstructured, and hence correspondingly ambiguous mass of signs. A reader or decoder can only begin to make sense of it where it is possible to infer something of the context in which communication takes place and which determines meaning.

What we have said here about writing can be said of culture in general, that is, of the totality of cultural products. It would be a mistake to imagine that they contain meanings that are not only visible, but also durable, and that we need only to retrieve them or to reconstruct them using the tools of the historian. That would require quite different forms of long-term institutionalization than merely the institution of writing. The expanded context does call for writing—there is no question about that. In the absence of writing (or a corresponding system of notation) communication cannot be stretched in time and space. But that is only a necessary, not a sufficient precondition. Even less can we claim that writing can of itself initiate such a process of stretching and making permanent. Writing cannot ensure the permanence of meaning and knowledge. Where such knowledge disintegrates, writing is converted into the indeterminate mass of signs that we have described above. The readability of writing is not a characteristic of the writing, but of those who make use of it. This fact cannot be repeated often enough.

At this point in our discussion I would like to introduce the term *memory-based culture* [*Erinnerungskultur*],[7] to refer to the set of circumstances that ensures that writing retains its long-term readability and gives the communication situation its elasticity. We have said that writing is in its origins largely a medium of memory and not of communication. It is a system of notation in the service of memory, a data-storage system, and it functions only in conjunction with an appropriate memory-based culture that ensures the enduring readability of texts—one might even like to call it the quality that makes it possible for us to inhabit the texts. For it is this quality of being fit for habitation that is at stake here. After all, we are talking about a symbolically constructed environment that man creates, in the shape of cultural products, in order that people may inhabit it together and live in a human community.

3. Connective Memory

If someone wishes to emigrate to a foreign country and acquire its citizenship, he must study the history of that country. Many countries make the approval of an application for citizenship depend on the proof of sufficient knowledge of their history. For countries like the United States, the citizenship rules represent the most important use that is actually made of history. The past is the decisive resource for the consciousness of national identity. Whoever wishes to belong must share the group memory. We have already discussed this normative aspect of collective memory in the Introduction, where we were concerned with the close link between religion and memory, and which we illustrated with reference to the exodus of the Israelites. Here we shall look at the social importance of the same link, independently of that religious dimension, and we shall do so in the context of ancient Egypt.

As we pointed out earlier, it was above all Friedrich Nietzsche who first drew attention to the bonding memory that constructs communities and makes them possible.[8] Society is based on the fact that people "have memories." Nietzsche developed this idea on the foundation of a distinction between natural memory that works hand in hand with forgetting, and an artificial memory that excludes forgetting in certain eventualities. Nietzsche calls this the "will's memory." He derives this concept from the model of an obligation that leads to future undertakings, and defines the human being that is capable of remembering as "the animal that can make promises."

And precisely this necessarily forgetful animal, in whom forgetting is strength, has bred for himself a counter-device, memory, with the help of which forgetfulness can be suspended in certain cases,—namely, in those cases where a promise is to be made: consequently it is by no means merely a passive inability to be rid of an impression once it has made its impact. . . . Instead it is an active desire to keep on desiring what has been, on some occasion, desired, it is in a real sense the *will's memory.*

This, says Nietzsche, "is the long history of the origins of responsibility."[9]

By the "will's memory" Nietzsche does not mean a memory of a shared history, but the memory of one's own promises and obligations. His "memory of the will," then, is not a collective memory (like the memory described by Aleida Assmann),[10] but an individual memory, and is the foundation of the moral reliability of the individual. The precise function of this moral memory, however, is to tie the individual to the community. For this reason it is "connective" rather than "collective."

Nietzsche has given the name of "memory technique" [*Mnemotechnik*] to this process of creating memory that underpins both culture and community. In doing so, he emphasizes the element of violence it contains. In the gloomiest terms, he describes this process, this civilizing process, by means of which human beings are bred into fellow human beings.

This age-old question was not resolved with gentle solutions and methods; perhaps there is nothing more terrible and strange in man's prehistory than his *memory technique.* "A thing must be burnt in so that it stays in the memory: only something which continues to *hurt* stays in the memory"—that is a proposition from the oldest (and unfortunately the longest-lived) psychology on earth. . . . It never happened without blood, torment and sacrifices; the most horrifying sacrifices and forfeits (the sacrifice of the firstborn belongs here), the most disgusting mutilations (for example, castration), the cruellest rituals of all religious cults (and all religions are, at their most fundamental, systems of cruelty)—all this has its origin in that particular instinct which discovered that pain was the most powerful aid to mnemonics.[11]

Here, Nietzsche adopts the black-and-white evolutionist attitudes of the nineteenth century, constructing the course of human history as a road leading from the darkness of cruel obligations to the light of freedom based on reason. Two elements of this bloodthirsty picture appear to me to be significant for our own arguments: the "connective," that is to say, socially binding nature of this memory; and second, its "artificial" character. We are concerned here with a kind of memory that has to be practiced and therefore cannot survive without a memory technique.

In his book on forgetting, which is by the same token just as much a book about remembering, Harald Weinrich emphasizes the pioneering nature of Nietzsche's analysis of morality. It is to be distinguished, Weinrich writes,

from other explanations of morality such as are to be found from Aristotle to Kant, essentially by the fact that in Nietzsche morality is based on what we might call, in modern terms, a communicative foundation. In the sphere of debt at least two people communicate with each other, a creditor and a debtor, and the medium of their communication is memory. The same claim may be upheld in the sphere of law with its criminological understanding of debt and atonement, and in the same way these two phenomena are also treated communicatively, that is to say, in the oral dialogue of court proceedings. If morality is made of the same mental stuff as debts and guilt, then it too is communicative in nature and presupposes in everyone who comes in contact with it a memory that is willing and able to function.[12]

Weinrich has brilliantly put his finger on the crucial point. Nietzsche's morality is an ethics based on relationships. In this respect it contrasts with the Western tradition of an ethics of individual happiness or individual striving, going back to Aristotle. All the more important, however, is it to realize that this is not a discovery, but at best a rediscovery. Like Nietzsche, the ancient Egyptians based morality on the relationships that bind human beings to their community, and defined memory as the decisive precondition of human association. Memory makes people capable of binding commitments. As we have seen, Nietzsche maintains that man needs this "connective" memory in order to be able to make promises and to enter into commitments. Unlike Nietzsche, the Egyptians do not develop the concept of responsible (conscientious) action from the special case of promises (i.e., with a view to the future), but from that of gratitude (or, more generally, as a response to earlier action, i.e., as a reaction to the past).[13] The man who has become predictable by virtue of his memory will be the same man tomorrow as he was yesterday and today. The remembering self is the locus in which society is inscribed, along with its claims and obligations.

The Egyptian concept for this connective memory that establishes individual identity and membership of the community is called *maat*. *Maat* even promises to confer immortality on this identity, in the form of survival beyond death in the social memory of the group. "The memorial to a man," the proverb runs, "is his virtue. The man of bad character will be forgotten."[14] It is to this principle that we owe the institution of the monumental Egyptian grave, and with it not only thousands and tens of thousands of the most magnificent wall paintings, sculptures, and buildings, but also hundreds of important biographical inscriptions. In them the owner of the grave gives accounts for his life to posterity. Nowhere does the link Nietzsche established between morality and memory appear more clearly than here. Life organizes itself in the past tense of a narrative, but only under the pressure of a moral judgment that adjudicates between remembering and forgetting. These inscriptions are not the product of an effusive desire to talk, a naive pride in one's own life achievements, or a natural feeling for history and the past, but the pressure to provide an apologia, a response to a tribunal-like situation that demands an explanation and calls memory to account.

Thus the Egyptian texts are in a position to illustrate and confirm the link Nietzsche observed between memory and society, time and morality. Nietzsche, however, goes one step further. Unlike the Egyptian authors, he is opposed to memory, opposed to the principle of a normative recollection that commits the individual to a social identity. He regards this linking of time and morality as a malign construct that he wishes to destroy with the methods of genealogy. He does not want his fellow man, but the superman; he wants to emancipate the individual from the shackles of his interpersonal relationships and free him to achieve a higher form of individuality. This is why he emphasizes the violent nature of the moral or connective memory.

The Egyptians describe their concept of humanity, *maat*, as a gentle yoke. This is understandable since we are faced with a body of hortatory literature that wishes to enlist our support of *maat*. But basically, they agree with Nietzsche when they proceed from the assumption that *maat*, our common humanity, social memory, cannot exist among human beings without the state and its agencies of compliance. The state exists to enthrone *maat* on earth, that is to say, to create the framework for teaching and remembering it. For it too, then, this memory is no autopoetic system, it is nothing that develops and regulates itself in the course of living interaction between human beings. Memory is a system that is imposed from outside and can only be sustained by state power. Without the state that penalizes forgetting, the "laws of the *maat*" would not be remembered. Hence, here too only things that continue to hurt remain in the memory. The only difference is that the Egyptians had already reached a stage of civilization where the pain of memory is no longer burned directly into the flesh, but is displaced into the symbolic forms of state institutions and laws, literary texts and school instruction manuals—in short, a symbolic world of markers that take the place of the body. Memory is no longer inscribed in the skin, but is instead engraved upon the heart.

The concept of writing is a convenient handle by which to sum up this symbolic world of signs, the different codes of a cultural memory technique. Writing now takes the place of the body. The Egyptian youth no longer has to undergo the torture of a rite of passage; instead he learns to write.[15] But by learning to write a boy acquired not just an important cultural tool, as is the case with us, but also cultural knowledge, the same kind of knowledge that was burned into the tribal novice during his initiation, that is, the cultural memory of the tribe. Through writing the Egyptian went a stage further, opening up a realm of public permanence in which he could inscribe himself, together with his "virtue." In his eyes writing had a redemptive dimension: it redeemed him from the curse of transience.

Writing and the state belong together and form the symbolic system of cultural memory, as well as the framework in which this can be stabilized. The state, and therefore inequality, subordination to a hierarchical system of commands and obedience: that is the price that mankind had to pay for the humanization of cultural memory. With the displacing of markers into writing, or, as Aleida Assmann puts it, with the "excarnation" of a cultural memory technique into symbolic forms, we find a change in the sense of belonging transmitted by such a process of remembering.[16] It becomes abstract, widely dispersed, and hierarchical. Egalitarian village communities make way for tribes headed by chiefs, kingdoms, and shortly after that, full-fledged empires. Fellow human beings are transformed into subjects.

We saw how writing and the state came to replace brute force in the course of the institutionalization of a social memory. In the same way, with the development of the history of religion in Egypt, the idea of a tribunal of the dead, and hence religion, comes to take the place of the state. The emergence of this idea coincides with the disintegration of the state. In a sense it becomes its successor-institution on the plane of morality and normative memory. The state with its agencies of compliance is now replaced by a divine tribunal to which every man must answer. Here he will be examined to see whether he has lived according to the laws of *maat*. The form this takes is that his heart is weighed on a balance against a figure representing *maat*. Simultaneously, he recites a long series of sentences all of which begin with the words "I have not . . . " and in which he exonerates himself from a corresponding list of possible offenses. If the scales are balanced his self-exoneration receives divine sanction. If not, he falls victim to the "devouring goddess," the monstrous personification of forgetting and oblivion.[17] We can, of course, go along with Nietzsche and regard this devouring spirit as the demonic mask of violence that beats memory into man and forces him to remember yesterday and answer for it. Conversely, however, we could also regard it as the fury of destruction against which all culture struggles and against which man erects the markers of cultural memory in order to endow his own existence with meaning and permanence. That is the ambivalence of cultural memory. From one side it appears as the means of violent disciplining, from the other, as the means whereby we can be rescued from oblivion. In the light of Nietzsche's thinking it is the wound that compels man to remember as long as "it does not cease to hurt"; seen by the light of Egyptian philosophy it is an imperishable world in which man can inscribe himself and thereby ward off oblivion forever.

In Egypt, the normative memory, *maat*, is not only the medium through which the individual fits into society and through which society reproduces itself; it is not only the glue that holds culture together.[18] Over and above that it is a redemptive force.

4. Memory as Defined by Halbwachs and Warburg

The link Nietzsche established between cultural memory and violence stands as a highly illuminating contrast to the idea of memory developed by Maurice Halbwachs with his notion of "collective memory."[19] Regrettably, Halbwachs was unfamiliar with Nietzsche, so that he never became aware of this fundamental divergence of views. Halbwachs agrees with Nietzsche that memory is a social phenomenon. However, for Halbwachs it is not linked to force of any sort or the intervention of any third party; it is not "made" or "bred into us." Instead, memory arises and develops in a manner that Halbwachs would undoubtedly have described as "autopoetic," in the sense of "self-generating," if the conceptual apparatus of modern systems theory had been available to him.

For Halbwachs, memory is developed in individuals in proportion to their communication with others and their membership of social constellations. In the absence of such membership and communication, the individual is unable to organize his internal images and shape them as memories. Memory is a parameter of social organization—Halbwachs uses the word *frame*, thus anticipating Erving Goffman's concept.[20] This social parameter is transmitted to the individual through his association with other people, and it introduces structure into his chaotic inner life. Frames are spatio-temporal schemes which enable the individual to organize his incoherent images. They are rationalizing categories that provide the individual with structure and coherence. Remembering is a self-objectifying and self-structuring organizing process. In our dreams this organization is dissolved; the dreaming self is asocial.

For Halbwachs the past is not an objective given, but a collective reconstruction. It does not survive as such, but has constantly to be reconstructed anew, in accordance with its function for a given present. It is only remembered, that is, reconstructed insofar as it is needed. Unlike Nietzsche, Halbwachs avoids sharply contoured statements, but this is what he means when he insists—incidentally, without referring to Proust—on the distinction between *reconstruire* and *retrouver*. The past is not "rediscovered," but reconstructed.

The past is needed because it imparts togetherness. The group acquires its identity as a group by reconstructing its past togetherness, just as the individual can use his memory to convince himself of his membership in the group. In this sense, we could speak of a normative past in Halbwachs, even though he himself never stressed the binding character of this memory. At this juncture, however, it is easy to extend his line of thought to Thomas Luckmann's concept and theory of "invisible religion" (on this point see Chapter 1).[21] Luckmann is concerned with knowledge that unites people and with the memory that creates community. He has shown that this knowledge has definite normative, in his word, *binding* features. This is why Luckmann calls it religion, more specifically "invisible religion," in contrast to the visible religion of the institutionalized churches. Luckmann's thesis is that precisely because of its invisibility, invisible religion resists secularization. That is obvious, for what we see here is in fact the cultural memory which comes into view in the course of the neutral, unpolemical perspective of sociological analysis.

For Halbwachs, however, there is no such thing as "cultural" memory, and he avoids any mention of the normative nature of collective memories. On this point he is at the opposite pole from Nietzsche. The principle he sees at work in the formation of memory is not violence, but love. He insists on the affective nature of collective memory. The individual's belonging to the different social constellations and the internal cohesiveness of these groups are represented as affective bonds. Not violence, but feelings, hold culture together. Feelings shape our memories, and give them color and definition. It is tempting in this context to remind ourselves of Aby Warburg's concept of the pathos formula. Here, too, we are looking at emotionally tinged concretizations of collective memory.

For Warburg, whom I would like to introduce here as the third member of our triad of founding fathers of a sociology of memory, this cultural collective memory has an emancipatory, rather than an enslaving function. In this he stands in direct opposition to Nietzsche. With the assistance of cultural objectifications, man is able to free himself from the phobic pressures of reality. He can free himself from his fear of demons and of being overwhelmed by the senses. Warburg's concept of the phobic is closer to Freud's theory of trauma than to Nietzsche's bloody memory technique. But it cannot be denied that the motifs of anxiety and terror amount to a common denominator and that they are completely absent from Halbwachs.[22]

Between Halbwachs and Warburg we find the same dividing line as between Halbwachs and Nietzsche. It is the line between "communicative" and "cultural" memory,[23] between memory as an autopoetic system and memory as a cultural institution made visible in signs, symbols, images, texts, and rituals, that is, in "writing" in the broadest possible sense. Warburg is interested in the "road map of the images in the European memory," in the interconnections between images, image formulas, themes, in short, in objective cultural forms not psychological contents. Halbwachs, in contrast, avoids as far as possible all reference to objective cultural forms. There is a dividing line for him here beyond which we have to speak not of memory, but of tradition, historiography, and the like. He stays within the framework of psychology. The power and persistence of memories come not from tradition, but from feeling, from the individual's need to belong to one or more groups.

Today we are able to realize that all these thinkers are right in their own way, and we can bring all these different approaches together to form a general theory of cultural memory that can be made productive for a typological description of different cultures. We can make use of the systemic and autopoetic connection between memory, consciousness, and communication that is emphasized by Halbwachs.[24] But equally, we can also make use of the objectifications of communally remembered knowledge in the shape of cultural forms, and the displacement and making visible of collective memory into writing in the broadest possible sense. We use *writing* here as a general term encompassing all the systems of notation that mankind has ever used to fix the contents of memory, from cave paintings to computers.[25] It makes sense to think of writing, as does Warburg, as a form of liberation and the gaining of distance, but it is also sensible to emphasize its *prescriptive* aspect, as does Nietzsche, the element of obligation, taming, disciplining, and indeed subjugation of human beings. All these things make sense because cultures differ among themselves and because spectra containing varying options continually open up.

5. Freud's Concept of Obsessive Memory

The fourth theoretician of memory who must be mentioned in this context is Sigmund Freud. Like Nietzsche, he correlates memory with guilt and conscience; he too regards this link as a malign syndrome and steps upon the stage with the pathos of a liberator aiming to free mankind from its toils. However, the object of his criticism is not morality but religion. He combines the methods of genealogical reconstruction—in this he resembles Nietzsche—with the goal of critical deconstruction. Just as Nietzsche emphasizes the element of violence, Freud stresses the dimension of compulsion in memory. For both Nietzsche and Freud, the decisive aspect of this violence or compulsion is the inscription of memory in the innermost recesses of the self. What for Nietzsche is "the wound that does not cease to hurt," is the concept of trauma in Freud. Only those traditions that "must have undergone the fate of being repressed, the condition of lingering in the unconscious, can display such powerful effects on their return as to bring the masses under its spell."[26] In Chapter 2 we examined Freud's doctrine of the return of the repressed as he elucidated it in his book on Moses, so we can be brief here. Freud enriches the theory of cultural memory by adding to it the dimension of the unconscious. While the concept of tradition extends only to *conscious* cultural labor and the technology of the reception and handing on of the heritage, the concept of memory also includes the *unconscious* spiritual life of the group. According to Freud, monotheistic religion represents the return of a repressed memory. The decisive triggering factor of this repression was the murder of Moses.

Neither conscious nor unconscious denial of the deed could eliminate the presence in the psyche of the act or guilt, but would merely intensify the unconscious store of guilt and anxiety; indeed Freud maintains that this obsession with this unrecognized remorse drove the perpetrators and their heirs to compensate for their sin and that of their primitive forefathers by becoming increasingly more devoted to the God and religion of Moses.[27]

This guilt feeling and the ethics of bad conscience nurtured by it possess, in Freud's words, "the characteristic—uncompleted and incapable of completion—of obsessional neurotic reaction-formations"[28] For Freud this is the wound that "does not cease to hurt."

However, this trauma that forms the basis of memory does not affect a man's skin, but his unconscious. In Nietzsche, social memory is constituted as the site in which society inscribes its own norms. That would be the superego, in Freud's terminology. Freud, however, situates collective memory in the unconscious. These deep layers of the mind are the place in which universal human experience etches its traces. In this way, Freud arrives at a conception of collective memory that is a precise contradiction of Nietzsche's "memory of the will." In his view, monotheistic religion is far from being the "going on wishing for what you have once wished." It is a compulsive "passive inability to rid oneself of an impression once received," the consequence of a compulsion that traumatic memories keep imposing on individual souls. Where Nietzsche emphasizes the normative nature of memory, Freud substitutes their compulsive character.

Freud dismisses as "superficial" the explanations for Israel's guilt that are advanced in the Bible itself. The word *superficial* is key. Freud operates here not just with the distinction of outer and inner—tradition and memory—but with a distinction between surface and depth. Surface: this is the realm of consciousness. To Freud's way of thinking this no more suffices to explain the phenomena of religion than does the outer dimension, the realm of tradition, of objective cultural products and institutions. "Depth" designates the realm of latency that is cut off from consciousness. It is here that religious motifs develop their oppressive dynamics, their coercive character. The theoretical construct of depth implies a devaluation of the surface, that is, of the texts, the explicit cultural objectifications and self-descriptions that in Freud's eyes are no better than "clever disguises." In Chapter 2 I attempted to show that Freud's judgment fails to do justice to the "surface," the texts. The texts contain all the themes that Freud addresses in his discussion of the deeper layers of the psyche that he postulates.

What is interesting about Freud's reconstruction is his use of biblical texts in support of a general theory of culture and religion. Basing himself on the Hebrew Bible, and, we may add, on Jewish experience, he develops a general theory embracing religion, culture, and memory, in which religion and culture are interchangeable concepts. In other words, he scrutinizes the Hebrew Bible with the eyes of a cultural theorist, rather than with those of a theologian or historian. I would like to follow him down this path and attempt to use the same texts to produce an entirely different theory of culture. The crucial difference between the psychological theory of memory and one based on cultural theory is that the latter denies the distinction between surface and depth asserted by the former. The realm of cultural objectifications and self-descriptions is not denounced as a disguise, but taken seriously as an authentic medium of cultural memory (a "medium" in the literal sense of something "between" inner and outer).

These descriptions are to be found above all in the corpus of biblical texts known as "deuteronomist" and they comprise, in addition to Deuteronomy itself, the deuteronomist chronicles. The latter prophets are close to this school and in part share their view of the world. This is exactly the same body of biblical texts that Freud had in mind in speaking of the "superficial motivation" of the Hebrew consciousness of guilt. There are two aspects of interest in a study of these texts from the point of view of cultural theory. First, it seems to me undeniable that they represent a new stage in Israel's advance to a written culture, a decisive step toward a writing-based cultural tradition. Second and most importantly, the theme of memory is central in these texts. They portray the history of Israel, from the exodus from Egypt down to the Babylonian captivity, as a kind of drama of memory that can be divided up, much as in Freud, into the three acts or phases of "experience," "repression," and "return of the repressed." The stage of "experience" consists of the story of the exodus beginning with the flight from Egypt, advancing to the arrival in Canaan, and culminating in the story of the revelation on Mount Sinai. This revelation is repeatedly invoked in Deuteronomy. The process of repression is described in the deuteronomistic historiography as a lapse from the Law and a turning to idolatry. The "return of the repressed," lastly, comes in the Second Book of Kings, where it is embodied in the unforgettable scene of the discovery of a forgotten "book of the Torah." During building works in the Temple, the high priest Hilkiah finds a book (Deuteronomy, in fact) which provokes sadness and consternation when it is read out in public [2 Kings 22].

The story of the book found by chance directs our attention to an unusual aspect of writing: writing as a locus of latency. This is the point at which my view diverges most sharply from Freud's. The step-by-step transition to a written culture points to a growth in conceptual complexity. In oral societies whatever is handed down coincides with whatever authoritative and useful knowledge is actually made use of within the horizon of a given present. Anything that is not used is forgotten, in accordance with the principle of "structural amnesia." Of course, such amnesia also exists in written cultures. Where we find it we speak of "rewriting history." It is even possible that memories that have been written down can be more easily disposed of than unwritten ones. Typically, however, forgetting assumes different forms in written cultures. If we ignore the special case of book-burnings, knowledge that has become useless and unfashionable still survives. We witness the buildup of outposts of cultural memory, dumping grounds of meaning and of texts that are unread and may even have become unreadable. Writing is a storage system, not a means of communication. It acts as an intermediate storehouse over and above actual communication processes. Communication through writing, as in writing letters, is actually the exceptional case. With the transition to a written culture, this realm beyond cultural communication grows more or less incalculably. Culture becomes many-layered, complex, and full of tensions. In writing, what is no longer of its time can endure and speak. It becomes a place of refuge to which the repressed and the inopportune can retreat, and a background from which what is forgotten can reemerge, a place of latency.

The prophet Isaiah is told: "Now go, write it before them on a tablet, and inscribe it in a book, that it may be for the time to come for ever and ever" (Isa. 30:8).[29] And the Lord says to Jeremiah: "Thus speaketh the LORD, the God of Israel, saying, 'Write thee all the words that I have spoken unto thee in a book'" (Jer. 30:2). The prophets regard writing as a place of refuge in which they can preserve their message from the obduracy of their contemporaries, hoping for better times when later generations will read the book and take its lessons to heart. Writing gives men of the period the opportunity to speak to subsequent generations, and they avail themselves of it. In writing, a memory that is no longer opportune can survive.

The motif of the rediscovered book is a literary fiction which articulates a consciousness of the specific complexity of the written culture. We call such works pseudepigrapha and so relegate the phenomenon to the realm of "pseudos," of lies and deceit. But this is hardly to do it justice. Even a book that first came into being around 622 is not unjustly presented as a work that has emerged from total oblivion. That is a legitimate strategy in the battle of memories. The memory reclaimed in Deuteronomy feels itself to be out of key with its time and is made to prevail in the teeth of the predominant state of forgetfulness. With the pseudepigrapha we seem to be confronted with a type of oppositional and reform literature. What is new legitimates itself as the old that has been forgotten.

This new phenomenon, the monotheistic idea of the Covenant with God, has a highly explosive political potential and religious power. The question is whether this idea is as old or as young as the texts that present it, or whether it extends back into a quite different era and really was repressed, as Freud believes. The very fact that we are speaking of an idea that was so revolutionary both politically and religiously might well incline us to Freud's view. I shall not attempt to answer this question, but wish instead to reopen it as a question by emphasizing the aspect of memory, as opposed to evolution. In this respect I take Freud's side, even though I prefer to reconstruct this memory in the forms of cultural, rather than collective, memory. The question, then, if I may conclude by formulating it one last time, is whether the monotheistic and theocratic idea of a covenant and chosenness belongs to the basic core of normative and formative knowledge of Israel, that is, of its cultural memory, and whether it can actually be traced back to the religious and political conflicts in Egypt of the late Bronze Age. Alternatively, did this idea only develop in exile, or did it come about in the period immediately preceding the exile under the pressure of a threatening political situation? Modern Old Testament studies lean fairly generally to the second alternative, to the assumption that the complex of monotheism, the idea of a covenant and the chosen people, was something absolutely new that presented itself, by a kind of literary fiction, as something old that had been forgotten. My own view, however, is that it quite conceivably is an ancient, primordial memory. It may have survived in part by virtue of its intrinsic power and unforgettability, not indeed in the collective unconscious, but in cultural forms and in cultural locations in a state of latency. Such forms or localities include the oral or written traditions of marginalized groups. This would mean that the legend of the discovery of a book does in fact contain an element of truth.

With the appearance of writing on the horizon, tradition increases in complexity. It ceases to be based exclusively on memory, but with the assistance of the media of external storage, it also acquires new forms of forgetting and re-remembering, of displacement and renewed access, of latency and return, of renaissance. Given the vast possibilities of storage, writing opens up a space of cultural latency that transforms the process of culture into a memory drama. And it does so parallel with how the labor of handing down a tradition becomes emancipated from memory.

Cultural Texts Suspended Between Writing and Speech

1. The Concept of the Text: Text, Transmission, and Expanded Context [*zerdehnte Situation*]

In anticipation of a more detailed examination of the topic, I would venture the assertion that the Latin word *textus* has no equivalent in other ancient languages, such as Greek, Hebrew, Egyptian, Akkadian, and others. As is well known, *textus* comes from *texo*, "I weave," and means "fabric," connection, coherence. Starting with this metaphor, Quintilian uses the term *textus* for the interconnections between words (*verborum*), the structure and coherence of speech. We shall call this concept of text the rhetorical concept.

Rhetoric distinguishes between information and communication, content and "linguistic manner," a distinction that is absent from the Oriental languages. The Egyptian *mdt* and the Hebrew *dabar* signify without distinction both the word *and* the thing, the subject matter that the word expresses. Whoever refers to something that has been said is unable to state whether he means the form or the content of what has been said. There is no distinction between words and things. However, it is this very distinction that counts in rhetoric, and this explains why rhetoric developed the notion of a text that refers precisely to linguistic manner, not the content of speech.

Philology subsequently took over the new concept of *textus* from rhetoric and applied it to the object of its own labor. *Textus* here stands in opposition to *commentarius. Textus* can be called a linguistic utterance to which one then relates in the form of a *commentarius; commentarius,* conversely, is the form of utterance that has a *textus* as its object. *Textus* and *commentarius* are correlative concepts. A linguistic utterance becomes a *textus* when it is the object of philological work: textual criticism, the production of a text, an edition, a commentary on a text. And, we may add, translation. As a rule, a linguistic utterance is not intended as a "text"; it begins life as the object of enjoyment of every kind, pleasure, instruction, and admiration, but not as the object of philological work. That belongs on a horizon that is secondary and retrospective in comparison to the original linguistic utterance. Thus, as a concept, the text does not occur naturally on the primary horizon of linguistic communication. We only speak of texts on the secondary horizon of a culture of philological interpretation. This arises where we are concerned with linguistic utterances that have become difficult to comprehend, either because of their great age or because of some other intercultural otherness, and this applies with particular force to the texts of antiquity. An ancient work may have become problematic, and stand in need of philological labor, because of the fragmentary nature of tradition, the large number of errors that have crept in through faulty copying, or because the context within which it was formerly understood has now disappeared. But even more importantly, because it may be thought of as having *merited* such attention, the word *text* becomes a badge of honor, and in the Trecento, at the dawn of modern philology, many works by modern authors laid claim to the title of text as a counterweight to the oppressive authority of the ancient classics. The commentary, a kind of secondary horizon that turns the work into a text, appears like an aura; even Dante, Boccaccio, and other writers are wont to clothe their works in the form of self-commentaries.[1]

The concept of the text passed from classical philology into ordinary language. Here, it lost the link with commentary and other forms of philological work and retained only the sense of a written product. In ordinary usage a text is a piece of writing.

In linguistics, especially text-based linguistics, this insistence on the written form has been abandoned. Here *text* is the term used, on the one hand, to describe the supreme linguistic unit above the sentence, and on the other, to designate the natural and concrete form of linguistic utterance. To put it in the words of Peter Hartmann, one of the fathers of modern textual linguistics, "When people speak, what they utter are texts."[2] Text is the form in which language occurs in nature; all other units, such as sentences, clauses, words, and morphemes are artificial definitions and analytical constructs.

However, this concept of the text seems altogether too general and vague. In contrast, the ordinary usage still contains an element of the original meaning of the term *textus*. We are indebted to the linguist Konrad Ehlich for having meaningfully preserved this crucial semantic element in a new form acceptable to linguistics.[3] Ehlich defines a text as a "retrieved communication." In this definition, what is commented on is not the original form of the text, but the transmitted message. However, the common element, namely the element of retrieval [*Wiederaufnahme*], is obvious. What is decisive for the genesis of texts is the separation from the immediate speech situation. This means, according to Ehlich, first, that the simultaneous presence of speaker and listener is no longer required, and second, that the acoustic dimension becomes problematic as the route by which an utterance is transmitted. The separation from the immediate speech situation becomes inevitable if the speaker has to overcome distances in space and/or time in order to reach the listener. For that means that the speech act has to be preserved at a distance from the immediate situation and must be transposed into a second speech situation. Ehlich explains this with the example of a messenger who learns his message by heart in order to be able to reproduce it in a different place for the benefit of the intended listener. Here we are fully justified in speaking of the "text" of the message. It is not the written form that is decisive, but the act of storage and transmission. The two speech situations, speaker and messenger on the one hand, messenger and listener on the other, are separated in time and place and yet in communication with each other through the text and the manner of its transmission. The *immediate* situation of copresence is replaced by "the *expanded* context," in which from two to virtually an infinite number of individual situations can unfold and limits of which are set only by the availability of the text and the manner of its transmission.

The original correlation of the concepts *textus* and *commentarius* has given way to the conceptual pair of text and transmission. In expanded contexts texts are speech acts. This definition of text has two advantages.

On the one hand, it frees text from the everyday, theoretically undesirable link to writing and makes room for the concept of an oral text. On the other hand, thanks to its link to the concept of transmission, this definition takes up a crucial element of the philological tradition. Not every utterance is a text, but only a linguistic utterance that is linked with a need for transmission on the side of the speaker and a need for retrieval on the side of the listener. In short, they must be utterances that are designed with a certain effect at a distance, whether in time or space, and to which people only have recourse when such distances are present. There is an echo here of the badge of honor that once surrounded the term *textus*. Cohesive forces are at work that not only bind the individual words into the "fabric" of the text, but that can forge links at a spatio-temporal distance between speaker and listener. It is not inappropriate, therefore, to refer to their "binding nature." Texts are utterances whose binding authority is intensified. If we intensify the word still further, we arrive at the concept of the cultural text which we adopt with gratitude. Following Aleida Assmann, by *cultural* texts we understand texts that possess a special normative and formative authority for a society as a whole.[4] *Normative* texts codify the norms of social behavior; they include everything from proverbs via wisdom literature down to the Shulkhan Aruch, to the Conduct Books and Knigge.[5] *Formative* texts formulate the self-image of the group and the knowledge that secures their identity. They include everything from tribal myths and sagas of origin down to Homer and Virgil, Dante, Shakespeare, Milton, and Goethe. Formativity and normativity always go together in these texts; only the emphases shift. There is no need to explore this further here. What matters is solely the concept of the intensified binding authority that characterizes the cultural text. It refers both to time and space, and in particular, to social space. Cultural texts lay claim to an overall social authority; they define the identity and cohesiveness of a society. They structure the world of meaning within which communication takes place, and the consciousness of unity, sense of belonging, and particular character is reproduced through the generations in a way that recognizably maintains the identity of the group.

Konrad Ehlich's concept of the text, which defines it in terms of the need for transmission, is subsumed into the concept of the cultural text and may be said to potentiate it. Through its link with transmission, it highlights the fact that the medium of storage and the institutionalization of the expanded context have a crucial importance for the shape of the text. Above all, however, it ties the quality of textuality to the act of retrieval. It is the element of retrieval that constitutes an assemblage of linguistic signs as a "text." In what follows, I would like to build on this concept of text and show that these three aspects, the storage medium, the institutionalizing of the expanded context, and the act of retrieval are closely interrelated. At the institutional level, the opposition of orality and writing appears as the opposition between festivals or ritual and schools, and at the level of retrieval as the opposition of repetition and variation.

2. Institutional Forms of Expanded Contexts

a. Expanded Contexts in the Framework of the Culture of Memory: Festivals and Rituals as Oral Forms of Institutionalization

The Order of Retrieval

With cultural texts that are designed not for a single act of reception, like a message, but for virtually endless acts of retrieval, it is not sufficient to store the texts. Storage is merely the precondition of their retrieval. Provision must be made for the act of retrieval. This problem takes quite a different form in the oral tradition than in literate cultures.

The concept of the expanded context does not apply to the *storage*, but to the *communication* of a message. It refers to the majority of concrete communication situations in which the communication is uttered. Compared to this communication, the question of storage is superficial. The essential distinction between the oral and written transmission of cultural texts consists, therefore, not in the storage medium or technology, but in the form in which the expanded context is institutionalized. In the case of oral transmission, the expanded context calls for a far more intensive formalization than in developed written cultures, and it generally assumes the character of a ritual. Festival and ritual are the typical forms in which societies without writing institutionalize the expanded context of cultural texts.

Ritual ensures the retrieval of a communication, the communicative presence of the text. Storage, once again, is not a form of presence but rather of displacement to a realm external to the communicative process. This remains true for cultures based on memory, albeit in a different fashion and perhaps to a lesser degree than for written cultures. Admittedly, it may seem to make no sense to speak of "externality" with regard to texts stored in the memory. We must remind ourselves, however, that in societies without writing it is far from being the case that everyone has the texts in their heads and can retrieve them at any time. On the contrary, the precise knowledge of the texts is reserved for specialists, and in a sharper form than in written cultures. This point is often overlooked. With the rise of writing, particularly in the early stages of literacy, we tend to think of societies divided into a small elite of writers and an illiterate mass. This is no doubt accurate, but the position with regard to the oral transmission of cultural texts forms an exception to this. For even in the most narrowly elitist of writing-based societies there is always a greater proportion of writers, taking society as a whole, than there are memory specialists in oral societies. The task is incomparably harder and brings with it a higher social rank, even in otherwise relatively unstratified groups. The huge gulf, both hierarchically and numerically, between the memory specialists and representatives of cultural tradition, on the one hand, and the participants in the expanded context of cultural communication, on the other, shows that here, too, storage and communication are two very different things. For those engaged in cultural communication, cultural texts are normally inaccessible, at least in any professionally polished form; they only know them in those rough outlines that are memorable to the untrained memory. They have to wait for the next presentation in order to be able to appreciate the text again and embark upon the process of communication. Otherwise, they cannot get near these texts at all. But they can acquiesce in this situation because they can count on the return of the performance, since the ritual cycle of the festival calendar ensures it.

The text as we have defined it is a retrieved communication, the recourse to a linguistic utterance through the hiatus of a temporal or spatial distance. If the text is available in written form, then the form of that retrieval can be more or less arbitrary. However, if it is available only in the form of a memory store, then it can be reintroduced into the communicative process only with the aid of fixed social agreements and guarantees. The messenger—if we may return to our initial example—must be able to arrive at his destination without let or hindrance; he must have access to the recipient and be recognized as the sender's representative.[6] Even this implies that a fair amount of institutionalization, framing, and legal guarantees is necessary if communication at a distance is to succeed. The effort required increases enormously if we find ourselves no longer concerned with the simple case of a messenger, and where the expanded context communicates simply between two concrete speech situations. This occurs when we are confronted with the highly complex example of cultural texts without either sender or receiver, but which a society uses, as it were, to communicate with itself by holding at the ready an authoritative corpus of normative and formative knowledge through the generations for a virtually infinite supply of communicative situations.

For this, oral societies don't merely need a technique of memory storage, they need a ritual order for presenting them. The infinite supply of communication situations must be organized into a chain that repeats itself at regular intervals. The ritual form ensures that oral cultural texts remain present to the mind. In this respect, the great tribal festivals are the equivalent of the role played by the book market and the reading rooms of national libraries in literate societies. The mere existence, the communicative presence of cultural texts, is possible only in a discontinuous way in oral traditions. It can occur and recur only in the fixed rhythms of a society's rituals. The rituals ensure that the tradition remains coherent. Cultures based on memory are built on ritual coherence.

Storage Methods

We must cast a glance at the typical techniques of memory storage. The situation here is that the majority of cultures based on memory make use of specific systems of notation that antedate writing or substitute for it. Among these we may mention the knotted strings of the Incas or the Australian *tchuringa* stone engravings. Likewise, the Sumerian counting stones constitute a notation system that antedates writing. It is from this that writing developed. But this system was not used to transmit cultural texts; it was concerned with economic transactions. We shall return to this important distinction later. In early written cultures writing is rarely used to store cultural texts. Preliterate notation systems, in contrast, are commonly used both for economic purposes and above all for cultural communication. There is a huge variety of such systems. Taken together with a memory technique almost anything can serve as a memory aid, from signs and notched sticks, via rituals and their associated props, to entire landscapes, as in the Australian "song-lines." This decisively enlarges the realm of linguistic codification, and opens up a variety of sign worlds that appear to be close to language and can even be construed as "texts." Because of this it does not seem in the least misguided for the bibliographer Don McKenzie to devote himself to the question of how to catalogue these song-lines for library purposes.[7] These are not texts in our sense, but they are mnemonic aids for storage purposes; for that reason, they are something like "text-related sign complexes." The text, then, is what enters into a person's consciousness in a way that is accessible and stands ready to be retrieved once the person reaches a certain stage. In this sense we might call the Rhine in the age of Romanticism a song-line and a cultural, text-related sign complex, just like other cultural landscapes, such as Rome, Paris, or the Gulf of Naples; such a phenomenon is perfectly possible at the heart of a fully developed literate culture. For, as we shall discuss further later on, when we are discussing cultural texts writing and memory always go together.

The cultural text that has been stored under the conditions of a memory-based culture and communicated under those of ritual coherence confronts us with a problem that is not normally present in a literate culture: the question of what constitutes the text. It is only in exceptional cases that the text is memorized verbatim. The best-known example of this is the Vedic tradition. The normal case involves the memorizing either of coherent narratives or else of formulas. Now, which shall we call the "text"? The stored deep meaning that is reproduced and filled out through improvisation, or the superficial form that will vary from one occasion to the next? Our definition, which defines the text as a retrieved communication, permits only the first option. The text is the sum of its variations, it is in flux. Paul Zumthor calls this *mouvance*.[8] The text that is not fixed, has a deep structure, and manifests itself in an ever-changing set of appearances—that is the form in which the cultural text exists in an oral culture.

Mouvance and Literal Wording:
Cultural and Sacred Texts

The idea of ascribing *mouvance* to the oral tradition and literal wording to the written tradition seems obvious but can be misleading. For literal wording can be found in the oral tradition and *mouvance* occurs in the written tradition.[9] The principle of literal wording is at home in the realm of sacred texts, not among cultural texts. I would like to begin with this distinction.

By the term *sacred texts* I mean linguistic utterances that are linked with the idea of the presence of something sacred. There are sacred places that are experienced and separated off as zones of contact with the sacred, and that may not simply be entered ("Draw not nigh hither: put off thy shoes from off thy feet, for the place whereon thou standest is holy ground;" Exod. 3:5). In the same way, there are speech forms that are designed to establish contact with the sacred and are not to be uttered casually. Simply to know them brings about a certain proximity to God; how much more so if they are expressed. Among sacred texts we include hymns, incantations, magic spells and magic formulas, cult recitations, and also certain prayers, as well as a host of other things that are linked with the idea of magical effects or a divine presence. In such cases it is self-evident that the transmission and reproduction of the communications depends on literal accuracy. These texts need not be understood, what counts is that they are reproduced or recited as accurately as possible. There is no room here for improvisation.

This immediately explains the distinction between the *mouvance* of heroic epic in Homeric Greece, in the modern Balkans, and medieval Europe, on the one hand, and the word-for-word oral tradition among the Indian Brahmans (the carriers of the Vedic scriptures), or of the *ubwiiru* in Rwanda of which it is said that the officials entrusted with their preservation and verbatim repetition were the most exalted dignitaries of the realm, and the three highest among them, the only ones who knew the entire text of all eighteen rituals, even shared in the divinity of the monarchy. Memory lapses could be punished by death.[10] In these and many other instances we are confronted with sacred rather than cultural texts. The storage of sacred texts typically goes hand in hand with a duty of secrecy, and with their reproduction and utterance we find the phenomenon of strict ritual shaping and observance.[11]

Text and ritual stand in inverse relation to each other in sacred and cultural texts. With the sacred text the ritual is the essential part, and the discourse during the sacred ceremony is only a part of the whole. In the cultural text, in contrast, what counts is the reproduction of the text, and the ritual merely provides a framework for it. The embedding of text and action is different in the two cases. With the sacred text it has the function of a performative speech act. When the right words are spoken at the right time and in the right place by the right speaker in accordance with the rules, these words do not refer to a meaning, they create it. Examples are the "Yes" spoken by the bridegroom, the words "In the name of the people," as spoken by the judge, or "In the name of the father . . . ," as spoken by the priest. Thus the sacred text becomes associated with the idea not simply of pointing to what is sacred, but, in a sense, of producing it ("theurgically"). This explains the exclusivity, secrecy, and ritualistic nature of sacred texts. None of that has any force with cultural texts, or not to anywhere near the same extent. If they were secret, how could they exercise their normative and formative power and authority on behalf of society as a whole? It is true that in cultures based on memory the need to store and present them is usually reserved for a few specialists, but that is connected with the rarity of the memory capacity needed to transmit them, not with the need to keep them secret.

b. The Expanded Context in the Framework of a Literate Culture

School and Scriptorium as Institutional Forms of Writing: The Stream of Tradition

In early literate cultures it is precisely not the sacred and cultural texts for which writing was invented or first used. For these texts will have long had a firm place in the memory of specialists. Solutions to the problems of codifying, storing, and performing these texts were already established. Writing developed in the context of new problems for which solutions had not yet been devised. In Mesopotamia, this was the realm of the temple economy with its constant stream of new data that no human brain could retain.[12] In Egypt, in addition to the central activity of bookkeeping,[13] there was a further factor: the new state's need for visibility and eternity. Writing conferred permanence on political decrees and acts. In early written cultures, then, writing develops in the two realms of archiving and representation.[14] Cultural texts, in contrast, maintain their place in the memory. It takes centuries of writing for the archival and representative functions to be joined by a third realm, for which the Assyriologist Leo Oppenheim coined the phrase *stream of tradition*, or the stream that carries the cultural texts.[15] What this involves—as a rule—is *not* the writing down of a living, oral corpus. The oral tradition remains unaffected.[16] What develops in the medium of writing by way of cultural texts is something quite different. Instead of proverbs we have wisdom literature, instead of myths, elaborately artistic and highly didactic narratives, like the Gilgamesh epic or the Story of Sinuhe. We are looking at texts that are conceived as written, not with traditional works subsequently put into writing.

In Oriental studies the texts of the stream of tradition are normally grouped together under the heading "literary texts," contrasted with temple texts, on the one hand, and bureaucratic, archival texts, on the other. In the temple, writing is used to preserve the verbatim texts of the rituals; the archives store the files, letters, documents, and other texts of daily use that no memory can retain. Writing is needed for the cult and for preservation. Is there a third realm called "literature" alongside these two functional spheres?

When I asked myself this question thirty years ago, I felt that I should answer it emphatically in the affirmative. I defined this realm through the negative characteristic of an absence of succinct functional definition.[17] I classified texts that served bureaucratic or cultic purposes under the heading "practical literature," and contrasted this with the less obviously functional "belles lettres." Today, I see the matter differently, especially in light of the distinction between cultural and literary texts. The so-called literary texts evidently satisfy important needs. This is connected with writing itself. It therefore has an element of authorial reflexivity that brings it closer to the aesthetic and the concept of belles lettres. The literary texts are the texts that the Egyptians and Babylonians used in order to learn writing. Primers did not yet exist at the time. The assumption was that the best way to learn to write was to practice on the kind of texts that should be learned by heart, that is to say, cultural texts. Existing scribes instructed new scribes in how to write. Following the model of the cultural texts passed on via the memory, but adapted of course to the world of writing, new texts were composed as if born from the spirit of writing itself. These texts had to be learned by heart in order to school the mind, transmit knowledge, exercise social attitudes and norms, and to practice writing by writing down material learned by heart. Of course, "writing" at the time was very different from what we understand by that term today. Writing was the most important means by which to control the world. Being able to write and able to administer were one and the same thing. The purpose of learning to write was to become not a calligrapher or author, but a priest or an official. Apart from the bureaucracy and the temples, there was no call for books, nor was there a market in books. Whoever did not write for bureaucratic or cultic purposes, wrote to sustain the stream of tradition, but also by the way, or at an advanced age, with the aim of contributing to the art of writing, to the knowledge of God and the world, man and society, that was always linked with the ability to write. Writing was an act of socialization, the education of man as a civilized and social being. It was not a question of acquiring a technology, but rather of education in a very comprehensive sense, of *sbōjet* in Egyptian, *musar* in Hebrew, and *paideia* in Greek.[18] Literary texts were educational texts with a spectrum running from simple school textbooks to ambitious wisdom books. They were all destined to be learned by heart—*par coeur.*[19]

To begin with, the bard and the scribe are nothing more than conduits, agents of a tradition, the living embodiments of an expanded context. Both have the task of ensuring the continuity of a communicative process that consists in the encoding, storing, and retrieval of the linguistic utterances that have been consolidated into "texts." The differences between them arise from the fundamentally distinct ways in which the expanded context has been institutionalized. I would like to highlight two of these. One consists in the different forms of retrieval. In the case of the oral tradition it is based on the discontinuous rhythm of the ritual repetitions that bring bard and public together in the alternations between festivals and everyday life. In the case of the written tradition it consists in the continuous, day-to-day labor of copying and learning the texts by heart, and passing them on to pupils who also copy them and learn them by heart. In this way, they acquire not only the art of writing, but also the techniques of administration and the principles of civilized behavior. The second distinction consists in the professionalization of the carriers. In the world of oral transmission, the memory specialists, the bards, shamans, and minstrels, generally create their own profession, devoted exclusively to the conservation and performance of cultural texts. Teachers in the written tradition, in contrast, the "wise scribes," as they are called in the Bible (*soferim hachamim*), did not create an institutionalized profession; they were officials, and the pupils they instructed were the assistants who had been assigned to them (the intern system).[20] Schools in our sense, with professional teachers, did not exist. The Mesopotamian "house of tablets" was a comparatively small room that might well be linked to private houses, and probably also to offices, temples, and palaces where learning to write could go hand in hand with the business of maintaining the stream of tradition. Apart from this cultivation, enrichment, and transmission of the stream of tradition, there was no institutionalized method of literary communication, there were no libraries, bookshops, book markets, or private readers. Literary communication took place in the narrow framework of education and training.

This means that ancient Oriental literature is restricted and conditioned to a degree alien to us. It is restricted, on the one hand, by the parallel existence of an oral tradition, now lost, together with its culture of festivals and the ritual repetition of specific performances, and on the other hand, by the functional context of education, of practicing the writing culture. This writing culture, however, stood for culture in general, and the scribes, far from being a special guild, were the representatives of Egyptian culture as such. In this sense, the texts used to educate them should be regarded as cultural texts in the full meaning of the word.

Alongside these texts, however, there were texts of quite a different sort. It must be assumed that the business of maintaining the tradition was a full-time occupation for the scribes. We must distinguish between the didactic literature to be learned by heart and the corpus of knowledge to be consulted. This comprises "factual knowledge," such as medical, astronomical, and administrative reference books and lists. We must further distinguish the literature for recitation on ceremonial occasions ("sacred texts"). Only the didactic literature can be classed among the cultural texts, since it alone has a universal normative and formative authority. In contrast, the literature for reference and recitation is associated with the idea of secrecy; it is there only for specialists. Of course, the boundaries are ill-defined and a cultic text may easily be thought to be so exemplary or important in some other respect that it is taken up into the mainstream of the tradition, among the cultural texts. And beyond the narrow framework of literary texts in the wider sense, there is also the broader expanse of bureaucratic writing ("files"), and in Egypt there is in addition the entire complex of the so-called literature of the dead. Cultural texts amount to no more than a comparatively small portion of this extensive body of writing. But we should remind ourselves yet again that alongside it the oral tradition of myths and legends continues to thrive, and that cultural coherence in Egypt and Mesopotamia is still based to a great extent on the repetition involved in the rituals.

Repetition, Variation, and Innovation:
On the Differing Dynamics in Oral
and Written Culture

The most important distinction between an oral culture based on memory and the written stream of tradition is the element of variation or innovation. Only the written tradition, not the oral one, is subject to the constant pressure of change. The chief difference between the written and oral traditions is that the oral tradition is based on repetition, in other words variation is ruled out, whereas the written tradition allows for variation and even promotes it. This may seem puzzling at first glance. We might rather suppose that variation would dominate in the world of oral tradition, the world of rituals and the narrating of myths, because the words are not fixed and every performance of the text is different, whereas in a written culture the text is fixed once and for all and every reading or act of copying can only repeat it. Looked at superficially, that is of course quite correct. In reality, all the versions of a text handed down orally differ from one another. But these variations only become manifest once they have been recorded—taped, for example. They remain undetectable in the inner experience of listeners to an oral performance. Looked at from the inside, such performances are concerned with repetition, the re-presentation of a past, invisible, and otherwise inaccessible communication. Conscious variation in the sense of a controlled deviation can only be found in a written culture, where a text can be compared with an original version.

In the world of oral tradition the potential for textual innovation, and hence of information, is slight. Texts can survive in the cultural memory only if they mainly articulate what is already known. The alternation between absence and presence, weekdays and feast days, between deep-structure storing and superficial, concrete performance is completely adequate to the task of satisfying our psychological and neurological dependence on variety.[21] In the world of the written tradition, the situation is reversed. The only text that will be absorbed into the stream of tradition and will have a chance of being borne along by it over the centuries will be one that says something new and enriches existing texts in a decisive way. There is no more eloquent testimony to the written tradition's pressure to innovate than the complaints of Khakheperre-sonb referred to above from the Egypt of the Middle Kingdom ("Had I unknown phrases / Sayings that are strange, / Novel, untried words, / Free of repetition," etc.), a moving lament about the pressure to vary and innovate that is inherent in a written culture, a problem unique to the writer.[22] From bards, the public expects the familiar, from an author, the unfamiliar.

Of course, we must add at once that the authority and the institution of the author had not yet come into existence in this early stage of a written culture. The scribe and agent of tradition is expected to keep the tradition going by transferring texts from papyruses, or clay tablets threatened with decay to new ones, by his skill in restoring passages that have been destroyed, by comparing variants, explaining passages that have become incomprehensible, and by knowing enough about the corpus of writing to be able to expound it to his pupils. But he is not expected to "publish" new works. There was as yet no public for such works in the ancient Oriental world. Thus the scribe and agent of tradition embodies the tradition preserved in the mind just as much as the bard, but with the difference that his creativity is realized in the reproduction of texts, not in using improvization to fill the gaps in traditional deep structures. It is therefore only in exceptional instances that he takes up his quill to enrich the stream of tradition himself. If he does, he dons the disguise of a teacher of wisdom, he places his own words in the mouth of an authority who passes it on in the fictional situation of a father instructing his son or a pupil. This means that the author is first a literary fiction and second an orator, not a writer. Even the complaints of Khakheperre-sonb are a speech, but here we are not dealing with a father and his son, or a teacher and his pupil, but a sage communing with himself. The "Complaints" enlarge the concept of fictional authorship behind which the genuine authors lie hidden.

Only one writer succeeded in emerging from behind the mask of an oral teacher and acquiring some authorial individuality: Khety, the scribe of whom it is said in a wisdom text of the New Kingdom,

Rising up and glimpsing the sun for Khety the scribe
And a sacrifice to the dead made of bread and beer
before Wennofer [a name for Osiris],
Libations, sacrifices of wine and linen for his spirit and his disciples,
For the influential man with select proverbs!

. . .

It is he who made a book with the teachings of King Amenemhet I, after his death,
When he joined with the heavens and went among the lords of the necropolis.[23]

There is a clear distinction here between the author, Khety, and the fictional authority, Amenemhet I, who is credited with his doctrine. But this attribution is not taken too seriously. In another chapter the same wisdom text contains an encomium of the ancient "authors," and here we find Khety along with a series of other authorities of framing narratives:

Is there one here like Hardedef?
Or is there another like Imhotep?
None of our kin is like Neferti
Or Khety, the first among them.
I give you the name of Ptah-emdjehuty
And Khakheperre-sonb.
Is there another like Ptahhotep
Or the equal of Kaires?[24]

This text, too, expresses the tension between old and new that belongs among the typical tendencies of a writing culture in an expanded context: the overpowering influence of the old which prevents the new from asserting itself on equal terms. In the oral tradition, there can be no such breach between old and new because the maintenance of the tradition and the reproduction of what has been handed down is enacted in the form of (ritual) repetition. Repetition, however, means total congruence between "then" and "now," old and new, past and present. Here, *repetition* is not a problem but a structural necessity. Without repetition the process of preserving a tradition collapses. *Innovation* would mean oblivion. Repetition becomes a problem where a tradition can be perceived from outside as a visible, quasi-reified stock of knowledge. This visibility means that the difference between old and new becomes apparent. Only when writing comes into being does a tradition acquire a form that enables its representatives to regard it critically and to introduce innovations. Only through writing does the representative obtain the freedom to present his own contribution as something novel, strange, and unprecedented, in contrast to the old and familiar: *unknown songs, strange utterances, original speech that has never yet been heard, free of repetition.*

3. Canon: The Origins of Textual Coherence

a. Center and Periphery in the Stream of Tradition: The Canonization of the Classics

It frequently happens that the spoken language diverges from the language of the texts that have been handed down, to a point where the language of the ancient texts is no longer perceived as a dialect of the spoken language. It appears to be a completely different language that retains a family resemblance but still has to be learned independently. It is only where this occurs that the distinction between old and new becomes palpable and undergoes a qualitative change.[25] In the history of the Egyptian language, this rupture occurs in the fourteenth century B.C. At that point, the stream of tradition breaks down not just into old and new, but also into center and periphery. Thus at this stage there is an ancient body of writing that has receded into the past and whose language has become alien and has to be learned independently. The center is now occupied by an authoritative, as it were "classical" selection of texts from this tradition. It is from this period that we have the text we have cited about the impossibility of retrieving the ancient authors. The polarity of old and new now becomes dramatic; it acquires the idea of an irretrievable loss. The expanded context makes a qualitative leap; the act of reproduction is now conceived as a return to the past that involves crossing the threshold of an era.

The typical cultural response to this experience is to canonize ancient texts selectively and to revere them as classics. Looked at in retrospect, this often appears as a natural process in which certain texts simply come to predominate. In literature, as with wine, the best is the most suitable for storage. In reality, however, decisions often intervene in a way that has little to do with "quality." By common agreement, the two most important texts of Egyptian literature are *The Dispute Between a Man and*

His Ba and Akhenaten's *Great Hymn to the Sun.*[26] Both of these, however, are documented in only a single contemporary manuscript or inscription, and evidently never entered the *stream of tradition.* In the case of the *Great Hymn* this is readily comprehensible: it fell victim to the persecution that resulted in the obliteration from memory of every recollection of the Amarna period. In the case of the *Dispute,* the reasons for this oblivion are inexplicable. An astonishing number of texts that seem important to us and do not seem in any way inferior to the works of recognized classics have been preserved only in a single manuscript.[27] These include *The Tale of the Shipwrecked Sailor,* the Papyrus Westcar, and *The Admonitions of Ipuwer.*[28] This fact shows clearly that the creation of a tradition involves a process of selection, and that the "aging" of texts, their growth in time, value, and authority, depends upon such selection processes and their criteria. Writing as such, and this is what I wish to emphasize, does not guarantee continuity. On the contrary, it conceals risks of being forgotten, of disappearance, of aging and being left to gather dust that are alien to the oral tradition. It may point to rupture more often than continuity. We must always bear in mind that the storeroom of writing is a form of displacement. We find ourselves in the anteroom of communication. Orally transmitted texts have the rituals and festivals that constantly ensure their reproduction in the communication process. Books must first develop the institutions that ensure that their stored-up communications can be reproduced. As yet, there are no libraries and bookshops, and no isolated readers, and hence there are no institutionalized ways of ensuring that texts can last and be reproduced, outside the school tradition. Whatever is not absorbed into that tradition disappears.

b. Bringing the Stream of Tradition to a Standstill

The rule about verbatim reproduction exists, as we have seen, as far back as memory-based cultures, and is linked there with the exceptional case of sacred texts. In contrast, the customary method of handing down cultural texts involves the preservation of deep structures and filling in the details. This freedom in the process of reproducing texts is maintained in the written culture. In the history of the Egyptian, Mesopotamian, and biblical traditions we note an astonishing degree of *mouvance.* Texts continue to be added to over centuries. The enlargement of the Book of Isaiah with Deutero-Isaiah and even Trito-Isaiah is typical. Passages are inserted, the texts are rearranged and updated by modernizing editors. We might mention the Egyptian Instruction of Ptahhotep as one example typical of many. The millennia-long history of the Gilgamesh epic, from its Sumerian beginnings to the neo-Assyrian twelve-tablet epic, combines all the forms of amplification, accommodation, glossing, and translation. The stream of tradition is a living process that retains a considerable degree of *mouvance*, even in the conditions obtaining in a written culture. We must not forget that we are still within the realm of an essentially memory-based culture, despite some written support. The texts are meant to be learned, and for many of them ceremonial recitation is the customary form of communication reproduction, alongside their didactic function in schools. *Mouvance* belongs among what might be called the natural fundamental structures of the expanded context. The principle of "times change and we change with them" is not invalidated by the arrival of texts. In the oral tradition, this process takes place imperceptibly, and hence does not enter into consciousness. In the written culture, in contrast, it becomes visible and is not necessarily regarded as progress by those involved.

From a certain point in history, we repeatedly observe attempts to bring the stream of tradition to a halt and to stabilize the texts. Rules for conserving and reproducing them are introduced; verbatim accuracy is made into the cardinal principle. "Add nothing, move nothing, and take nothing away" is the watchword by which to put a check on the tendency inherent in the expanded context of adjusting texts to fit the times. We first encounter this formula in connection with the institution of messengers, in dealing with weights and measures, in the preservation of contracts, and later on, in the institution of testimony where the faithful account of an event was in question—that is, in all situations where absolute reliability was indispensable.[29] The decisive turning point was when this virtue was transferred to the examination of texts and thereby *from the concern with content to a concern with the language employed.* The earliest proof of this can be found in a Babylonian colophon.[30] The principle has its roots, then, in the written culture of Babylon. But its locus classicus is to be found in the Bible, in Deuteronomy (4:2 and 12:32). Admittedly, the focus here is also a contract whose text not only needs to be preserved in its integral shape, but also is supposed to be put into practice. But there is a clear shift of attention from the content to the language employed.

With regard to this history of canonic formulas, we should observe that the canonization of the shape of the text and the obligation to guarantee that it will be passed down with absolute fidelity to the word has a two-fold root. The first undoubtedly lies in the need to deal with sacred texts. For sacred texts, a punctilious fidelity to a verbatim record was already of paramount concern in the oral tradition. The second root, however, is to be found in the law. The meaning of the canonic formula is simply that the expanded context is underpinned in two different ways. There is a *ju-ridical* underpinning, on the model of a contract, and a *sacral* underpinning, on the model of a rite. The duty of the copyist is to proceed with the reliability of an official, and with the religious vigilance and attentiveness of a priest.

c. Tradition as Interpretation and the Cultivation of Meaning

Through the process of canonization, cultural texts are treated as sacred texts. This gives rise to tension, since it means combining two opposites. The sacred text is subject to tight restrictions on access and rules relating to purity. Cultural texts, in contrast, insist on universal normative and formative authority. They aspire to be known and taken to heart by everyone. This sets the stage for a conflict which the canonic cultures have attempted to resolve in a variety of ways.

1. The Jewish solution: The text remains in the sacred language and is endowed with all the marks of holiness. However, the priestly restrictions on access and the rules relating to purity are extended to the entire nation.

2. The Catholic solution: the text remains in the sacred language and is endowed with all the marks of holiness. Its normative and formative implementation is entrusted to a hierarchically organized institution, the Church, within which the priestly rules on access and purity only hold good for a representative group.

3. The Protestant solution: The text is translated and made accessible to all, and its normative and formative claims are given a higher value than its sacred character.

It would be interesting to add to this list the various solutions provided by Islam and Buddhism. But what is common to every solution is the insistence on interpretation. The position of the canonical text differs from that of the sacred text that is fulfilled through recitation, but is identical with the cultural text since it, too, demands to be taken to heart and put into practice. It is no magic formula, in the sense that knowledge of it and recitation brings a proximity to God, although it can also be used in this way. Far more decisive is its claim to establish identity and its assertion that it will ensure membership in the group if you take it to heart and abide by it: membership in the group of Jews, Christians, Muslims, Sikhs, Buddhists, Jainists, and so on.

What we might call the primal scene of this intrinsic link between canonization and interpretation can be found in the scene at the Water Gate in Jerusalem, as described in chapter 8 of the Book of Nehemiah. This took place during the seven days of the Feast of Tabernacles when Ezra read out aloud to the assembled people from the book with the Law of Moses, the Pentateuch, and when the Levites explained what had been read, "so that the people were attentive unto the book of the law." Canonization, reading aloud, and interpretation belong together and form the three pillars of a new constitution of the expanded context. With this the principle holding culture together is fundamentally changed and transformed from a ritual coherence to a textual coherence.

In the world of ritual coherence, cultural texts structure reality because they are communicated in the rhythm of group festivals and rites. In the world of textual coherence, life with texts is structured very differently. Since the texts do not exist in living memory, but have been displaced into thinglike pieces of writing, they assume one form when latent in a state of stored presence and another in the act of communicative reproduction. This form is no longer defined by time and obedient to the rhythm of workaday and feast day, but differentiated functionally into foreground and background, or, as in the terminology proposed by Aleida Assmann, into a functional memory and a storage memory. The transfer from latency to presence, the reproduction of the displaced memory-store, is enacted chiefly in the form of interpretation, the effort to reconstruct meaning. After all, as we have already stressed, what is being stored is not the texts themselves, but assemblages of linguistic signs which can only be reconstituted as texts through the act of reproducing them. The reproduction of texts handed down orally is accomplished in a discontinuous manner through ritual repetition; the reproduction of texts handed down in writing tends to be a process of continuous "cultivation of meaning," of interpretative work on texts.

Text and Ritual: The Meaning of the
Media for the History of Religion

I think that the changes in written characters in different periods of culture have always played a very important part in the revolutions in human knowledge as such, and particularly in the manifold changes in the opinions and concepts of religious questions.

—MOSES MENDELSSOHN[1]

1. From Ritual Coherence to
Textual Coherence

It has often been proposed that there might be a connection between the histories of religion and the media. As early as the eighteenth century, a link was perceived between monotheist religion and the invention of the alphabet, and the connection between Protestantism and the printing press is a long-standing commonplace. The present chapter aims to explore such issues with reference to the ancient world and to establish a link between the origins of the book-based religions and changes in the history of the media. In the process I make use of ideas that I developed at length in my book *Cultural Memory*, and shall only allude to here.[2]

In the relationship between text and ritual, the history of religion marks a turning point that amounts to a complete reversal. Where, previously, the text was embedded in the ritual and subordinated to it, now the text, in the shape of a body of canonic writings, becomes the pivotal factor, and ritual is left with only a framing and accompanying function. This turning point is a watershed, and separates two types of religion. We may differentiate these as cult religions and book-based religions. Cult religions

are the primary phenomenon everywhere. They arise seamlessly from tribal religions, branch out into the complex and complicated polytheisms of
the early high cultures, and can still be found in the Asiatic world down
to the present day, frequently in a state of peaceful coexistence with religions that stand on a very different footing. Book-based religions, on the
other hand, all arise from a radical rupture with tradition. We may follow
Theo Sundermeier in characterizing religions at this stage as "secondary religions."[3] This concept includes all religions that do not trace their origins
back to the mists of time, but claim to be the product of historical acts of
revelation and creation. They include the three Western monotheisms, Judaism, Christianity, and Islam, as well as Buddhism, Jainism, and the Sikh
religion. All secondary religions are book-based religions. They are founded on a canon of sacred writings, such as the Hebrew Bible, the Christian
Bible, the Koran, the Jain canon, the Pali canon, and the Adi Granth.[4] The
change of medium that formed our point of departure has its corollary in
a structural change in the nature of religion. On the side of the secondary
religions we find writing and transcendence, while on that of primary religion we find ritual and immanence.

This transformation is accompanied by a transformation of "cultural memory." In the cult religions, the "connective structures" that ensured
the identical reproduction of the culture down through the generations
were based primarily on the principle of ritual repetition. In the case of
book-based religions, they are founded on the principle of interpreting the
canonical texts. I would like to make three additional points in support of
this assertion: first, with regard to the distinction between cultural and canonical texts; second, in relation to the "expanded context" and its institutionalization in the oral and written traditions; and third, with reference
to the change that takes place in the question of who participates in the religion, a situation that changes drastically in the development from ritual
to textual coherence.

By "cultural texts" we understand all sign complexes, that is, not just
texts, but also dances, rites, symbols, and the rest, that possess a particular normative and formative authority in the establishment of meaning
and identity.[5] Cultural texts lay claim to an authority that embraces society as a whole; they determine its identity and coherence. They structure
the world of meaning in which society makes itself understood, and also
the sense of unity, belonging, and individuality that can be handed down

through the generations, thus enabling a society to reproduce itself as a recognizable group.

Cultural texts change with the changing context of a changing present, and it is precisely the cultural texts that are subject to the most radical editorial modifications.[6] This is because it is they, above all, that are concerned to adapt themselves to a changed reality. It is they that must be continually added to and accommodated because they have to be transported from one generation to the next and because they keep finding themselves in a changing environment. Such *mouvance*, to use Paul Zumthor's term, is the fate of texts destined for repeated use; it is the form in which they are adapted for constant reuse, and the typical form of organization of the "stream of tradition" (in the sense used by Leo Oppenheim) in Mesopotamia and Egypt. The earliest and most widespread form of the cultivation of meaning consists in alterations to the text. Such alterations are forbidden wherever the literal word is sacrosanct and where neither "jot nor tittle" can be altered. That is the step that we call canonization.

As noted earlier, we owe the concept of an "expanded context" to Konrad Ehlich, who applies it to a communication situation in which, thanks to the existence of the appropriate cultural institutions, it is possible always to recall communications that have been stored. Therefore, the principal difference between the oral and written transmission of such communications or cultural texts does not lie in the medium and the technology of storage, but in the way the expanded context is institutionalized. The position with oral transmission is that the extended context calls for a far more radical shaping process than is required in developed written cultures, and it normally takes the form of ritual. As we have seen, festivals and rituals are the typical ways in which societies without writing institutionalize the expanded context of cultural texts. Ritual ensures that a communication will be recalled; it guarantees the communicative presence of the text and thus the ritual coherence of the culture. Despite the growing quantity of written matter, early written cultures are decisively based on such ritual coherence.

The possibility created by writing of storing linguistic utterances in their literal form, so that they could be reproduced subsequently without the need to learn them by heart, was a development that liberated people from the repetition compulsion of ritual coherence. What mattered now was understanding. This is the place where Hans-Georg Gadamer's principle of "merging horizons" comes into its own. This principle represents the *unio mystica* of text and reader, a process of merging achieved in the realm of ritual coherence by ritual itself. The classical example is the "dream time" of the Australian Aborigines. With every new celebration mythical time comes into being yet again, and the clock of everyday, linear time is put back once more. In the realm of textual coherence, such mystical fusion can only be achieved with the aid of an elaborate art of interpretation. The hermeneutics of the merging horizon described by Gadamer is only valid in the framework of canonical texts, and then only for this exceptional case of the expanded context. Admittedly, it provides an outstanding description of this context. However, far more is called for simply than "intrinsic textual markers," to which Gadamer ascribes "eternal expressive power." What is needed is the entire apparatus of a culture of learning, exegesis, understanding, and internalization with all of its highly complex set of assumptions.

The transformation from ritual to textual coherence implies a change in the *structure of participation*. For textual coherence to exist, knowledge of the text has to be as widely disseminated as possible. Ideally, every member of society should be able to read the texts, and even learn them by heart, as well as having access to an interpreter from whom he or she can seek advice. In the case of ritual coherence, the opposite participation structure obtains, one based on the principle of secrecy. Cult religions are religions concerned with mysteries, just as book-based religions are religions of revelation. They are dominated by the pathos of proclamation and explanation; cult religions, in contrast, are dominated by the opposite pathos of keeping secrets, exclusivity, and esotericism. I shall discuss this in greater detail in Section 3. The increased participation of the entire nation made possible by the book-based religions implies that the sacred is constantly present and accessible. In the primary religions, the sacred was much more evident to the senses, in a variety of ways. In exchange, however, the sacred occasions when the holy made its appearance were spread much more abstemiously over the whole year. Flavius Josephus, the Jewish historian, drew attention to this important distinction between pagan cult religion and Jewish book-based religion in his polemic *Contra Apionem*.

Can any government (says he) be more holy than this? Or any religion better adapted to the nature of the Deity? Where in any place but in this, are the whole

People, by the special diligence of the Priests, to whom the care of public instruction is committed, accurately taught the principles of true piety? So that the body politic seems, as it were, one great *Assembly*, constantly kept together, for the celebration of some sacred *Mysteries*? For those things which the Gentiles keep up for a few days only, that is, during those solemnities they call MYSTERIES and INITIATIONS, we, with vast delight, and a plenitude of knowledge, which admits of no error, fully enjoy, and perpetually contemplate through the whole course of our lives. If you ask (continues he) the nature of those things, which in our sacred rites are enjoined and forbidden, I answer, they are simple and easily understood. The first instruction relates to the DEITY, and teaches that GOD CONTAINS ALL THINGS, and is a Being every way perfect and happy: that he is self-existent, and the SOLE CAUSE of all existence; the beginning, the middle and the end of all things, etc."[7]

2. Ritual and Immanence: The Changing Structure of the Sacred

The principle of ritual coherence is combined with the idea of the need to maintain the world. Ritual cultures or cult religions typically assume that the universe would suffer or even collapse if the rituals were not performed in an orderly manner. The ritual always serves to maintain an overall unity that is threatened by decay. The emphasis on textual coherence grows as this idea fades. For the Bible, this change is brought about by the emergence of a theology of creation and a theology of the will. The world does not owe its existence to rituals, but to the sustaining will and activity of a transcendent God. For the tradition of classical humanism, the Platonic theory of the world-soul (as formulated in the *Timaeus*) and the Aristotelian idea of the unmoved mover signify a comparable revolution in the relationship between man and the world. These philosophies likewise remove from man the burden of keeping the world going and represent the cosmos as an ordered, living totality that exists independently of man. This did not indeed have any further implications in the practices of the Greek cults, but it did for Greek culture which, unlike that of ancient Egypt, did not disappear along with the rituals, but survived in the texts.

The principle of ritual coherence and the need to maintain the world is connected further with the social type of the priest, much as the notion of text-interpretation implies the social types of the interpreter, the scholar, and the priest. The priest is separated from the community by strict rules about purity; he becomes qualified by virtue of a ritual cleanliness that is achieved by means of washing, fasting, sexual abstinence, and other forms of what Max Weber terms "magical asceticism." Priestly competence is in the first instance a physical matter; the body is much more directly involved than in the case of book religions. With the institution of celibacy, this was given such decisive form in Roman Catholicism that even today we tend to talk more of priests than of parsons and pastors. In addition, of course, there is an emphasis on knowledge in the shape of ritual and liturgical competence. The priest has to know how, when and where specific actions are to be performed, and which words have to be spoken or chanted. The whole business of keeping the world going, with all its assumptions, can only succeed if a plethora of rules are followed all of which have to be known and mastered. Success or failure are proved through the direct interaction with nature, through the fact that the sun rises or sets, that it rains, that the seed blossoms, the cattle thrive, the army is victorious, the storm passes or the calm comes to an end, the pregnant woman gives birth or the invalid recovers, etc., etc. The sacred realm with which the priest is concerned and for whose sake he must purify himself exists within this world; it is attached to a particular location or is vividly present to the senses, and it is separated from the profane world of everyday by very high barriers. This contrasts starkly with the situation of the interpreter or preacher. The sacred realm with which the latter is concerned is radically separated from this world. Within this world it is present exclusively in written form. For this reason both in Judaism and Islam, writing is invested with ideas and regulations that have manifestly been imported from the world of ritual. Thus a Jew may not put a Bible on the floor, and a Muslim is forbidden to destroy any piece of writing in the Arabic script or language. He may not even take it to read in unsuitable places, even if it is only the newspaper. Christianity, and especially Protestantism, has done away with even this vestige of ritual. The interpreter or preacher becomes qualified for his office through his knowledge of the scriptures. He knows how to read them and to read them aloud, he knows them by heart and is able to use one passage to shed light on another. Above all, he knows how to make them relevant to particular situations in the present. Here, there is no direct interaction with nature. The success of his calling is measured by the degree to which his sermon is taken to heart, that is, by the translation from text to practical life.

The transition from cult religion to book religion is accompanied by a structural change in the nature of the sacred to which the Greek specialist Albrecht Dihle has drawn our attention on the basis of semasiological observations.[8] Greek and Latin distinguish between two concepts of the "holy" that exist in only one form in Hebrew as well as in modern languages. The first term, *hieros* in Greek, and *sacer* in Latin, designates "the holiness that exists objectively in many places in the world." The second term, *hosios* or *sanctus*, signifies "the qualification of a person or of circumstances that is necessary for dealing with the holy."[9] Primary or cultic religions are concerned with the holiness that exists visibly in the world (*hieros*). Priestly dealings with this holiness call for holiness in the sense of *hosios*. This signifies a condition that is segregated from the profane sphere. Secondary religions, on the other hand, abolish this distinction because holiness is no longer to be found anywhere in the world. The only thing that can still pass as *hieros* or *sanctus* is the holy scripture, *biblia sacra*.

The expulsion of the holy from the world, into a transcendental realm on the one hand, and into scripture on the other, leads to a fundamental redirection of attention. Previously, all eyes were focused on the phenomena of this world and the holiness that was manifest in them. Henceforth, attention is concentrated exclusively on scripture. Everything else is stigmatized as idolatry. The things of this world, images above all, are snares and pitfalls that distract attention from the scriptures. Man must free himself from any entanglement with them. The denigration of images and the visual in general is accompanied by a form of discourse that desensualizes religion and dismantles the theatricality of ritual. Moses Mendelssohn, incidentally, saw the danger here with particular clarity. "We are literal people," he complains, "our entire nature depends on letters."[10] Accordingly, he praises Judaism for prescribing so many rituals because they enable the aesthetic dimension of religion to be preserved even in the context of a book religion.

3. Ritual, Text, and Mystery

The principle of ritual coherence is based on the media that make the sacred visibly manifest in the world. These media include holy places, trees, sources, stones, grottos, groves, but also and above all, images, statues, symbols, and buildings such as temples, pyramids, and stupas. The priest has to adapt himself to these evidences of the sacred. "Put off thy shoes from off thy feet," it says in Exodus 3:5, "for the place whereon thou standest is holy ground." Where the holy is present in corporeal and visible form, other laws obtain and to ignore them can be fatal. This holds good also for the sacred texts that are embedded in the rituals for the purpose of recitation or already in recitable form. They too make the holy present. To have them recited correctly in the right place, at the right time, and by the right speaker unleashes cosmic energies that keep the world in order. In late Egyptian civilization, these texts were brought together under the generic title "The Power of Re," which means something like "solar energy." The Egyptian priest had to chew sodium and cleanse his mouth before reciting these texts. These utterances had to be protected from profanation just like the holy places, images, and symbols, and hedged around by all the rules of secrecy.

I would like to illustrate this with a number of examples from Egypt. Ancient Egypt can be regarded as the prototype of a religion based on mystery.[11] In a text from the Middle Kingdom, "The Admonitions of Ipuwer," we hear the following lament:

> Lo, the private chamber, its books are stolen,
> The secrets in it are laid bare.
> Lo, magic spells are divulged,
> Spells are made worthless through being repeated by people.[12]
> See, the secret of the land, its limits are unknown,
> If the residence is stripped, it will collapse in a moment.
> . . .
> See the serpent is taken from its hole,
> The secrets of Egypt's kings are bared.[13]

Thus great emphasis is placed on extreme confidentiality in ritual texts:

> You shall accomplish this without allowing any man to watch,
> Apart from your true confidant and a lector-priest.
> Let no other person watch and let no servant enter from without.
> . . .
> This script is truly secret.
> Profane persons may not watch
> At any place and any time.[14]

Or again: "Now when this is recited the place is to be completely seclud-ed, not seen and not heard by anyone except the chief lector-priest and the *setem*-priest."[15] In the crypts of the temple of Hathor in Dendara, it is said that entrance is forbidden to foreigners in particular:

> The hidden place of the powerful in the sistra house
> If the destroyers invade Egypt.
> The Asiatics do not enter there,
> The Bedouins do not harm it,
> The profane do not walk around there.
> Whoever recites a spell against it,
> May the milk of Sekhmet be in his body.[16]
>
> . . .
>
> The place whose secret is hidden
> Against the day that the Asiatics invade the fortress.
> The Phoenicians do not approach it,
> The Aegeans do not enter,
> The lizards do not crawl around there.
> A magician does not perform his rites.
> Its gates are not opened to those without authority.[17]

A ritual book from the Late Period with the title *The End of Work* is de-scribed as follows:

On this day (1 Achat 20), the book entitled *The End of Work* is examined. This is a secret book that foils magic, that formulates the incantations, establishes the in-cantations and keeps the whole universe in check.

It contains life and death. Do not make it known, since whoever makes it known will die a sudden death and will be murdered on the spot. Keep away from it, for it contains life and death.

It is (only) the scribe of the administration of the house of life who recites it.[18]

The ritual takes place in the house of life, of which it is said:

> It shall be very, very hidden.
> No one shall know it, no one see it
> Apart from the sundial that gazes on its secret.
>
> . . .
>
> The officiating priests . . . shall enter silently, their bodies veiled,
> So that they shall be protected against a sudden death.
> The Asiatic may not enter, he may not see anything.[19]

The priest who is able with his words to release cosmic energies intervenes in the cosmos in a supportive way, but he may also intervene menacingly if the situation calls for it and a crisis has to be averted. Thus he may threaten to halt the bark of the sun in its tracks if a particular patient is not instantly cured. This is discussed by Porphyry, the Neoplatonic thinker, in his letter to the Egyptian priest Anebo, known to us from the response written by Iamblichus. Porphyry is scandalized by the idea that the priest could have an effect on the cosmos simply through the act of recitation. "For the reciter threatens to shatter the heavens, to make public the mysteries of Isis, to reveal what is hidden in the abyss (of the universe), to bring the bark to a standstill, to cast the limbs of Osiris before Typhon and other things of this sort."[20] Such texts do in fact exist in large numbers. It would be hard to reproduce more precisely Egyptian notions of the power of cultic language. Porphyry has in mind threats of the kind that occur frequently in Egyptian books of spells,[21] but it also gives a much broader sense of the performative power of cultic language in general. The sacred texts are able to generate such effects—effects that are also to be feared if they are profaned, if they fall into the wrong hands and their mysteries are revealed. The "power of Re" is, as we have said, the generic name for such "sacred texts" that have to be protected and kept secret because they contain cosmic knowledge. The ritual incantation of this knowledge keeps the world going because it joins in the cosmic work of the journey of the sun. In Egypt, a sacred text was thought to be a linguistic repository of the holy and was subject to the same restrictions and regulations with regard to access as the cult image. The recitation of a sacred text produced the same corporeal and visible realization, the "making present" of the "godly," as the holy image. This literature was secret because it formed part of the cult mysteries of objects that had to be protected from profane defilement and from being deprived of their power by the external world. Whatever had been desecrated was no longer able to make the godly present and real.

4. The Foreign-Language Dimension of Sacred Texts

In his reply to Porphyry's accusing the priest of blasphemy, Iamblichus too turns out to be extremely well informed. For he writes that the priest or magician does not utter such threats in his own interest and by his own responsibility, but that he moves onto the same plane as the gods, assumes the identity of a god, and only resorts to such extreme measures while acting in this role, and not in his own person.[22] Nor did he desire to create havoc; on the contrary, his intention was to ward it off. These threats were intended apotropaically, to ward off evil demons. The magician speaks to the gods as a god, and in the last analysis it is their cause he is defending, since they too want to prevent evil demons from gaining the upper hand. This brilliantly encapsulates the principle of cultic language. Elsewhere, however, Iamblichus discusses this principle even more explicitly.

I am thinking here of the famous chapter in which Iamblichus responds to the question Porphyry had posed about the meaning of meaningless formulas or names.[23] *Ti gar bouletai ta onomata asema?* What is the purpose of invocations without meaning? What are being referred to are the so-called *onomata barbara* or magic words that are to be found, above all, in the Greco-Egyptian magic papyri. These formulas, Iamblichus replied, are not actually meaningless; they only seem so to us because we have forgotten their meaning. They are not meaningless to the gods to whom they are addressed. What we find here is a divine language that we have forgotten but which the gods still understand. Even if it has become estranged from us, when we speak it, it is still able to raise us to the level of the gods. Thus Iamblichus conceives of the language of the Egyptian cults in a mystical sense: it is less concerned with the impact of speech on the hearer than on the speaker. By speaking the divine language, he himself becomes a god, even though, or rather because, he does not understand it. This mystical interpretation of cultic language is of course a misunderstanding. Nevertheless, Iamblichus correctly understands the divine character of cultic speech, which the priest recites not in his own identity but in the role of a god.

Iamblichus's theory of a mystical language of the gods is so interesting, for all its misunderstanding, that I would like briefly to summarize it here. According to Iamblichus, we harbor in our souls mystical and mysterious images of the gods. This internal iconography is activated when we utter the foreign-language formulas, helping us to raise our souls to the gods and thus to approach them as closely as we can. The very fact that we do not understand these formulas is what makes them seem sublime. Precisely because we do not understand them our uttering them brings about our inner transformation. It is their foreignness and their foreign-language nature that helps us to transcend our own nature.

Iamblichus's mystical account of the effect of the speech on the speaker is precisely the principle that underlies the Egyptian cult. It consists in the ability to encounter the gods not as man but as a god, to communicate with them on the same plane. This presupposes that in his commerce with the gods the priest makes use of the language of the gods, and not that of man. For its part, the language of Egyptian cult recitation is often obscure, but for quite different reasons. We are not concerned here with foreign-language formulas or senseless abracadabras. The cultic recitations are couched in a divine language, not in the sense of a foreign language, but as divine language mediated by masks and roles. This speech has a transformative power, a power not concerned, or less concerned, with transforming the speaker than with transforming the listener.

What is crucial is that the priest encounters the gods not as a man, but in the role of a god. Iamblichus rightly insists "that the workings of the gods are not achieved by two different parties confronting one another (man and god), but that this kind of divine activity is brought about in agreement, unity and consent" (4.3).[24] "The theurgist issues his commands to the cosmic forces by virtue of the power of the secret symbols, no longer as a man and no longer as exercising power over a merely human soul, but as if he now belonged in the ranks of the gods. These commands are more powerful than those available to him by virtue of his own actual nature" (6.6).[25] The fundamental idea of the ritual practices of the ancient Egyptians could not be formulated with greater clarity. This "theurgical" principle applies to action and in particular to language that cannot be separated from action. The recitation accompanying the actions contains the transformative, transfiguring power. This explains why the priest is always on hand with his scroll. He administers the linguistic side of action, the recitation that becomes divine speech in the mouth of the priest at the moment of the cultic act. When the priest speaks, one god speaks to another, and the words unfold their transformative, performative, and "presentificatory" power.

By its meaning and nature, therefore, sacred recitation is divine speech, stored in the medium of writing and realized in the context of cul-

tic role play. The priest does not speak in his own person; he does not encounter a divine image as a human being. Instead he slips into a role in
the context of a combined divine and worldly "constellation." Cultic language is language of the gods,[26] a language that also treats script as belonging to the gods. The Egyptian word for hieroglyph means roughly "God's
words." The failure to distinguish between script and language in the expression *mdt ntr*, "God's words," for hieroglyphic script, is symptomatic of
the close link between script and cult in the Egyptian mind and remained
decisive for modern theories about hieroglyphs. Giordano Bruno's understanding of hieroglyphs evidently was inspired by Iamblichus:

The . . . "sacred letters" used among the Egyptians were called hieroglyphs which
instead of individual signs [*designanda*] were specific images taken from the things
of nature, or their parts. By using such writings and voices (*voces*), the Egyptians
used to capture with marvellous skill the language of the gods. Afterwards, when
letters of the kind which we now use with another kind of industry were invented
by Theuth or some other, this brought about a great rift both in memory and in
the divine and magical sciences.[27]

Admittedly, the turning point did not come, as Bruno believed, with the
invention of the alphabet, but with the shift of emphasis from sound to
meaning in the definition of sacred texts, from expression to content, from
ritual performance to the need to heed the texts as a guide to living, and
from cultic theatricality to hermeneutics. This turning point is the subject of the correspondence between Porphyry and Iamblichus, in which
the older man is already reasoning on this side of the threshold, while the
younger man persists in the older view.

5. Mysteries of Reading and Intellectual Rituals

It was Bernhard Lang who coined the concept of "intellectual ritual."[28] Following up Robert Ranulph Marett's claim that "primitive religions are danced rather than thought," he draws attention to a fundamental change that leads from rites that are danced to rites in which "only the
word still dances," while the participants devote themselves to reciting and
interpreting, listening to the word and taking it to heart. His thesis is that
this change first took place in early Judaism, during the Babylonian exile.

From these origins, it spread throughout the entire ancient world, together with a prehistory in the rejection by the prophets of orgiastic cults and sacramental magic, and a long posthistory in the religion of what Lorenzer termed the "bookkeepers."[29] Lang has the same change in mind here as we have described in terms of the concepts cult religion / book religion, primary/secondary religion, and ritual/textual coherence. Lang, too, places the invention of paganism and idolatry in the same context. Moses' anger at the sight of the orgiastic dance round the Golden Calf captures this polarity with the succinctness of a primal scene. The scriptures in his hands (the tablets with the Ten Commandments) and the scene before his very eyes prove to be incompatible. *This* script and *this* cult form an irreconcilable antithesis.

The Egypt of the Ptolemaic and Roman periods provides us with a late illustration of the primary, cult-oriented religious experience and of a culture given coherence by ritual. The cult here produced more and more writing, so that it ended up with a whole library of sacred writings in and around itself. Even so, the library remained subordinate to the cult, and the shift from a cult religion to a book religion did not take place. Clement of Alexandria describes not just the structure and composition of such a library, but also the mode of its cultic integration in the shape of a procession that we might describe as the typical Egyptian form of an "intellectual ritual." In Chapter 3 I gave a detailed account of Clement's description. It consists of the solemn procession of five priests or representatives of five different categories of priest: singers, astrologers, scribes, stole-keepers, and prophets (high priests). A particular group of books is assigned to each of these priests or priestly orders, whose task is to learn them by heart and master them perfectly. This gives rise to a canon of books whose internal arrangement and hierarchical structure reflects precisely the hierarchy of the priests in the temple. Thus the procession of the priests makes visible the hierarchic ordering of the canon of sacred books. In total, the books to be mastered by the priests or priestly orders amount to thirty-six—the number of the decan stars, that is, the totality of time. In addition, there are a further six medical books to be mastered by the image bearers, the *pastophoroi*, which brings the total up to forty-two, the number of Egyptian provinces and at the same time, the number of the limbs of Osiris's body that had been torn in pieces and scattered throughout the provinces. This latter, then, is the totality of space. The procession of priests demonstrates in impressive fashion the interconnections between ritual, script, and memory that characterize the Egyptian cult. The books must be learned by heart; they are not meant for reading, but as the foundations of a specialized priestly memory. The entire canon, which is staged and activated by means of a procession, in its turn provides the foundation for the ritual process of sustaining the world.

6. Writing and Revelation

In Judaism the relationship between writing and cult is turned on its head. The scriptures, ceasing to act as something that precedes or follows a cultic act, are the heart of the matter. The cultic act is reduced to something that comes after the scriptures, in the form of communal readings, memory, internalization, and interpretation. This amounts to a complete reversal. The scriptures do not give permanence to the ritual, they replace it. It is one of the most remarkable coincidences of history that the Temple of the Jews was destroyed at the very moment when the internal development of the religion had rendered it superfluous and undermined the meaning of the rituals. This was when Titus destroyed the Temple in A.D. 70. The Jesus movement was just one of a number of Jewish (and Greek) trends that sought to do away with the fundamental idea of the cult, namely blood sacrifice and ritual killing, and replace it with a process of sublimation, moralization, and internalization. If Titus had not destroyed the Temple they would have had to close it—or else Judaism would never have come into being, and Christianity and Islam along with it. The Temple had in a sense outlived its usefulness, since the cult had long since found its death in the scriptures.

There is much to be said in favor of the idea that Jewish monotheism, the principle of revelation, and, arising from it, the constantly increasing loathing of traditional cult forms, were born from the spirit of writing, or at least were bound up with the medium of writing in a profound way, very much in the spirit of Moses Mendelssohn, who more than two centuries ago postulated a link between media revolutions and religious transformations. The step to a transcendental religion was a step out of the world—we are tempted to speak of an emigration, an exodus—into the world of writing.[30] Ultimately, the canonized scriptures replace art, public life, and the world. The world is itself declared to be an object of idolatry and is thus discredited. The reverence now being paid to the Creator must not be allowed to become ensnared in His creation. God's radical positioning outside the world goes hand in hand with the radically scriptural nature of His revelation.

With this we touch upon a link between writing and transcendence that Friedrich Kittler has summed up with inimitable succinctness. "Without cultural techniques, . . . no one would know that there is anything apart from what there is. The sky would just be sky, the earth earth and so-called human beings would simply be men and women. But the revelation of the sacred leads to knowledge or (to put it more precisely) to artificial intelligence."[31] Kittler establishes a link between the "artificiality" of writing, in which the sacred becomes revealed, and the principle of the asemanticity of the texts that we discussed in connection with Iamblichus. Kittler, too, is thinking of the *onomata asema* of the Greco-Egyptian magic texts.[32] Admittedly, the very distinctions I am concerned to draw become confused here. The sacred texts of which Iamblichus speaks are quite different from the Bible and the Koran texts which Kittler has in mind, and the boundary that separates these worlds is the question of meaning. In Iamblichus, meaning plays no role at all because the texts are not supposed to be understood by men, but by gods, and the less meaningful they appear to men the more divine they are. In the Bible and the Koran, in contrast, meaning plays the central role. This explains why there are no commentaries on the Egyptian "transfigurations" and "demonstrations of solar power," while a vast, even limitless tradition of commentary exists about the Bible and the Koran. This is why we have priests and cultic communities on the one side and teachers (rabbis, mullahs) and learning communities on the other. The Bible and the Koran did not grow out of cultic formulas, but out of laws and narratives. The norms that govern them have their ultimate roots not in theurgy, but in morality and law. They form the basis for human conduct, not cult practices. It is in this context that we must view the writing that opposed the cult and led to its overthrow.

Nevertheless, I would like to express my agreement with Kittler on the point of the writing-based "artificiality" of revelation. Without the techniques of writing and hermeneutics it would be impossible to conceive of what the eighteenth century called "positive religion" and thought of as something artificial, in contrast to natural religion. There is no natural evidence in favor of prophetic monotheism, which, as St. Paul says, walks by faith not by sight. Faith is based on writing, on the attested covenant and the law. Cults are based on the act, the performance, on sight. Writing leads to a de-ritualization and de-theatricalization of religion.

Officium Memoriae: Ritual as the Medium of Thought

I. Cosmology and Religion: The Case of Akhenaten

Around the middle of the fourteenth century B.C., King Amenhotep IV of Egypt, who later called himself Akhenaten, did away with Egypt's traditional polytheistic religion and replaced it with the cult of a single god, the sun. This is the first occurrence of the foundation of a religion that we hear of in the archives of human history. Akhenaten appears as the first in a line that continues in Moses, Zoroaster, Buddha, Jesus, and Mohammed. However, when we look at the texts in which this new theology has come down to us, we feel tempted to place the king in a completely different context, namely that of Ionian nature philosophy. For in reality our concern here is not the revelation of a new truth which leads men to conduct their lives according to a new set of rules, but a new cosmology, a theory of origins and fundamental principles, or "archai," as the Greeks would have called them, on which the world is based. Akhenaten made the discovery that the sun creates light and heat through its rays, and that without this there would be no life on earth. Hence, so much depends on the sun that even traditional religion acknowledges the sun god as the creator and supreme god. But over and above that, through its motion the sun also creates time, so that—and this seems to have been the king's crucial discovery—absolutely everything that appears by the light of day and that unfolds in time seems to be explicable as the work of the sun. These ideas are familiar to us from the Ionian nature philosophers, who, however, express them in a completely different medium. Instead of writing his thoughts down on a scroll of papyrus and depositing them in the temple, that is to say, in a place that is both sacred and public; instead of using his theory to establish a new form of discourse, or to intervene in a preexisting one, the king built giant temples and then, in a second stage, moved on to a more general and very radical reshaping of culture as a whole. The most drastic element of this revolution was the abolition of the traditional cults. Akhenaten thought of his theory as the discovery of a new god who demanded exclusive worship. He destroyed the traditional world of the gods by using the medium of cult and rituals to express the cosmological idea that the whole of reality depended upon the activity of the sun. To illustrate his cosmological theory, the king was able to make use of the medium of the didactic poem, but what he lacked was a distinct discursive framework in which this didactic poem might have been produced without severely damaging the overall religious, political, cultural, and economic life of the nation. The only conceivable framework for this didactic poem was the cult in which it could be recited as a hymn to a new god, which he tried to erect on the tabula rasa of a tradition that had been repudiated. The Ionian nature philosophers put forward questions that were just as radical, but their answers led them to different conclusions, and they invested in writing, while Akhenaten strove to implement his ideals within the realm of ritual.

One of the central implications of the new worldview lay in the perception that the world had no need to be kept going by human beings, since it arose solely from the activity of the sun god. This activity could not be influenced by cult ritual; the only possible option was gratefully to accept and confirm it as the expression of a benevolent and charitable concern for mankind. This gave the rituals an entirely new meaning, one that made the sacramental magic of the traditional rites, with their interest in keeping the world going, seem unacceptable and intolerable. In Egypt the rites were the medium of cosmological thinking. The form of their world picture was directly translated into ritual acts. We might also say that for the Egyptians ideas concerning cosmological discourse had a hortatory force that led to their issuing in ritual action, and not, as would seem natural to us, to critical reflection. Put abstractly, thought among the Egyptians was still subject to the pressure of action from which Ionian nature philosophy had already become emancipated.

Akhenaten was approximately eight hundred years ahead of his time, so his efforts to do away with the traditional picture of the world proved futile. His revolution remained a mere episode; after his death religion quickly reverted to a belief in the old gods. This traditional world picture was based on the idea that the world required the assistance of ritual in order to keep functioning. The role of ritual in maintaining the functioning of the world took place in three media: recitation, the provisioning of the gods, and the annihilation of enemies. Ritual recitation is comprehensive and dominant; it accompanies both the rituals of provisioning and those of annihilation. As to these rituals, the crucial distinction between them has largely been overlooked because German uses the same concept, *Opfer*, to include both sacrifice and offering. French is more discriminating here because it distinguishes between *sacrifice* and *offrande*. The word *sacrifice* succinctly defines the bloody victim, while *offrande* designates all other votive gifts, such as water, bread, vegetables, flowers, and incense. I only grasped the importance of this distinction when I had to lecture in French on the results of my research on the Egyptian cult of the dead. That, too, is an instance of the relationship between thinking and medium. In the Egyptian cult, *offrande*, that is to say, a nonbloody offering, always serves the purpose of sustaining the world by providing for it; *sacrifice*, a bloody offering, in contrast, keeps the world going by annihilating the enemy. To slaughter is to punish. That becomes unambiguously clear in the accompanying recitations that are always the decisive factor. The relations between language and ritual oscillate in the sense that sometimes the speech accompanies the actions and sometimes it is the other way around, but the two always go together. There are rites in which the accompanying action is reduced to sprinkling a few drops of water or burning a few pieces of incense, but cuts are never tolerated in the verbal side of the proceedings. This principle is also familiar to us from the Communion service. The action, namely the distribution of bread and wine, can be reduced to minimal indications, but a similar reduction in the accompanying words is inconceivable.

2. Cosmological Constellations

What is this traditional world picture and how should we imagine the ritual process of sustaining the world? I have already suggested that traditional religion, too, assigns to the sun god the supreme position of a god of creation and the state. We must now attempt to conceive of this idea in polytheistic terms. The creative and governing functions of the sun god are made manifest in the constellations of a world of gods that he brings forth from within himself and that, as ruler, he attaches to himself. He carries out his world-creating and world-sustaining tasks at the head of this pantheon in the shape of the "course of the sun," the apparent motion of the sun around the earth. Creation is nothing more than "the first time" that this revolution occurs. The expression *the first time* in Egyptian corresponds to such concepts as *be-reshit*, genesis, and *creatio*, creation. But this also implies that there is no bottom line; the creation keeps on repeating itself through all further "times," down to the present. Cosmogonic energies are continuously at work and maintain the world by constantly re-creating it. *Creatio* is *regeneratio*.

What is there here for human beings to contribute? If the world could come into being for the first time, all further occasions ought surely to be likewise possible independently of human intervention. Why do human beings have to become involved? Did they seriously believe that the sun would come to a standstill without their assistance? Surely not. Rather, their concern was probably to mobilize the energies of the cosmos for the success of their own projects, the state, the community, healing and health, birth and death. Nothing is more dependent on regeneration than mankind. Not only does man live in a world of decay and wear and tear, but he also wears himself out and moves inexorably toward his own demise. By intervening in cosmic processes in which creation could be seen to be at work, man could believe that he was taking part in the creative renewal of the sun. Just as today's astronomers imagine that they can hear the echo of the Big Bang in the background noises of the cosmos, and that they can observe its continued effects in the frenetic expansion of the universe, the Egyptians experienced the cycle of night and day and the apparent motion of the sun around the earth as a mighty action that sustained the world, created order, and prevented chaos. They differ from modern cosmologists, however, who if they are not acting on instructions from NASA and in the interests of military control, are acting in the cause of science and from theoretical curiosity. The Egyptians' interest in the course of the sun arose from their yearning for regeneration. Just as the sun overcame the darkness every morning, so too the Egyptians desired to conquer their enemies. And just as the sun went down in the west every evening in order to rise again in the east the following morning, the Egyptians wished to experience their own death in the west. And the rituals were needed to establish this connection, to tie human concerns into the cosmic work. The world they sustained was a symbolic world of meaning in which gods and men, the state and the cosmos, nature and society, human action and cosmic cycles formed a totality. The task was to sustain this meaning-filled world through ritual. Had the rituals ceased, the sun would not have come to a standstill, but the creative and regenerative energy it liberated in its motion would have ceased to benefit human beings. Pharaoh would have ceased to prevail over his enemies, his laws would no longer be obeyed, the sick would no longer be healed, and the dead would no longer be regenerated in their graves.

There are many texts that clearly express this connection between ritual action and political, social, and individual well-being.

> If the Osiris ceremonies are neglected
> At the appointed time in this place . . . ,
> Then the land will be robbed of its laws,
> And the mob will abandon its superiors,
> And there will be no commands for the people.
> If we do not behead the enemy we have before us in
> Wax, on papyrus or in wood, according to the rules of the ritual,
> Then the foreigners will rebel against Egypt
> And civil war and revolution will arise in the land.
> No one will listen to the king in his palace,
> And the land will be robbed of its defences.[1]

So we are looking at a magic causality that does not function automatically, but has to be set in motion by a ritual. The link between cause and effect is not self-evident; it must be articulated linguistically and represented in cultic terms.

Thus we find here a type of thought that is powerfully interest-led. As we have said, this type of thinking is under pressure. Its conclusions call for immediate implementation, and to be translated into cultic, ritual action. Ritual action, however, is necessarily repetitive and so requires precision. Rites are not constantly being reinvented and so new ideas are not constantly being produced. The question the cult answers, or the problem the rituals solve, disappears in the solution. That is the great difference be-

tween this way of thinking and the philosophical discourse of the pre-So-
cratic philosophers, whose answers or solutions call not for ritual action
but for contradiction. In their responses the questions do not disappear,
but are in fact posed or set free among the rituals and myths they had oblit-
erated—rituals and myths, that is to say, that had been repressed into the
body of implicit cultural knowledge.

I would like now to take a further step and inquire into the knowledge that has been inscribed in these rituals and that underpins them.
It is not entirely the case that we are confronted here only with implicit knowledge. There are certainly extensive explicit codifications of this
knowledge, of which I have already mentioned two examples. One is the
Great Hymn of Akhenaten, in which he describes his new cosmology; the
other is the Papyrus Jumilhac, a monograph on the eighteenth province of
Upper Egypt, which not only lists the chief places, gods, rituals, sacred objects, and so on, of the region, but also comments on the necessity of the
rituals in a way that we can only describe as theoretical. Such codifications
exist in significant numbers, and we must regard this wealth of documentation as the tip of the iceberg that was undoubtedly over a hundred times
larger than the remnants that have come down to us.

I would like to single out one classical work that illustrates this codification of knowledge. This is the Amduat, a maplike representation of
the night phase of the course of the sun. The netherworld is divided up
in the Amduat into twelve sectors: the twelve hours of the night. The picture reproduces both space and time, but time is the dominant principle.
The sun god crosses the netherworld in a boat. The sun bark is present in
all twelve sections, so that we see not a particular moment, but the overall course of the sun. The hour is subdivided horizontally into three reg-
isters. In the middle section the sun bark is shown sailing on, mainly on
a strip of water but sometimes pulled across the sand. In the upper and
lower strips the various creatures that the sun god encounters on his journey are depicted and described.[2] The emphasis is placed on their speeches
and actions. We are confronted here less with the cartography of a space
than with a choreography of a ritual. Hence the division into hours and
the consequent dominance of time. But it is in this respect that this description corresponds to the structure of the Egyptian picture and knowledge of the world. The world is chaotic by nature. The cosmos comes into

being—in the world of both men and gods—through the communal celebration of the cosmic ritual.[3]

The picture given in the Amduat is based on the idea of the "course of the sun" as a ship's journey through heaven and the underworld, and elaborates it in two directions. The first can be called a *specification*, the aim of which is precision and wealth of detail. Magic is an exact science. This is the aspect of magical knowledge that we find so disconcerting. It is not simply that spaces are depicted that are beyond the scope of any process of observation or experience. What is so strange is to see the *precision* with which they are described. Thus the measurements of the hourly segments are given exactly. The breadth is in each case 120 *jtrw* (1 *jtrw*, Greek *stadion*, corresponds to ca. 10.46 km), the length is 309 *jtrw*. We may ask ourselves how the Egyptians can have arrived at such figures. Is it a question of speculations about number symbolism? Or were they based on calculations and extrapolations from known geographical measurements? It is well known that in antiquity the art of surveying was regarded as the great achievement of the Egyptians;[4] the real focus of interest, however, is not the specification of space, but of action. The nocturnal journey of the sun is divided into *phases* that are pictured in the shape of *scenes* and *constellations*. In the event of the sunset alone 124 different beings take part and are identified by name. These beings and their names are nothing but personified components into which a ritualized "science" breaks down the event of the setting sun.

The Amduat distinguishes 908 beings involved in the nocturnal journey of the sun. The "Litany of the Sun," another of these "books of the netherworld," distinguishes seventy-five shapes that the sun god adopts in the night. The "hourly ritual" and related rites of the sun divide the course of the sun into twenty-four phases, corresponding to twenty-four shapes of the sun god. As a specifying device, this optical presentation of ritual functions like a microscope: it breaks down the cosmic process into what seems like a fantastic wealth of differentiated components.

The other direction taken by magical knowledge aims at *concentration*. By this I mean the way in which the entire panoply of figures and scenes is consistently related to a few "ideas of redemption." It is this relation to the *redemptive efficiency* of the action as ritualized that gives the entire project a *meaning* in the first place and the specifying description the character of an *interpretation*. In the center there stands the idea of a two-fold process of overcoming that is brought about by the ritual of the sun's journey through the night: the overcoming of *evil* that assumes the shape of the water-dragon Apopis and threatens to bring the sun bark to a halt, and the overcoming of *death*. Both are manifestations of chaos; they are in fact twin aspects of the same process. The overcoming of *evil* is the active, transitive aspect that faces outward. Here, the sun god appears as the king of worlds who creates order through his royal commands, dispenses justice, and makes provision. In this aspect, the course of the sun is a "process" in a legal sense, a court hearing in which evil is dealt with and the sun god is "vindicated." In the course of this process the "divided" world that has been made ambivalent by the presence of evil is brought back to a single meaning, that is to say, it is governed, made safe and inhabitable. The overcoming of *death* is the passive or intransitive aspect of the nocturnal journey. Here the action appears as a life process that the sun god himself undergoes as he ages, dies, and is reborn. The mystery of solar rebirth stands at the heart of all these books of the netherworld; it is the central fact about salvation in the Egyptian religion as such. Through this vanishing point the entire cosmos appears in a kind of soteriological perspective, as a process of salvation. Once again, we see that time has priority over space. While the Greeks admired the harmony of the whole, the Egyptians were fascinated by the continuous process of vindication and rebirth. It is this process, the course of the sun, that reveals to them the meaning of the world. In this process the sun appears to them as the quintessence of the plenitude of life that can overcome death and of an ordering power that banishes chaos.

3. Forms of Knowledge for Sustaining the World

What kind of literature are we discussing here? It might be thought that we are concerned less with the codification of knowledge than with statements of faith. For it is after all the invisible and unknowable that is displayed to us in such detail. However, the title "Amduat" [i.e., "what is in the netherworld"] makes it quite clear that this work sets out to impart knowledge.

To know the beings of the netherworld,
To know the mysterious beings,
To know the gates and the paths on which the Great God
(The sun god) travels,
To know what is done,
To know what is in the hours, and their gods,
To know the course of the hours and their gods,
To know their transfiguring names for Re,
To know what he calls to them,
To know those who thrive and those who have been destroyed.

The word for *to know* occurs nine times in the title. This so-called book has been handed down to us in a form that serves a quite specific purpose and again makes clear to us in whose interest and under what pressure this thinking and codification took place. For it forms the decorated painting of the sarcophagus chamber of the royal tombs of the New Empire, on the walls of which it is unrolled like a giant papyrus scroll. This knowledge is supposed to be at the disposal of the dead king in the next world. Furthermore, since it surrounds him on all sides, the depiction of the nocturnal journey of the sun is supposed to place him at the center of this process. Thus this is no reference book. The magical causality of the rituals has here passed over into the medium of writing.

However, there are good grounds for believing that we are dealing here with something that has changed its function. The very stylization of the narrative that results from presenting it as the unscrolling of a papyrus manuscript suggests that a transposition has occurred, a transcodification. There is another text, which treats of the role of the living king as the priest of the sun god, that gives us some hints as to the true place of this literature. Here too there is constant talk of knowledge, and it seems quite unambiguous to me that the knowledge under discussion is the kind of knowledge that is codified in writings like the Amduat.

The king
Prays to the sun god at dawn
As he arises, as he "opens up his sphere,"
As he flies up to heaven as a scarab
He enters into the mouth,
He emerges from the thighs

At his birth in the eastern skies.
His father Osiris raises him on high,
The arms (of the gods of the air), Huh and Hauhet,
receive him.
He takes his place in the morning bark.

The king knows
The secret speech spoken by the "eastern souls,"
When they make festive music for the sun god
As he rises, as he appears on the horizon
And when they open up the doors
At the gates of the eastern horizon,
So that he can journey forth on the paths of heaven.

He knows their appearance and the forms they assume
Their dwelling places in god's land.
He knows their locations,
When the sun god embarks on his journey,
He knows the words spoken by the ship's crew
When they draw the bark along the horizon.

He knows how Re is born
And his transformation in the flood.
He knows the secret gate from which the Great God emerges,
He knows the one who is in the morning bark,
And the great image in the night bark.
He knows his landing places on the horizon
And thy journeys in the goddess of heaven.

This text enumerates everything the king has to know for a single, albeit crucial act: the worship of the sun god at dawn. He is familiar with the nature of this cosmic event, its different phases, the scenic, constellational form it takes, and its soteriological significance as a rebirth; he knows the participants, their actions, their speeches, their living conditions; and he is familiar with the spatial setting of the process: the gates of heaven, barks, landing places, pathways. He has to know all these things with precision so that his reverential speech can intervene effectively in the cosmic process. He desires to contribute to the success of this process and to participate in it in order to bring the world of men into a state of harmony with the cosmos, and contributes to this success by knowing the soteriological meaning of the event and by articulating it through the cult.

The king gleans this knowledge from a cosmological literature. One side of this literature has survived in the netherworld books from the kings' tombs. This is the side concerned with the nocturnal phase of the sun's course. The Amduat is only the earliest, classical example; there are a number of other netherworld books and even a few dealing with the diurnal phase. We must imagine all this literature to have been located in the temple library; from there it is drawn on both for the purposes of recitation and for the decoration of the kings' tombs.

Nothing illustrates the magic nature of this knowledge more clearly than the generic name for these "sacred books" that came to be accepted in the Late Period: *b3w R ᶜw*, which means roughly, "the proofs of the power of Re," in other words, the solar energy that is liberated in the course of the sun's journey and that sustains the world. In this solar energy the magical causality that the Egyptians wish to copy and enact becomes manifest to their ritualistic way of thinking. Hence we should think of this literature as, on the one hand, "the sun's energy," in the sense of a codification of what holds the world together and keeps it going from one day to the next, and on the other hand, as the basis for a ritual practice that aspires to nothing less than to make use of this solar energy for the salvation of the state, society, king, and individual.

This example may perhaps have clarified the principle of a ritualistic way of thinking led by fascination, identification, and the desire to participate. Here the world does not confront the human being as the object of his investigations. Instead, this mode of thinking becomes involved in the processes it is concerned to understand in a symbiotic or constellational way, and it expresses itself through the ritual that aims to make this involvement real in a practical manner. I have confined myself to a discussion of the course of the sun, and would like, by way of conclusion, to give a brief account of two further examples: the cultic geography of the Late Period temples and Egyptian ideas about the flooding of the Nile.

The temples of the Ptolemaic and Roman periods confront us with a vast corpus of knowledge about the forty-two provinces of Egypt, on the one hand, and a huge quantity of rituals activating this knowledge through cultic practices, on the other. In the Late Period, a time of foreign domination and internal disorder, the Osiris mysteries developed into the supreme festival of Egypt. In the course of the celebrations a corn mummy was assembled and a procession took place representing the search for, the finding, and the gathering together of the limbs of the god Osiris that had been scattered throughout the forty-two provinces. The god's body was reassembled from these limbs, enacting the idea of the unity and wholeness of the nation as a cultural and political identity that was threatened by decay and oblivion and that was remembered and celebrated annually by means of these rites. The land of Egypt with its forty-two provinces is thought of as the body of a god who has been torn in pieces by an enemy and who is put together again in the course of rites that are performed annually, but also far more frequently (for these political and geographical semantics undermine great sections of the traditional rites). This takes the form of a procession of vases. We have already discussed this in the Introduction (3b) and can express ourselves more briefly here. Forty-two priests, representing the forty-two provinces, bring water in a canopic jar representing one of the forty-two parts of the body. The crucial connection between the offering, the body of the god, and geography is established by language in the form of an accompanying recitation. This is what transforms the water into Osiris and into the land of Egypt. In these verses it is said, "I bring you forty-two cities and provinces that are your limbs; the entire land is founded for you as the site of your body," or "the forty-two provinces are your limbs."⁵ It is evident that the reassembling and animation of the scattered body of the god signifies the restitution of the Egyptian world. Here too, precisely as with the cult of the sun, we perceive the interplay of action, language, and knowledge. Action includes the recitation of extensive geographical litanies, and these in their turn include an even more extensive cultic geographic literature. This literature has compiled for each of the forty-two provinces a particular limb, the chief temple, the priestly titles, the sacred tree, the eating taboos, other rules and prohibitions, and festivals and mythical traditions.

A third example relates to Egyptian knowledge about the nature of the flooding of the Nile. The interest of this example is that it occasioned a particularly lively confrontation between Greek and Egyptian thought. The Greeks showed no interest in the trajectory of the sun and Egypt's forty-two provinces, and therefore ignored the relevant Egyptian sciences and their ritual practices. They were fascinated, however, by the flooding of the Nile, and could not contain their astonishment that the Egyptians took no interest in it.

We already find Herodotus complaining that he "could get no information from the priests or anyone else about why the Nile behaves precisely as it does."[6]

What I particularly wished to know was why the water begins to rise at the summer solstice, continues to do so for a hundred days, and then falls again at the
end of that period, so that it remains low throughout the winter until the summer
solstice comes round again in the following year. Nobody in Egypt could give me
any explanation of this, in spite of my constant attempts to find out what was the
peculiar property which made the Nile behave in the opposite way to other riv-
ers, and why."

He regarded the answer he received from a scribe in Syene as a joke. "He
told me that between Syene, near Thebes, and Elephantine, there were two
mountains of conical shape called Crophi and Mophi; and that the springs
of the Nile . . . flowed out from between them. Half of the water flowed
northwards towards Egypt and half southwards towards Ethiopia."[7] Strabo, too, records his astonishment that unlike the Ptolemies,

the ancient kings paid little attention to such inquiries (as the causes of the flooding of the Nile), although both they and the priests with whom they passed the
greater part of their lives professed to be devoted to the study of philosophy. Their
ignorance, therefore, is more surprising, both on this account and because Sesos-
tris had traversed the whole of Ethiopia as far as the Cinnamon country of which
expedition monuments exist even to the present day, such as pillars and inscriptions. . . . It is surprising how, with such opportunities of obtaining information,
the history of these rains should not have been clearly known to persons living in
those times, especially as the priests registered with the greatest diligence in the
sacred books all extraordinary facts, and preserved records of everything which
seemed to contribute to an increase of knowledge.[8]

Needless to say, the Egyptians had a very lively interest in the flooding
of the Nile, but their answers to the questions put by the Greeks seemed to
them so strange that they did not recognize them to be answers, or alternatively, they did not recognize their own questions in them. We see here
not simply a different level of knowledge, but two entirely different forms
of knowledge.

We can compare Herodotus's report with an inscription on a large
rock on Sehel Island at the First Cataract. Admittedly, this stems from the
Ptolemaic period, but it claims to have been erected by King Djoser (ca.

2750 B.C.). The text is concerned with the same question that interested Herodotus, not inspired, however, by a theoretical desire for knowledge, but by an urgent practical need. The king reports that the Nile has failed to flood for the preceding seven years and that in consequence there has been a catastrophic famine. "So I decided to turn to the past and I asked a member of the priesthood of Isis, the supreme lector-priest Imhotep, the son of Ptah to the south of his wall: where is the source of the Nile? Who is the god there?" Imhotep does not equip any scientific expedition to the interior of Africa, but consults the sacred books ("the proofs of the power of Re") in the "house of life" of Hermopolis (?). It emerges from these books with great clarity that (against all the evidence) the flood began in Elephantine and that Khnum, the lord of that city, was the god in charge of the sources of the Nile.

There is a city in the midst of the water, Elephantine by name, from which the flood arises. It is the beginning of the beginning, the primordial district opposite Wawat (Lower Nubia). It is the union of the land, the primordial hill, the throne of Re. . . . "A pleasant place to live" is the name of his dwelling, "the two caves" is the name of the water; they are the two breasts from which all good things flow. Here is the bed of the Nile in which it rejuvenates itself. . . . Khnum is the god there.

When the king learns this, it is true that in Greek terms he has been badly misinformed about the source of the Nile and the cause of its flooding. But from an Egyptian point of view he is in possession of all the necessary facts and knows precisely what to do. He knows now to which god he must turn in order to come to grips with the catastrophe. Satisfied, he falls asleep and Khnum, the god in charge, appears to him in a dream:

I am Khnum who gave you shape. . . . I know the Nile. When it is introduced to the fields its introduction gives life to every nose, just like the bringing of life to the fields. . . . The Nile will pour water out for you without missing out a year or failing any land. Plants will grow and bend under the burden of fruit. The goddess of the harvest will be at the head of everything. . . . Those who are dependent will fulfill their heart's desires, as will the masters. The year of famine will pass . . . and contentment will return to people's hearts more than before.

Everywhere we encounter the constellation of sacred writings, ritual action, and a type of thinking that seeks to articulate and gratify existential needs and yearnings through the medium of ritual. Countless examples of this could be adduced. Instead, however, I would like to conclude by citing a text that is concerned with the question of what will happen if the day comes when the rituals are no longer performed.

> And yet the time will come when it looks as if the Egyptians had worshiped the godhead in vain with a pious heart, unceasing devotion, and all holy attentiveness, and will be robbed of all its fruits. For the godhead will once again rise up to heaven from the earth and will abandon Egypt. This land, once the seat of religion, will now be deprived of the divine presence. Strangers will people this land and the ancient cults will not only be neglected, but even prohibited. Of the Egyptian religion only fables will remain and stones with inscriptions. . . . In the days to come men will weary of life and will cease to admire and venerate the cosmos (*mundus*). This totality, so good that there neither ever was, nor is, nor shall be anything better, will be in danger of perishing; men will regard it as a burden and will despise it. They will cease to regard this world as God's incomparable world, they will no longer love it, this glorious edifice, built from an infinite diversity of forms, the instrument (*machina*) of the divine will that unstintingly pours out its favor into its creation, where everything that is deserving of reverence, praise, and love shows itself in harmonious diversity as the one and all. Light will be preferred to darkness and death to life. No one will lift up his eyes to heaven. The pious will be thought mad, the godless wise and the wicked good. . . . The gods will take leave of men—O painful leave-taking!—and only the wicked demons will remain behind. They shall mingle with men and drive the wretched into all kinds of crime, into war, robbery, and fraud, and everything that is repugnant to the nature of the soul.
>
> In those days the earth will no longer be firm, the sea will cease to be navigable, the heavens will no longer hold the stars in their course; every godly voice will inevitably fall silent. The fruits of the earth will rot, the soil will be barren, and the air itself will be stale and heavy. That will be the old age of the world: the absence of religion (*inreligio*), order (*inordinatio*), and understanding (*inrationabilitas*).[9]

What this text communicates is the idea that the world will "grow old" and become uninhabitable if it ceases to be contemplated through the medium of ritual, that is to say, observed, interpreted, venerated, and animated by ritual speech. Ritual as a form of thought is an *officium memoriae*, a cultic memory service that daily sets a vast store of knowledge of the world in motion. Its purpose is not just to interpret the world, but to take the meaning it has elicited and to feed it back into the world to strengthen, foster, and rejuvenate it, through liturgical words of comfort and enactment of the ritual.

As long as people lived in a world which they imagined they had to sustain, through their thought and memory as well as through their ritual action and speech, no conditions could be created for the production of the media of thought familiar to us, that is, for scientific, philosophical, and artistic discourse. What was required for these to emerge was the emancipation from the need to sustain the world and the gaining of distance and perspective. This was achieved in the West by a double breakthrough of two very different processes, which, however, converged in their effects. One was the monotheism of the Bible with its sharp separation of God and the world, creator and creation. The other was Greek metaphysics with its no less sharp distinction between the world of the senses and the world of the mind, the world of becoming and the world of being. Together these two steps liberated man from the business of sustaining the world, and we need to unthink both these processes if we wish to understand the Egyptian mentality.

A Life in Quotation: Thomas Mann and the Phenomenology of Cultural Memory

1. Thomas Mann's "Teaching"?

a. Approaches

Up to now, Thomas Mann has not figured in the debates about the nature of myth and mythical thinking. Yet few have contributed as much as he has in the twentieth century to our understanding of this form of thought, to the clarification of the way it works, to the reconstruction of its various historical strata, and to the perception of its metahistorical and above all its contemporary relevance.[1] Not even his friend Karl Kerényi found it necessary to include one of Thomas Mann's pioneering texts in his anthology *Die Eröffnung des Weges zum Mythos* [Opening a Path to Myth].[2] The reason for this neglect is that where the interests of creative writers go beyond the realm of the aesthetic they are not taken seriously as "secondary literature." There is an unbridgeable gulf separating the discourses of scholarship and literature. As a theoretician and phenomenologist of myth, Thomas Mann has not just been forgotten, he was not taken cognizance of in the first place. This criticism does not of course apply to the Germanists, who have always insisted on the central importance of myth in Thomas Mann's work. It is aimed at the religious scholars, philosophers, and specialists in cultural studies who have attempted to grapple with approaches to myth. The problem is how to stimulate a response to Thomas Mann in the first place, and this chapter is intended as an initial contribution. My thesis is that in his *Joseph* novels Thomas has not simply created a work of literature worthy of analysis by literary scholars, but that he also follows a specific purpose that cries out for a critical discussion by students of religion and cultural philosophers.

To explain Thomas Mann's purpose it is necessary to take a step back and look at the broader context. Mann entitled his speech in celebration of the seventh centenary of the city of Lübeck, "Lübeck as a Spiritual Form of Life," and he described this as the real theme of his novel *Buddenbrooks*. A similar purpose, namely the reconstruction of spiritual forms of life, seems to be a feature of all his major projects. This addresses such questions as the experience of time, individual consciousness, the conception of human beings and their sense of the world, that is to say, categories of vast anthropological scope and profundity. Could it be the case that what he had in mind with the *Joseph* novels was the attempt to bring to life the idea of "Egypt as a spiritual form of life" through the medium of fiction? Erich von Kahler understood the novels in this way. On May 9, 1943, in his letter thanking Mann for sending him a copy of his lecture "Joseph and His Brothers," he included a quotation from Jacob Burckhardt's *Observations on the History of the World*: "It is very painful to have to lament the impossibility of a spiritual history of Egypt which could at best only be provided in hypothetical form, such as a novel."[3] He obviously intended to suggest that Thomas Mann had succeeded in achieving this in the *Joseph* novels.[4]

I am not entirely clear that Thomas Mann would go as far as that. He himself speaks in this context not of Egypt, but more generally of "antiquity." "Antiquity lived in this way," he states in his lecture on Freud—and by "in this way" he means as he described it in the *Joseph* novels. For this generally antique or archaic way of life he coined the term *a life in quotation*. Hence I shall work on the assumption that the theme that is being treated in the "hypothetical form" of the novel is something like "antiquity as a spiritual form of life" (and by antiquity Thomas Mann meant not just classical antiquity, but the ancient biblical, Oriental, and Egyptian worlds, the worlds of the early cultures in general). I assume further that it is not just permissible but a matter of justice to take the text at face value and subject it to an analysis with this project in mind; in other words, to take up the threads of the dialogue that Thomas Mann had sought in his essays and correspondence (above all, with Karl Kerényi who was a specialist in religious studies). There are two reasons for proceeding in this particular way:

First, the student of antiquity, unlike the literary scholar, finds himself dealing with the same subject matter and the same problems as Thomas Mann. We too are grappling with the recuperation of past forms of life, and by this we understand the same questions concerning the sense of time, the concept of the human being, images of the self and the world, notions of value, the construction of meaning, and so forth, that Thomas Mann raises in his novel. We do not, indeed, make use of the hypothetical form of the novel, but the form of scientific argument is likewise hypothetical and we too never achieve more than plausibility.

Second, Thomas Mann himself evidently set great store on being taken seriously in his project of depicting spiritual forms of life. He particularly wished to be taken seriously as a scholar. Thomas Mann's scholarship operates on two planes that must be clearly distinguished so as not to throw the baby out with the bathwater. As far as the details of his stories are concerned, and the scenarios in which facts are incorporated, we are confronted with a playful manner, "amusing precision" and "fictionalized science"—a graceful game that eludes the grasp of scientific criticism. Running alongside that, however, there is an utterly different stratum of intellectual reflections, concerning consciousness and religious history, that does not just permeate the novel but also pervades the letters, speeches, and essays. It would be a great mistake not to take these passages seriously or to dismiss them as ironical disguises and bantering self-dramatizations.

On the contrary, it is here that he demands to be taken seriously. That emerges very clearly wherever he claims to have discovered something before the scholars. One example can be seen in a statement about *Buddenbrooks* in connection with the bourgeoisie as a spiritual form of life, or, in Max Weber's terminology, with the link between the "Protestant ethic and the spirit of capitalism." He says of Werner Sombart, "That he is largely in the right emerges from the fact that I dramatized his theory in my novel twelve years before he formulated it."[5] Here, then, we have in his own words his claim to have formulated a doctrine of his own. Moreover, it is the same doctrine that the scholars arrived at by their own route some twelve years later. Thus with *Buddenbrooks* Mann found himself facing the same problem as Max Weber and Werner Sombart, social scientists with whose work he became acquainted only at a later date.

This is the sense in which I would like to examine the "teaching" that

Thomas Mann has presented in fictionalized form in the *Joseph* novels. As a first step I shall summarize the teaching without attempting to look at it from outside or describe it in my own words. I shall keep to Mann's own account of it. Then I will move on to the second stage and attempt to examine this teaching from the standpoint of the problems raised by Mann, but which lie beyond the horizon that he staked out.

b. "A Life in Quotation": The Freud Lecture of 1936

"A life in quotation" is a phrase used by Thomas Mann in his lecture "Freud and the Future," which he gave in Vienna in 1936 on the occasion of Freud's eightieth birthday.[6] Mann used this phrase in connection with a specific aspect of his *Joseph* project, one that seemed to him to come closest to psychoanalysis. In so doing he took up a suggestion that had come to him from the psychoanalytical camp. Ernst Kris had sent him an offprint of his essay "The Psychology of Older Biographies," from the journal *Imago*, in which he had pointed to the parallels between his own argument and specific themes in the *Joseph* novels. Thomas Mann acknowledged the parallels and called them "extraordinarily legitimate." What was at issue here?

In his essay Ernst Kris had developed a principle that he called "a lived *vita*." He began with the observation that in older biographies, especially those of artists, the same motifs, patterns, and typical developments recur. This led him to conclude that it was the subject of the biography who had lived his life in preformed patterns, rather than the biographer who had imposed such patterns on his life. Thus it was not the description that was shaped by formulas, conventions, and patterns, but the experience itself. "Many of us live today," Ernst Kris claimed, "a biographical type, the destiny of a class or rank or calling. . . . The freedom in the shaping of the human being's life is obviously connected with that bond which we term a 'lived *vita*.' "[7] This idea of a succession and an identification with a previously set pattern was, Kris claimed, the fundamental motif of Thomas Mann's *Joseph* novels.

The connection between myth and psychology in the work of Thomas Mann is one of the aspects that have been exhaustively investigated not just by him, but by Germanists more generally. *Depth* is the keyword here. "The word 'deep' psychology," Thomas Mann wrote, "has a temporal significance: the primitive foundations of the human soul are likewise *primitive time*, they are those profound time-sources where the myth has its home and shapes the primeval norms and forms of life."[8] These depths are invoked in the Nekyia, the descent into hell with which the novel opens. As with an apostrophe to the Muses they are regarded as the sources of inspiration and imagination of hidden knowledge.[9] What is at stake here is the way cultural patterns date back to time immemorial; it is simply impossible to probe so far back in time. The paths we tread are lost in the mists of time, as are the influences that give depth to our souls and meaning to our lives. Time appears here as the psychologically internalized dimension of a vertical anchoring process of human life, and this vertical axis reaches down into depths that are infinite. Historical narratives like the *Joseph* novels or the Babylonian *Gilgamesh* epic turn out to be no more than a stage set behind which further vistas of memory open up. No one can say where these tracks or paths come from in which our lives disappear.[10] The principle of this vertical anchoring of human life without beginning, or with an age-old beginning, is what Thomas Mann calls "myth" or "mythos."[11]

Thomas Mann's theory of myth divides naturally into its parts "myth" and "bios" or "track" and "quotation." One refers to the age-old pattern, the other to historical appropriation, repetition, and reimagining (*Vergegenwärtigung*). Between the two lies the mystery of mediation. How does the imprinting attach itself to the individual? Through descent, blood, and heredity, or through association, language, instruction, and education, or through both? The cogency of these questions forces us to divide our topic into three parts: imprinting, mediation, and appropriation. There is no need for us to explore the individual mythical images and motifs—such as the descent into hell and resurrection, the mother-godhead and the redeeming child, or the hostile brothers.[12] These motifs have been investigated at length in scholarly monographs. We shall confine ourselves to the theory.

2. Vertical Anchoring: Myth as a
Spiritual Form of Life

a. Imprinting

Before all action and decision making, all conscious shaping of one's life, it is the primeval stories that leave their mark on our lives. Thomas Mann calls them "primeval norms, primeval forms."[13] Without such primeval influences, time, history, and reality are inconceivable. All events are a fulfillment, as it says in the introduction to "The Great Hoaxing."[14] Prior to all history is the primordial scripture that is fulfilled in the events that come to pass, the "footsteps in which we all move."[15] That this imprinting is lost in the mists of time is crucial; it goes back far beyond the earliest horizons of the historical cultures. Before Mary there is Isis, Ishtar, Inanna, and ultimately all distinctions are blurred in the eternal feminine.[16] To come first and to be unique are mere illusions. Everything recurs. And yet the novel tells

of beginnings when everything happened for the first time. That was the attraction of novelty, it was what was amusing about this way of telling a story in a by no means ordinary sense, namely that everything was happening for the first time, that there was a whole host of new beginnings, the beginning of love, of hatred, of murder, and many other things. But this dominant uniqueness is simultaneously repetition, mirroring, reflection; the product of the motion of the spheres that turns what is above, the stars, into what is beneath, carries the earthly back up to the heavens, so that gods become men and men become gods once more, the earthly is prefigured in the stars and the individual character seeks his self-esteem in the fact that he descends from a timeless mythical pattern which he turns into a present reality.[17]

This densely packed sentence contains all the points that we would like to consider more closely in turn. Let us begin with the paradox of something happening for the first time, and repetition. The paradox is resolved if we distinguish the propositional content of myth from its mode of existence. The myth tells of first-time occurrences and inaugurations. It exists, however, in the form of repetitions, which themselves take two forms. It repeats "itself" in the event that takes its course "following a once-established pattern" and "is" repeated in the course of festivals and ceremonial recitation.[18]

We cannot describe the mode of existence of myth, the mythic organization of cultural memory, more accurately than by invoking such concepts
as recurrence, repetition, and reimagining. Myth constantly recurs and always as "*the one and the only time.*"[19] This brings us back to our keyword
festival. The image of the "rolling sphere" refers to the intransitive form of
mythic repetition, the form in which it repeats itself. In a very striking way,
this image gives temporal shape and dynamism to the vertical axis of Babylonian astral mythology, the correspondence of the upper world and the
lower one. It is an attempt to give shape to a mythic sense of time in a situation where a historical consciousness is completely absent. The contrasting image from within religious studies is Mircea Eliade's *mythe de l'éternel
retour.*[20] This mythic sense of time is simultaneity or "timeless present"—
concepts also to be found in Thomas Mann. "That all things may coincide
in time is of their very nature and essence; realities wear each other as disguises."[21] This explains why the only temporal form appropriate to myth
is the timeless present that includes "the fact of the revolving sphere."[22] Of
course, the theme of time is known to us from *The Magic Mountain*; it is
the aspect of myth which we understand better thanks to the subtle distinctions made by Thomas Mann. In the monotony of the cycles of nature, early man lives in a state of timelessness, just as Hans Castorp lives in
the monotonous world of the sanatorium.[23] The mythical is the timeless.[24]
Through the recurrence of the same, time constantly cancels itself out. But
what recurs in the flow of time are the patterns that have been created, the
primordial images of myth. For the mythic consciousness they are the only
true reality, while the contingent event that only happens once is dismissed
as unreal. Werner Frizen has shown that the veil—Rachel's *kitonet pas-
sim*—is a central symbol of this mythical experience of time in the novel.
The images woven into the veil symbolize the foundational acts that recur
throughout the action and fill it with meaning and significance in men's
eyes. It is these recurrent images alone that endow the texture of the passing of time with meaning and consistency.[25]

On the temporal plane we think in terms of simultaneity or timelessness, the merging of past, present, and future. The corresponding phenomena in the dimension of space are the way in which "above" and "below" mirror one another. Both time and space are merely the metaphorical
figurations of a fundamental distinction. The mythical or the real exists at
the beginning, and it comes from "above," it "returns" and "comes down"

to us. This provides the framework for a state of consciousness that knows itself to be dependent on something that is not-here and not-now, and is able to relate the present to a supreme not-here and to a prior or future not-now, and that is therefore constantly able to transcend itself. What Thomas Mann depicts so vividly in his novel is a life lived in two time dimensions: on the one hand, in the present with its bonds and commitments, immediate goals, joys, and travails; and on the other hand, in the past and the future, a different temporal dimension standing at right angles to the first. This latter dimension stretches back to the mythical traditions and images lost in the infinite depths of the past, and also extends into an equally distant future in the shape of hopes and promises.[26] The vertical temporal axis is always bipolar. What Thomas Mann calls myth is the cultural form it assumes; in the *Joseph* novels he shows how myth is experienced, practiced, and lived in the lives of individuals.

This vertical anchoring is an elitist principle. It is the mark of those who are born into it—kings, rulers, and other great ones of the earth whose lives are lived on a grand scale, thanks to their office. Second, it is the mark of those who are called and chosen. Max Weber calls them "religious virtuosos" and "people with a talent for religion" [*religiös Musikalische*], people characterized by a particular sensitivity to the resonances and transparencies of the present in relation to the not-now and not-here of a different reality.[27] And, finally, it is the mark of those who are brought up and educated to it, of the scribes and of those who know the myths. In the novel, the characters of Jacob and Joseph exemplify the distinction between mythical culture and the expertise of the scribe. Both are forms of vertical anchoring. Writing appears here as the agent of greater distance and consciousness.

b. Mediation

Thomas Mann outlined his conception of Joseph in a letter to Kurt Horvitz:

Joseph, the Amurru youth with the Babylonian-Egyptian education, knows of course about Gilgamesh, Tammuz, and Usiri, and he follows in their footsteps. A far-reaching and peculiarly fraudulent identification of his self with that of these heroes may be assumed, and the re-realization of what is essentially a timeless myth is a principal feature of the psychology that I am inclined to ascribe to this entire world.²⁸

This mythical lore is transmitted to the boy through two cultural agencies: festival and school. The connection established between myth and festival in the novel belongs to one of the profound and enduring insights of Thomas Mann's expertise in the science of religion. The festival makes the myth a present reality, and the myth represents the specifically oral organization of cultural memory. What is central here is experts in memory and festivals, instead of books and libraries, copyists and exegetes. Festivals guarantee the communication and circulation of myth—of formative knowledge—within the group, and are therefore experienced by the participants as the recurrence of a mythical present. "Repetition in the feast is the abrogation of the difference between was and is." This is how Thomas Mann describes the specific marriage that time and myth enter into in the feast.²⁹ The Australian Aborigines call it "dreaming." This word seems apposite in the present context as well because Thomas Mann too likes to use the word *dreamy* [*träumerisch*] to characterize the mythic and festive consciousness of time and the self. We always encounter the expression when a character finds that the contours of the present are becoming blurred or porous, exposing "the mythic," the higher reality, to view. The feast, and especially the Syrian Tammuz-Adonis mysteries, become for the young Joseph the medium of "inner appropriation," as Thomas Mann notes in connection with Merezhkovsky, "so that the mystery becomes the pattern of his life."³⁰ Joseph "knows the feast in all its hours."³¹ Familiarity with the myth, and hence with the established primordial forms and norms that give life a meaning and an orientation, is something that the individual acquires through the experience of festivals. Only a person who knows how to live in two different time frames, the (vertical) time frame of the feast, and the (horizontal) time frame of the everyday reality,³² is in a position to find his way around in time, and experiences "the repetition in the present of events whose foundation lay far back in the past."³³

The second agency of cultural mediation is the school lessons that Joseph received, chiefly at the hands of Eliezer, Jacob's "oldest servant."³⁴ At that time children did not learn to write with the aid of primers, but straight from the basic texts. The pupil had to learn these by heart and write down extracts from memory. Thus at the same time as learning to write, he also acquired a stock of basic cultural knowledge. This included, as far as cuneiform was concerned, the *Gilgamesh* epic as a text of central importance in the tradition. A similar process can be observed in learning the hieratic texts, in the Egyptian cursive script. Here, the pupil learned to write while at the same time being introduced to the classics of the wisdom literature, above all Kheti's "Satire of the Trades," the "Instruction of King Amenhemet I," the "Prophecies of Neferti," as well as "The Story of Sinuhe," the "Literary Controversy" (Papyrus Anastasi I), and many other texts, the majority of them translated and readily available in Adolf Ermans, *Literatur der Ägypter.*[35] The story of "The Two Brothers" was of fundamental importance for the *Joseph* novels because of its well-known parallel motifs, and was correspondingly used by Thomas Mann. However, it does not seem to have formed part of the school syllabus. Mann alludes on occasion to some of the other texts, but in general it is surprising to see what little use he makes of the original Egyptian texts. It would have been an enticing project to reconstruct the memory of a Syrian youth of the late Bronze Age who had received a comprehensive education in the cuneiform and hieratic texts. Even on the basis of the published sources available in the 1930s this could have been carried out in a much fuller and more precise way than Thomas Mann set out to achieve.[36]

Festival and school represent two mutually complementary educational worlds. A boy presumably learned about the Osiris myth less at school than from the different festivals. Myths were in something of a marginal position in the literature taught at school, at least in Egypt. However, as far as Joseph was concerned, there was also a third source of traditional knowledge, to be found neither in the Babylonian and Egyptian worlds, nor in the festivals and schools. This third source was the specifically Hebrew tradition, which at the time was just beginning to emerge. In the *Joseph* novels it is treated as a kind of family tradition. Here, too, Thomas Mann meditates on the form of transmission, and he comes up with the idea of a particular form of ceremonial that was destined to go down in memory theory as "conversational remembering."[37] He calls it "pleasant conversation" [*das schöne Gespräch*],[38] "in other words, conversation which no longer served the purpose of a practical exchange of ideas or of intellectual discussion, but consisted in the mere relation and utterance of matters well known to both speakers."[39] This is the spontaneous, intimate form of "ceremonial communication," in contrast to the institutionalized and public form of the feast. Mann's idea of "pleasant conversation" takes up a Jewish motif.[40] In Deuteronomy, conversation, "conversational remembering," is included among the different forms of cultural memory technique with the aid of which the Covenant with God will be preserved even after the death of Moses and the "wilderness generation."[41]

The great care which Thomas Mann devotes to the question of the cultural transmission of myths distinguishes his theory of cultural memory from those of Sigmund Freud and Carl Gustav Jung—in a very welcome way, I believe—even though his ideas resemble theirs closely in other respects. Both Freud and Jung accept the idea that mythical images and stories can be inherited biologically. Freud situates this faculty, which he calls "an archaic heritage," in the unconscious. While Jung goes so far as to posit a "collective unconscious," Freud thinks this unnecessary because in his view "the content of the unconscious, indeed, is in any case a collective, universal property of mankind."[42] For Freud, the idea that mythical formations can be inherited provides the key to the harmony he claims exists between individual and collective memory. "If we assume the survival of these memory-traces in the archaic heritage," he writes, "we have bridged the gulf between individual and group psychology."[43] Similarly, Thomas Mann's theory of memory also envisages a central role for the unconscious. Only because the formulations of myth arise from the unconscious can they gain such an influence over the lives of individuals that they can force its contingent elements into the coherent form of a biography. However, these mythical memory traces have not entered into the unconscious by way of biological inheritance, but through cultural mediation.

c. Quotation and Legitimation

I shall move now from the cultural to the anthropological premises of a "life in quotation." These can be divided into two groups, general and specific. The general assumptions relate to Thomas Mann's conception of an archaic level of consciousness and constitution of the self. The specific ones are concerned with Jacob and Joseph as exceptional, "chosen" figures with a very special predisposition for the perception of higher realities. Let us begin with the general assumptions, which are concerned above all with Thomas Mann's famous idea of the "self open to the past" [*das nach hinten offene Ich*]. He developed this concept above all in his essay "Freud and the Future," and more briefly, in "The Unity of the Human Spirit": "The ego of antiquity and its consciousness of itself were different from our own, less exclusive, less sharply defined. It was, as it were, more open to the past; it received much from the past and by repeating it gave it presentness again."[44] Thomas Mann's analyses of the archaic conception of the person are the most important contributions by far to this topic before Marcel Mauss, who gave his pioneering lecture "La Notion de personne" in London in 1938. The ethnologist Meyer Fortes was present at this lecture and, looking back on it after an interval of thirty years, referred to Marcel Proust as one of its literary antecedents. He had in mind Proust's definition of the kitchen maid as "an abstract personality, a permanent institution to which an invariable set of functions assured a sort of fixity and continuity and identity throughout the succession of transitory human shapes in which it was embodied; for we never had the same girl two years running."[45] This twin aspect of a person as timeless institution and as historical incarnation, with the predominance of the first over the second, was what concerned Thomas Mann, whose characters "did not quite know who they were, or who knew it in a more pious, more profoundly precise way than the modern individual: whose individuality was open to the past and incorporated elements of the past with which they identified, in whose footsteps they walked and that came to life in them once more."[46] This conception of the person is embodied with special clarity in Eliezer, the oldest servant, since the concept of "the oldest servant" represents an *institution permanente* comparable to Proust's *fille de cuisine*. The historical incarnations of this role are all called Eliezer and are so identified with their role that they speak of their predecessors in the first person. This is the so-called moon-grammar. In Jacob this openness to the past assumed a particular form that is called "worship" [*Feierlichkeit*, literally, "solemnity," "earnestness"]. Worship is defined as "the extension" of the self, and "its assimilation into the eternalness of being, which returns in it and wherein it recognizes itself. That is to depart from all singleness and limitation."[47] Of Isaac, too, it is said at one point that his ego "faded out and back into the archetype."[48] Translated into the language of modern psychology, this refers to "distinct forms of the cognitive development of the relation of the ego to the external world in the sense that human beings experience elements of their environment in different degrees as 'aspects of themselves' and hence draw demarcation lines that vary for different individuals."[49]

Thomas Mann's writing about "character" as "mythical role" is also relevant in this context. It is true that the individual imagines that he is able to act "on the basis of his own ideas and his own initiative," but his dignity and self-assurance come to him

out of the deeper consciousness that he represents something which was once founded and legitimized and that he conducts himself once more for good or ill, whether nobly or basely, in any case after his own kind, according to pattern. Actually, if his existence consisted merely in the unique and the present, he would not know how to conduct himself at all; he would be confused, helpless, unstable in his own self-regard, would not know which foot to put foremost or what sort of face to put on. His dignity and security lie all unconsciously in the fact that with him something timeless has once more emerged into the light and become present; it is a mythical value added to the otherwise poor and valueless single character; it is native worth, because its origin lies in the unconscious.[50]

This passage illustrates the analogy between temporal and psychological depth—the principle of "vertical anchoring"—with particular clarity. The mythical knowledge of imitation and inheritance is buried in psychological strata to which consciousness has no access. The mystery of mythic recurrence is enacted in the unconscious.

It is uncanny to see the mixture of free will and guidance in the phenomenon of imitation. In the end it is hard to tell whether it is the individual or the destiny that actually follows the pattern and insists upon the repetition. The inward and outward play into each other, and materialize apparently without act of will into the event which was from all time bound up with and one with the individual. For we move in the footsteps of others, and all life is but the pouring of the present into the forms of the myth.[51]

A present can only become reality if it relates to a past.[52] In his lecture "Freud and the Future" Mann developed this idea in connection with Schopenhauer.[53] "Myth is the foundation of life; it is the timeless pattern, the pious formula, into which life flows when it reproduces its traits out of the unconscious."[54] Also at stake in such mirroring and allusion is the legitimation of one's own conduct; at issue is man's need "to dignify his life by attaching it to the higher law and reality."[55] "Myth," Thomas Mann writes, "is the legitimation of life; only through myth and in it does life find self-awareness, sanction, consecration."[56]

Thomas Mann evidently formulated such statements with reference to myth in general. In this respect, however, Jacob and Joseph rise far above the world around them. They have "a talent for religion" to a quite extraordinary degree. The religious man experiences what happens to him as full of meaning, and for the mythic consciousness the meaningful is what recurs, the déjà vu. "Such a recognition," he remarks at one point, "can have its soothing as well as its disturbing side. A man says to himself: 'There it is again!'—with a sense of the solid ground, the shelter afforded by the myth, the reality, or even better, the truth of what is happening— all of which reassures him."[57] Joseph recognizes in Mutemenet the goddess Ishtar and "unconsciously" replies to her as Gilgamesh had done. And similarly, 130 pages later, Mann writes, "He knew his tears: Gilgamesh had wept them."[58]

What in Jacob's case is described as "worship," assumes in Joseph a much more conscious and playful form since, as Mann so neatly puts it, "Jacob's own settled paternalism had not yet arrived at the height of such complicated craftiness."[59] Both Jacob and Joseph are men of "mythical lore who always understood what happened to them, who in all earthly events looked up to the stars and always linked their lives to God's."[60] In Joseph's case, however, this is differently, less emotionally inflected, and assumes instead a wittier, more calculating character. Joseph wants things to be "full of allusions" "so that his life, so painstakingly introspected, seemed full of that quality, and its circumstances showed themselves suffused with correspondences to the motions of higher things."[61] Jacob is notable for his "obedience," Joseph for attentiveness and vigilance. These three expressions sum up the meanings of the Latin term *religio* as Kerényi once explained them in a letter to his friend.[62] Thus while it is true that in Thomas Mann's view, myth characterizes an early stage in human history, it is a late, mature stage in the development of the individual.[63] What is meant is the conscious understanding, deepening, and experiencing of the vertical anchoring of one's own existence, in fact, the life in quotation which alongside memory and an overview also requires a distance from the present, from the "horizontal network."

The idea of a life in quotation goes one step further beyond the stage of the semiconscious or "dreamy" life in myth. It refers also to the way in which myth becomes subjective or reflexive in the living self. The latter does not just act out the myth: it "celebrates" it, as Thomas Mann puts it:

But let us suppose that the mythical point of view could become subjective; that it could pass over into the active ego and become conscious there, proudly and darkly yet joyously, of its recurrence and typicality, could celebrate its role and realize its own value exclusively in the knowledge that it was a fresh incarnation of the traditional on earth? One might say that such a phenomenon alone could be the "lived myth." . . . For life in the myth, life, so to speak, in quotation, is a kind of celebration, in that it is a making present of the past, it becomes a religious act, the performance by a celebrant of a prescribed procedure; it becomes a feast.[64]

The examples that Thomas Mann adduces for this life in quotation are Cleopatra and Jesus. However, both cases are really instances of a death in quotation. Jesus dies with a quotation on his lips. *Eli, Eli, lama asabthani* is the beginning of Psalm 22, and Thomas Mann agrees with Max Weber that "his cry was evidently not in the least an outburst of despair and disillusionment; but on the contrary a lofty messianic sense of self. . . . Jesus was quoting, and the quotation meant: "Yes, it is I!" Precisely thus did Cleopatra quote when she took the asp to her breast to die; and again the quotation meant: "Yes, it is I!"[65]

3. Cultural Memory

Thomas Mann inserts myth into the framework of a "vertical anchoring" of mankind in the depths of time and hence into a context for which the concept of "cultural memory" has been devised.[66] The theory of cultural memory poses the question of the function of culture and seeks the answer in a direction that can be indicated with the keyword *memory*. Culture, and this is the assumption, achieves much the same for groups as memory achieves for individuals. This approach goes back to ideas of the 1920s that are associated above all with the names of Aby Warburg and Maurice Halbwachs.[67] The art historian Aby Warburg gave the title *Mnemosyne* to his ambitious project of collecting the image-memory of the West.[68] In terms of subject matter, he was concerned with the afterlife of antiquity; at the level of theory, however, this afterlife was seen as a kind of cultural memory work. The presence of the old in the new was in Warburg's view not a question of the sheer persistence of the subject matter, but one of spiritual appropriation and transfer. In culture we find the objectifications of human experiences which can spring into new life even after the lapse of thousands of years. Here, too, the depths of time and the

depths of the soul become intermingled. The sociologist Maurice Halbwachs has likewise shed light on the social—and hence cultural—conditions influencing individual memory, but from quite a different angle. His
book *Les Cadres sociaux de la mémoire*, which appeared in 1925, showed
that the past is never able to survive as such, but can only survive if it is
reconstructed within the framework of a cultural present. The past is a social construction. To sum up the two approaches succinctly, we might say
that Warburg explores culture as a phenomenon of memory and Halbwachs explores memory as a phenomenon of culture. Warburg was interested
in the ways in which culture was informed by memory, Halbwachs in the
way in which memory was marked by culture. Warburg spoke of "mne-
mic waves" that issue from the past and put their stamp on the present.
He spoke, too, of "engrams" and impulses that left their mark. Conversely,
Halbwachs spoke of reconstructions that start with the present and reach
back into the past. For Halbwachs, there was no such thing as objectifications of past events.[69] For him the past was always the product of cultural
projections back into the past. His keyword was *frame*. Only from within
the social and cultural frames of the present can the individual recollect
the past, and the only past events that he can recollect are those that can
be reconstructed within that framework. Being a sociologist, Halbwachs
had only a limited interest in the past, in the "vertical anchoring" of mankind. Sociology does not inquire into "vertical anchoring," but only into
the horizontal links between human beings and the network of systemic
functions into which the individual is inserted. The nineteenth century
was obsessed by the notion of diachronic time; everything was explained
genetically. In the twentieth century, the pendulum swung no less one-sid-
edly in the opposite direction. The keywords now are synchronicity and
system. Halbwachs's theory of memory is wholly under the spell of this
way of thinking. Warburg's interest in memory, on the other hand, was
exclusively concerned with the vertical past. This is also Thomas Mann's
approach since in this respect, as in so many others, he was the authentic
child of the nineteenth century.

In this context, Thomas Mann's doctrine of a life in quotation represents a third, independent approach to the mystery of the past. Why and
for what purpose does man need the past? And how does he relate it to the
present? The answers to these questions are provided by the categories of
legitimation and imagination. For Thomas Mann, too, the past does not

endure as such, but only as a cultural, symbolic form that he calls "myth." The past is the dimension of time, or rather, timelessness that characterizes the typical. The typical, in as much as it determines the present, also negates its temporality, elevating it into a timeless simultaneity. But this process in which the past influences and marks the present is achieved by recourse to memory. In this way the approaches of Halbwachs and Warburg converge in Thomas Mann. With Warburg he emphasizes the influential forces that issue from the past and provide meaning and guidance. With Halbwachs he stresses the imaginative power of the past, the past as a legitimizing fiction. In the process he does not simply counterpoise past and future, but instead contrasts vertical, diachronic time, which ranges into the heights and depths, past and future, with the synchronic, as it were "horizontal" present. Vertical time ensures that life has meaning, orientation, and coherence. This associates the past with depth and the future with height. The future is the realm of God. "God's concerns" are focused on the future, on what God intends for us, although it is worth noting that Thomas Mann's God is a god who is still in the process of becoming. This explains why Thomas Mann still has need of the Greek pantheon and the messianic God of Christianity, the latter of which forms a future horizon within the realm of myth. The dual blessing from above and below relates to these twin poles of vertical time. From beneath come the primordial mythical forms, the "binding patterns of the deep"; from above come the promises that guide us and the freedom of the individual. Whoever has no part in this vertical anchoring above and below, and who is absorbed in the present, that is to say, in what we nowadays would call the systemic networks of synchronicity, lives for the day like the dumb brutes.[70] Thomas Mann's vision of a vertical time-axis which stands at right angles to the synchronicity of the present as the source of meaning, orientation, and "blessing," can be read as a magnificent analysis of cultural memory. Among contemporary writers, it is Botho Strauss who has gone furthest in endorsing a comparable understanding of the function of cultural memory. Inspired by his concern that this vertical dimension of our lives is at risk of being undermined and of being doomed to disappearance, he writes,

And yet, wouldn't we like to distance ourselves more and more from these men of our own day, those who live wholly in the present. How unsatisfying it is to belong merely and utterly to the contemporary type. Passion and life itself call for returns (even more than anticipations), and collect their strength from empires that have passed away, from historical recollections. But where are we to find them? To belong to the surface life of networking has taken the place of the roots that have been severed; the diachronic, the vertical structure is left hanging in midair.[71]

4. Was "Life in Antiquity Really Like That?" Five Critical Observations from an Egyptological Standpoint

a. Not for Everyone—Perhaps for Individuals

It is difficult for an Egyptologist to avoid asking whether Thomas Mann's claim about a life in quotation can really have been as prevalent as he claims when he states apodictically, "This was how life was lived in antiquity." After all, we possess information about hundreds, if not thousands of ancient Egyptian lives in the shape of tomb inscriptions. Almost all of them are highly standardized, and follow preestablished models and stereotypes, walking in the footsteps of others, as Thomas Mann puts it. But these primordial images have little in common with myths; rather, they have to do with the norms of social behavior. These people do not think they are Horus or Seth, Osiris, Thoth, or Anubis, Isis, Hathor, or Nephthys. And the formulas they quote (if we can speak of "quoting") are not lost in the mists of time, but are precisely situated in the history of Egyptian ethics. The only Egyptians to whom Thomas Mann's idea of a life in quotation, mythic celebration, and the incarnation of specific roles might apply are the kings, and perhaps their immediate entourage. Pharaoh was the embodiment of Horus, the queen was Isis. In his position as regent and the designated successor of Tutankhamun, Horemheb compares himself on one occasion with Thoth at the side of the sun god, a comparison that corresponds exactly to Joseph's own mythical self-esteem. It is hard to say how their sense of self differed from that of nonroyal persons (whether "it was open to the past").[72] This life-feeling and sense of self-esteem applies with particular force to the Hellenistic rulers, including Cleopatra, and it was undoubtedly shared to a certain extent by the upper strata of society in Hellenism and pagan late antiquity in general. But Thomas Mann himself makes perfectly clear how amazed the people around Joseph were by his life in quotation and his mythical self-dramatization, even though their astonishment was reduced higher up the social scale, and grew the further down you went. The scribe Khamat is quite repelled by Joseph's way of "mirroring himself in the Highest." Even in Thomas Mann's Egypt, so much is clear, the ordinary man did not live in quotation or in myth.

b. Not Always, but in Particular Situations

But there are other, highly peculiar, and well-developed ways in which the ancient Egyptians did "walk in the footsteps of others," and did act or not act in accordance with preset patterns, and did seek to lend their present existence reality or success through their relation to higher things. These forms have come down to us in the so-called "choice of days," an Egyptian invention that was transmitted to Europe in the Middle Ages as *dies aegyptiaci* and has survived in modern Egypt.[73] In calendars every day was related to a mythical event and this event was used to determine whether the day had a favorable, uncertain, or dangerous augury. In many instances, this event represents the interpretation of a natural phenomenon, such as the beginning or the end of the flooding of the Nile, the ripening of the harvest, the equinoxes and solstices, the Etesian winds, and so on, so that attuning one's own personal life (*bios*) to mythological events (*mythos*) amounted to the adaptation of human life to the life of the cosmos. The myth interprets the cosmos and functions prescriptively, putting its stamp on the individual *bios*, so that man walks in the "footsteps" of a mythically interpreted cosmos.[74]

c. Things Were Different in Israel and Egypt

In Israel a turn of phrase like "a life in quotation" has a totally different meaning. Here it is a fundamental text that is being quoted. The quotations do not refer to collective knowledge, formulas circulating by word of mouth, figures of speech, myths, but to written texts with an intensified authority. Of course, this does not apply to the late Bronze Age. But presumably no one lived in quotations at that time. For can we call quotation what Thomas Mann has so convincingly shown to be "following in footsteps," to be the incarnation of patterns established in primordial times? Can we quote something that is not situated in time and place, and that comes from the depths of a mythical dream time? Does not this concept of a life in quotation simply obliterate what for human beings are the vital distinctions between myth and writing, as well as between myth and history? Quotations only exist in the world of writing where speech has to prove its credentials by basing itself on an authoritative text. That was the case in Israel, and Israel is special and perhaps unique in this respect. The step that Israel takes to the stage of writing and a life in quotation amounts to a revolution in the history of mankind. The life in quotation legitimizes itself in Israel because it relates not to myths, but to the written word.[75] The writing in question is God's word and as such it is the absolute, legitimizing authority on which everything is based. There is no truth that cannot be derived from quoting from this text and interpreting it. We find ourselves here at the very opposite pole to the world of myth. Scripture alone—and nothing else—is capable of being quoted. In contrast, Thomas Mann's conception of a life in quotation knows no limits to what can be quoted (and in this respect it is comparable to the thinking of postmodernism).

d. A Projection of Modern Artistic Trends onto the Past?

When all is said and done, what Thomas Mann calls "a life in quotation" does not really describe particular historical realities of the late Bronze Age or classical antiquity so much as a specific trend in the arts of the 1920s that Aleida Assmann has called "the memory of modernity." Myth loses the contours of a lived history and expands into a magmatic memory of mankind as a whole, in which images cease to be organized in coherent narratives. Instead, everything goes with everything else and is rearranged in the work of art as quotation and montage. Ezra Pound, James Joyce, and T. S. Eliot are the typical exponents of this trend.[76] Admittedly, in this context Thomas Mann still defends a position that resolutely clings to the Romantic privileging of the subject. The modernist interest in myth aims in precisely the opposite direction: away from the Cartesian subject/ object dichotomy, away from the making absolute of the ego, and toward overlapping agreements and dependencies. Thomas Mann's conception of the "self open to the past" belongs in this trend of relativizing and even dissolving the rigid boundaries of the self of the modern subject. On the other hand, the turn to the typical, mythical, and "human" that unites him with the antisubjectivist and antipsychologistic tendencies of European modernism is combined with the simultaneous emphasis on, and even apotheosis of, the individual and his subjective inner world. With respect to this latter he remains within the tradition of the nineteenth century that he so greatly admired. This amalgam of individualism and cultural memory or "vertical anchoring" that we find in Thomas Mann seems to me to be highly significant. In Thomas Mann, cultural memory is not made to serve the constitution of collective identity at the expense of the individual, but it quite definitely redounds to the benefit of the individual ego and the forms of its self-dramatization. In this respect Mann anticipates much of what Erving Goffmann describes as the "presentation of self in everyday life."[77]

e. The Myth of the Unity of the Human Spirit

The story of Tammuz-Adonis-Osiris-Joseph-Hermes-Christ presents the archetype of the Son and God who has died and has been resurrected as the primordial mythical foundation of the savior-renewer-redeemer. Not even Kerényi, who is normally far from being pedantic about establishing such comparative links, is willing to follow Mann here.[78] With Mann's inclusion of Egyptian, Jewish, and Greek myths, the pan-Babylonianism of Winckler and Jeremias is far surpassed. According to Mann's intention, such a programmatic syncretism belongs to

the overall character of a work that attempts to bring many things together and, because it perceives and imagines the human as a unity, it borrows its motives, memories, allusions, and linguistic sounds from many spheres. Just as the element of Jewish legend is constantly underpinned by other mythologies that are felt to be timeless, and is thus made transparent, so too is the titular hero, Joseph, a transparent figure whose appearance changes teasingly with the changing light: he is, consciously, an Adonis and Tammuz figure, but he then slips clearly into a Hermes role, the role of the worldly man of affairs and the clever bringer of advantages among the gods, and in his great dialogue with Pharaoh, all the mythologies of the world, Hebrew, Babylonian, Egyptian, Greek, all mingle so indiscriminately that we scarcely recollect that we are dealing with a biblical, Jewish storybook.[79]

The postulate—we might even call it the *myth* of "the unity of the human spirit"[80]—was concerned with overcoming cultural boundaries and making intercultural understanding possible, as well as the translatability of everything into everything else. The cultures are only "dialects of a single language of the spirit." Such ideas can be found early on in Thomas Mann's works, for example, in his review of Spengler in 1922. They have their source there in the writings of Count Hermann Keyserling, who as early as 1919 had produced his own idea of the *Logos spermatikos* in opposition to Spengler's morphology of culture. Keyserling defended the humanist unity of the spirit against the thesis of the mutual untranslatability of cultural formations.[81] In Thomas Mann, this syncretism is also directed against the fascist ideals of "purity and unity," which incidentally, also have a Jewish version in Oskar Goldberg's collectivist mysticism.[82] The myth of the unity of the human spirit also underlies the "phenomenological approach to religion," whose most important representative, Gerardus van der Leeuw, wrote his principal works at the same time as Thomas Mann. Carsten Colpe has been fully justified in describing the scientific consequences of this trend as an "unhistorical reduction to a uniform sameness" [*Vereinerleiung*].[83] This myth must have been in the air at the time as a pacifist antidote to fascist ideas. The same may be said of Karl Jaspers's great essay *Vom Ursprung und Ziel der Geschichte* [The Origin and Goal of History], which was inspired by the undoubtedly noble and worthy intention of elevating the Asiatic cultures into the aristocracy of Greece.[84] But in these works, good intentions go along with a blindness for the otherness of others and the foreignness of foreigners, which should not be fought, but should be simply accepted and respected, in the spirit of that *humanisme de l'autre homme* which Emanuel Lévinas teaches.[85] It is nowhere laid down that the experience of foreignness must go hand in hand with hatred and rejection. We can learn to respect otherness even while defining it as other. Thus it would be easy for us to imagine that the description of Joseph's encounter with Egypt might take the form of a hate-free experience of foreignness. But Egypt is instantly seen through and reduced to such formulas as Sheol, cult of the dead, senility [*Greisenhaftigkeit*], civilization, rococo, and so forth, and where foreignness survives, as with the Sphinx, it is given unambiguously negative connotations and decried as waste and void, savage and sterile. The myth of the unity of the human spirit prevented Thomas Mann from obtaining a view of the spiritual world of Egypt in its foreignness.

These five criticisms have very different weightings. They refer not to the novel as a work of art, but to its "teaching," something that Thomas Mann has expounded in other, nonfictional contexts. They must be understood in the context of a reading that sets out to give an appreciation of this teaching as one of the most important contributions to our understanding of myth and cultural memory. Such an appreciation can only be critical; that is the business of scholarship in whose discourse Thomas Mann intervened with the tools of the novelist and essayist. The importance of his contribution is far from being recognized at its true worth.

Egypt in Western Memory

"Every society," writes the great Mexican writer Octavio Paz, "is de-termined not just by its attitude to the future, but also by its view of the past; its memories are no less illuminating than its intentions."[1] This state-ment may serve to summarize the project of a history that can explore the history of such memories.

Memories that shed light on a society are different from those which Martin Walser described as a "private matter" in his Peace Prize speech in Frankfurt on October 11, 1998.[2] They are expressed publicly and enter into the symbolic forms of a culture. Arising from *within*, from the isola-tion of people's heads and hearts, they make their way into the *interstices* of communication and, if only they are significant enough, they end up in the visible *outer* world of symbols, texts, rituals, and monuments, and form the basis of a cultural memory that can last hundreds or thousands of years. This is how the material of the history of memory comes into be-ing. Walser claims that every man is alone with his conscience. And noth-ing is more alien to conscience than symbolism. But no one is alone with his memories; each man is always part of a whole. The more monstrous the memory, the greater the inevitability with which it finds its way into symbols and into the public sphere. The history of the memory of Aus-chwitz is only just beginning—after decades of silence, and it is not about to come to an end. For the events of Auschwitz do not concern just Ger-mans and Jews, but the whole of mankind, and because of their enormity they create a memory for the whole of mankind. Auschwitz has become part of a normative past from which future generations will derive values and guiding principles. Later still, the history of this memory will one day be written. And it will shed light on the society in which we have lived and which we were.

The past as it lives in our recollections and acquires form and shape in our cultural memory is very different from the past that is researched by historians. It is *our* past, it is what we once were. The horizon of historiography stretches as far back as there are sources; the horizon of cultural memory, however, extends only as far as a society can identify itself in the past and give an account of itself. Goethe put a figure on this of three thousand years.

> Those who cannot draw conclusions
> From three thousand years of learning
> Stay naive in dark confusions,
> Day to day live undiscerning.[3]

That leads us from, let us say, 1800 (when he was writing), back to 1200 B.C., the point in time in which we traditionally place the Trojan War and the exodus from Egypt. These two events mark the limits of European cultural memory. Both were acts of emigration, of breaking away from the Orient. The Israelites emigrated from Egypt and Aeneas fled from Troy in Asia Minor. For it goes without saying that throughout the Middle Ages and until far into the eighteenth century, people looked at the Trojan War through the spectacles of the *Aeneid*, and not of the *Iliad*. Moses and Aeneas, the two émigrés, were the foundation heroes of the West.

Both emigrations belong largely in the realm of fiction and not of history. Here, however, where we are concerned with memory, the distinction between fact and fiction is of no importance. The major difference between history and memory perhaps lies here.

This is why memory history, unlike historiography, must itself ignore the distinction. It must not treat memories as fictions, dismissing them with a condescending smile and confronting them critically with the facts that emerge from research into the past. For from the standpoint of the history of memory, these fictions are themselves facts, to the extent that they have defined the memory horizon of a society as it was, and have thus put their stamp on its particular character.

This fact points to a fairly radical change in our approach to the past. It we take Egypt as an example, this emerges very clearly. The Egypt that still lives, or lives again, in the memory of the West is very different from the Egypt that appears in the studies of Egyptologists. A remembered past has an appellative character, a "mytho-motor" quality. It is a source of claims and guiding principles, a foundation, but also a challenge to the present and a force propelling a society toward the future. This explains why Martin Walser perceives publicly proclaimed memories of Auschwitz as reproaches and accusations, as a "moral bludgeon." In the medium of cultural memory the past is never free from pain or value-judgments. Of course, it is instrumentalized, as Walser asserts. All sorts of things are the subject of research, but people only remember what they can use. They are not concerned with the past as such, with "what actually happened," but only with what it means for the present and how it continues to exist in it. What is important is to give an account, as Goethe says, to oneself and to others. Such considerations do not apply to historical research.

Thus we do not inquire here into the history of research on Egypt, but into the place of Egypt in our memory. This question is by no means self-evident. For what is abundantly clear is that there is barely any room at all for Egypt in our contemporary memory. Egypt belongs only in the researched past, not the remembered past. If a distinguished statesman of our day can play a central role in this festive occasion,[4] can write a book on "the states of early history," and can give a detailed account in it of the Egyptian state of the Middle Kingdom, he is writing as a historian who goes far beyond the conventional horizon of the educated public.[5] However, it would not occur to any politician to quote a pyramid text or a royal inscription in a speech as one might quote Homer or Isaiah. Egypt is still an object of our curiosity and specialized historical research, but not of our memory or general education.

The situation was different at a time when the hieroglyphs had not yet been deciphered and, from our modern point of view, our knowledge of Egypt was nonexistent. At that time, Egypt formed part of our own past. From a biblical standpoint, it could be said that "we" were *in Egypt*. At any rate, Egypt was the object of what was, if anything, a traumatic memory. As an image, Egypt was the antithesis of the biblical image that determined our own self-image. But antithetical images are just as important as models for our self-image. Egypt was the quintessence of idolatry and despotism, and it provided the mythic motor of emigration and resistance with which many groups still identify. These include the Puritans and the Boers, Jews in the Diaspora, slaves in the American South, and the liberation theologians of Latin America.

But there was also a contrasting image, to be found in the texts of the ancient Greeks, especially in late antiquity, and these texts were written not only by Greeks, but also by Egyptians, partly in reaction to the biblical view of Egypt. These texts were partly passed down during the Middle Ages and partly rediscovered in the Renaissance, and they unleashed what amounts to a revolution in memory history.

This image was as unambiguously positive as the biblical account had been negative. Egypt appears in it as an object of fascination. A remembered past always possesses strong emotional overtones, since it could not otherwise exert a powerful mythic influence on the present. In addition, it is always powerfully personalized. The biblical image of Egypt focuses on the figure of Moses as liberator, and the central figure of the Greek image of Egypt is that of Hermes Trismegistus. In the Renaissance, these two were regarded as contemporaries, and they marked the three-thousand-year boundary of cultural memory. In the mosaic in the floor of the cathedral in Siena, Hermes Trismegistus is referred to as Moses Aegypticus, the Egyptian counterpart to Moses. Both were teachers who proclaimed the knowledge of a divine revelation, the one in the Torah, the other in the Corpus Hermeticum. A memory returned when, in 1463, Marsilio Ficino was able to lay his hands on a comprehensive manuscript of the Corpus Hermeticum. We might almost speak of the return of the repressed. Marsilio Ficino interrupted the translation of Plato on which he was working at the time and began right away to translate the Corpus Hermeticum. In his eyes, the Corpus was far more important because it was so much older. This was the source at which Plato had drunk, and Moses too, when he was brought up as a prince at the court of Egypt. This was the true teacher of the West.[6]

What returned at this point and what had been repressed for more than a thousand years is something I would like to call "cosmotheism," to use a term coined in the eighteenth century.[7] This is the doctrine of the divine animation of the world, that is, the very thing that biblical monotheism fought against so vehemently and condemned as paganism and idolatry. Hermetic cosmotheism was much more than a philosophy. Its representatives were those "magi" who united the practices of doctors, healers, magicians, astrologers, enchanters, soothsayers, theologians, philosophers, and philologists in one person, and who were given a fitting monument by Goethe in the figure of Faust.[8] It is a miracle that this magical and mystical view of the world could survive alongside Christianity, and that they could combine in people's minds into a common memory horizon. This really was a case of two souls dwelling in one breast.

Now, it might be objected that my comparison of the Bible and the Corpus Hermeticum greatly exaggerates the new significance of Egypt in the memory horizon of the early modern period. The Bible is the universal authoritative text that serves as the basis for readings and sermons every Sunday in every church in Christendom, whereas the Corpus Hermeticum is the esoteric text of a small number of initiates. But that is the very point I am making. It was this esotericism that made possible the coexistence of revelation and cosmotheism. It is true that the Corpus Hermeticum was known only to a few, while in theory at least everyone knew the Bible. But these few Hermetic adepts had an effect that was disproportionately large, so that everyone knew that this world contains mysteries and that there were wise men who knew these mysteries. These Renaissance scholars did not sit in ivory towers. In the culture of knowledge of the early modern period, mysteries had a completely different place from the one they occupy today. Esoteric knowledge was held to be the most precious knowledge because it was the nearest thing to divine wisdom.

Egypt was the great model of this esoteric knowledge. This view of Egypt was not based just on the Corpus Hermeticum, but also on another text that was discovered in the fifteenth century and caused a great stir: the *Hieroglyphika* of the Egyptian author Horapollo Nilotes. Horapollo described the hieroglyphs as picture-writing that could encapsulate entire thought processes in a single picture, an extreme form of mental compression. Whoever had mastered it freed himself from the discursive and conventional complexities of language and intuitively grasped their content. These pictures were ideally suited to the goals of cosmotheism. By virtue of their direct involvement in nature, it was believed that they contained a magical ability to conjure things up and exercised a power over the objects that they depicted. Hieroglyphs were thought to be an esoteric script created to transmit Hermetic doctrines. Even today, in ordinary language, the word *hieroglyph* has something mysterious about it.[9]

The fascination exerted by hieroglyphs was also one of the main reasons why Egypt refused to disappear from the memory history of the West, when in 1614 the Geneva philologist Isaac Casaubon unmasked the Corpus Hermeticum as a text of late antiquity and denounced it as a Christian forgery.[10] On the contrary, it can be shown that the fall of Hermes Trismegistus inaugurated a new and even more influential chapter in the memory history of Egypt. This brings me to my own contribution to research in this area that can be found in my book *Moses the Egyptian.*

The pioneers of this new phase were of a quite different order from the Renaissance magician. They were Hebrew philologists, Hebraists, and their hero was not Hermes Trismegistus but Moses.[11] Their books did not mention Egypt in their titles, but were disguised as biblical commentaries and studies. This explains why this phase of the memory history of Egypt has remained more or less unknown to this day. The decisive impulse was given by the Cambridge scholar John Spencer, whose work bore the title *De legibus Hebraeorum ritualibus* or *The Jewish Ritual Laws.* This book set out to describe all those countless and evidently entirely irrational laws in Torah about sacrifices, ceremonies, the furnishings of the Temple, and dietary rules, and explain them in terms of the history of religion.[12] Who would have suspected one might find a book about Egypt in this? But we need to take a step further back in time.

With his project of providing a historical explanation of the Jewish ritual laws, Spencer fell back on the *Guide of the Perplexed* of Rabbi Moses ben Maimon, known as Maimonides, which was written toward the end of the twelfth century.[13] Maimonides, too, wished to give an explanation for the ritual laws which in Jewish orthodoxy are said to have no explanation, a circumstance which explains why the search for such reasons (*ta'ame ha-mitzvot*) is forbidden. Maimonides concedes the absence of rational grounds, but not the *complete* absence, because such an assumption would conflict with God's goodness. He therefore introduces the idea of a historical explanation. The explanation he cannot find in reason must be found in history.

The explanation that he provides runs more or less like this. When God gave His people laws through Moses, He saw that the world was already full of laws, rites, and customs. God's goodness, and the regard He had for the customs and the intelligence of His people, made Him refrain from simply abolishing these rites and creating a tabula rasa to write His own laws upon. Instead, He arranged His new writing so that it exactly overlapped with the old one. For every pagan rite, festival or custom He introduced a commandment that precisely reversed it. This normative inversion was designed in the long run to lead to the original one being forgotten. This explains why the ritual laws can only be understood in their original historical context, that is, in terms of the pagan laws which they have overwritten.

In his search for traces of this vanished pagan religion, Maimonides became the founder of the history of religion, and he discovered the Sabeans, the last pagans, who survived in Harran in Mesopotamia into the Middle Ages. They worshiped Sin, the Babylonian god of the moon, and for Maimonides, they were the very last representatives of a pagan religion that had once encircled the globe.[14]

When, after a gap of five hundred years, John Spencer took up Maimonides' project of providing a historical explanation for the Mosaic ritual laws, he replaced Harran and the Sabeans with Egypt since it was quite evidently Egypt and not Mesopotamia that supplied the historical context for the Mosaic law.

This change of place turned out to be decisive. We know more or less nothing about the Sabeans (and Maimonides deduced from this that the memory technique which had ensured that they were forgotten had functioned efficiently), whereas there was plenty of information about the Egyptians from biblical, classical, and patristic sources. So Spencer was in a position to replace the Sabeans, who really existed only in the imagination, with a highly informative account of the Egyptian religion. This led him to do away with the model of normative inversion borrowed from Maimonides and replace it with the model of *translatio*, of importing the Egyptian rituals into the new framework of the Hebrew laws. Where Maimonides had seen inversions, Spencer perceived analogies and correspondences. He saw them everywhere. He called the Egyptian rituals and the Mosaic laws "hieroglyphs," in the sense of a symbolic codification of sacred truths. What Moses did was to recodify the hieroglyphs of the Egyptian mysteries into the language of the laws of Hebrew monotheism. In this way, the historical explanation of the Mosaic laws tended toward a total relativizing and historicizing of the distinction between monotheism and the pagan religion.

However, Spencer did not go so far as to turn the Egyptians into monotheists. In fact, Spencer completely ignored Egyptian theology; he was only interested in Egyptian rituals. He left theology to Ralph Cudworth, a contemporary of his in Cambridge who taught Hebrew and who published an outline of the original and universal theology in his work *The True Intellectual System of the Universe.*[15] Cudworth took his documentation from classical writers and the Church fathers, including the Corpus Hermeticum, but supplemented them with a large number of Greek and Latin inscriptions from the Hellenistic cult of Isis. He accepted Casaubon's dating, but refused (and in this respect posterity is on his side) to regard these texts as Christian forgeries. They did not provide proof of the great age of this theology, but they did demonstrate its tenacity. In his view, the documents he was able to assemble all pointed in the same direction, namely to the idea of the One God who is everything, the One who is All, *hen kai pan.* Cudworth was able to show that the pantheism of the Hermetic texts was fully confirmed by the other, less suspect texts. And all these texts came from Egypt.

The place of Hermes Trismegistus was now taken by Isis. Cudworth appears to have been the first person to put the story of the veiled image in Sais, which had been told by Plutarch and Proclus, at the center of Egyptian theology, and therewith unambiguously declared Egyptian religion to be a mystery religion.[16]

According to Plutarch, the inscription on the image of Isis in Sais ran, "I am everything that was, that is and that will be; no mortal man has ever lifted my veil."[17] This phrase now became a credo, the central symbol of the Egyptian mysteries. The transition from Hermes Trismegistus to Isis also signaled a paradigm change from magic to mystery. The Renaissance magician was now replaced by the Freemason as the representative of the new paradigm for the preservation of memories of Egypt. The Freemasons, too, were of course the bearers of secrets, but they were far from living in an ivory tower. Their numbers included rulers and statesmen, artists, writers, and scholars who put their stamp on the intellectual profile of their age. The century of the Enlightenment was also the century of secret societies.[18]

The Freemasons and Illuminati thought of themselves as the legitimate heirs to those Egyptian initiates. They saw in Egypt the model of a two-layered religion that concealed the mystery of a primordial truth behind the allegorical facade of countless rituals, symbols, ceremonies, and festivals. Such acts of identification transmute a researched past into a remembered past, and transform history into myth.

Spencer's book was a work of baroque learning. It was certainly not designed to trigger a revolution in the history of memory. The fact that this was just what happened during the eighteenth century was due above all to another book about Moses, one that built on the work of Cudworth and Spencer. This was *The Divine Legation of Moses*, by William Warburton, Bishop of Gloucester.[19] Warburton describes Egyptian religion as a mystery religion, and like Clement of Alexandria, he distinguishes between greater and lesser mysteries. The lesser mysteries consisted of Spencer's hieroglyphic rituals with their pointers to the immortality of the soul and retribution in the next world. The greater mysteries built on this and were reserved for a very few members of the elect. Warburton now imagines—since the ancient texts are silent on this point—that these few chosen ones are informed that religion is a fiction and that there is only one single universal deity about whom nothing at all can be taught. "And the great mysteries," it is stated in Clement, are those "in which nothing remains to be learned of the universe [*ta sympanta*], but only to contemplate [*eptopteuein*] and comprehend [*perinoein*] nature and things [*pragmata*]."[20]

However, Warburton does not interpret the polytheism underpinning the state as a priestly fraud, but as an indispensable and hence legitimate fiction. In his view, a civil society could not be maintained in the absence of the assumption of national gods to preside over the laws and make sure that they are upheld. The boundary between fiction and truth, idolatry and revelation no longer runs between Egypt and Israel; it runs through Egypt itself, separating the mysteries from the popular religion. Initiation takes the place of revelation, it is what separates truth from the superstitions of idolatry. The initiate is told, "God is unique and of himself, and all things owe their existence to this unique being." This comes from an Orphic hymn that Warburton ascribes to the Egyptian initiation.[21] Initiation liberates people from the delusions of idolatry and leads ultimately to the vision of truth, albeit a truth whose veil no mortal man has ever lifted. The ultimate, supreme vision is the paradoxical, mystical knowledge of the Unknowable, the infinitely hidden all-oneness of the divine. The revealed religion of the Bible is reduced to a special variant of the one, original wisdom which among the Egyptians and all the cults derived from them is protected by the guardianship of the mysteries. This wisdom can only survive among men under the veil of secrecy as long as "the earth has not become heaven" and "mortal men like the gods."

These words from *The Magic Flute* mark the pinnacle of this second return of Egypt to the memory history of the West. In the same years, toward the end of the eighteenth century, a book appeared by the former member of the same Viennese masonic lodge with which Mozart and Schickaneder, as well as Haydn, were associated. It was a masonic tract that the young philosopher Karl Leonhard Reinhold published with the title "The Hebrew Mysteries, or the Oldest Freemasonry."[22] In this book, Reinhold draws out the implications of the books by Warburton, Spencer, and Maimonides, whom he faithfully cites. What Moses taught the Israelites was nothing other than what he had learned from his Egyptian teachers. Isis and Yahweh are the names of one and the same god. The words with which Isis introduces herself to the initiates—"I am everything that was, that is and that will be"—say the same as the words with which Yahweh reveals himself to Moses: "I am that I am," or in Reinhold's words, "I am the essential existing being."

Friedrich Schiller then helped to spread the fame of these words far and wide. Schiller was friendly with Reinhold and made use of his book not merely for his ballad "The Veiled Image at Sais," but also for his essay "Moses' Mission."[23] Three core sentences of the Egyptian religion, Schiller maintains, are identical with God's idea of himself according to the statement in Exodus 3:14, "I am that I am."

First, the Orphic hymn, "God is unique and of himself, and all things owe their existence to this unique being."

Second and third, the Sais inscription that Schiller and Reinhold have duplicated for unfathomable reasons, supplying it in a shorter and a longer version: (a) "I am what is," and (b) "I am everything that was, that is and that will be; no mortal man has ever lifted my veil."[24]

No less a man than Ludwig van Beethoven copied these three sentences out in his own hand, and put them on his desk in a frame behind glass where he had them constantly before his eyes in the last years of his life.²⁵ This tells us how widely known Reinhold's ideas became, thanks to their influence on Schiller. The religion of the European Enlightenment was Deism; at the same time, it was widely assumed that as early as the ancient Egyptians, Deism had been taken under the wing of the mysteries, and that from there it spread out through the West via Moses, Orpheus, Plato, and other initiates, in the form of Kabbalah, Neoplatonism, and Spinozism. Is it possible to conceive of a stronger identification with ancient Egypt?

This image of Egypt faded toward the end of the eighteenth century. Under the influence of Herder and Winckelmann, a new theory of culture developed, one which no longer inquired into common origins, but instead sought to explain every culture in terms of its own, original essence or national spirit. Europe's original essence was now located in Greece, and the emergence of Indo-Germanic philology afforded a glimpse of the Aryans, who were now perceived to be an even more ancient source than the Greeks. This put an end to the traditional constellation of Athens and Jerusalem, the two pillars on which Europe was based. By the same token, it also spelled the end of the rivalry which had been held at bay previously by the Egyptian civilization which had preceded them both, but which had nevertheless supplied the dynamism of European cultural memory. From this point on, Athens and Jerusalem became irreconcilable opposites and Aryan Europe was defined by contrast with the Semitic Orient. Egypt was reduced in importance to one of the many Semitic or Semito-Hamitic cultures that nineteenth-century Orientalists studied with a mixture of theoretical curiosity and patronizing arrogance.²⁶ Once it was possible to read the texts, thanks to Champollion's brilliant deciphering of the hieroglyphs, this value judgment was confirmed. Instead of profound truths people discovered either trivial or incomprehensible utterances, and monotheistic mysteries were ruled out entirely. There was no longer any room for the mysteries of Isis in the positivist culture of historicism. The entire vast edifice of knowledge that the scholars of the seventeenth and eighteenth centuries had assembled on the subject of the Egyptian mysteries fell into oblivion. As the newly emergent science of Egyptology gradually discovered ancient Egypt, Egypt itself disappeared from the general culture of the West. Every newly discovered text strengthened the feeling of otherness. The more the nineteenth century came to know of Egypt, the less Egypt was able to speak to it. Once it had removed the veil of the hieroglyphs from the image of Egypt, it found itself utterly unable to relate to what met its gaze.

There was one single text whose discovery gradually started to change the situation, and bring Egypt back onto the horizon of Western cultural memory. This was the great hymn of Akhenaten from Amarna.[27] This text from the fourteenth century B.C. seemed familiar and spoke to everyone. This was no surprise, since it had been taken up into Psalm 104. This text actually did testify to the existence of an Egyptian monotheism. It was not concerned with initiation and mystery, but was a revolution from above that vanished again as quickly as it had appeared. The texts that have survived, however, together with such sensational archaeological discoveries as the Berlin Nefertiti and the tomb of Tutankhamun, have at least made the Amarna period an object of fascination to Western culture, and triggered the creation of works such as Thomas Mann's *Joseph* novels and Freud's *Moses and Monotheism*. A turning point has been reached. The Western horizon of memory is gradually beginning to expand to include its Oriental roots and to extend beyond Goethe's three thousand years to around five thousand years. At the same time, Egyptology is starting to break out of its ivory tower and its discoveries are beginning to find a greater resonance in the public. It is ceasing to be an orchid that a few universities can stick in their buttonhole as a special decoration, but is becoming an indispensable component of our historical consciousness that helps to prevent us from living from one day to the next and remaining in the dark, deprived of experience. It dwells not in an ivory tower, but in a lookout post which gives us a historical vantage point that reaches into the depths of the past. From it we can glimpse the origins of our spiritual world and our cultural memory in a different light and see them with a sharper focus.

Notes

PREFACE

1. H.-G. Gadamer, "Wahrheit und Methode," in *Gesammelte Werke* (Stuttgart, 1975), vol. 1, p. 478.

2. K. Ehlich, "Text und sprachliches Handeln: Die Entstehung von Texten aus dem Bedürfnis nach Überlieferung," in A. Assmann, J. Assmann, and C. Hardmeier, eds., *Schrift und Gedächtnis* (Munich, 1983), pp. 24–43.

3. A. Assmann, *Erinnerungsräume: Formen und Wandlungen des kulturellen Gedächtnisses* (Munich, 1999).

INTRODUCTION

1. M. Halbwachs, *Les Cadres sociaux de la mémoire*, 1925 (repr. 1975); *La Mémoire collective* (published posthumously by J. Alexandre) (Paris, 1985). On Halbwachs, see V. Karady, in M. Halbwachs, *Classes sociales et morphologie* (Paris, 1972), pp. 9–22. See also Chapter 5.

2. In this context we can ignore a third type, motor memory, the type that is involved in walking, swimming, cycling, and so on.

3. On the general question of memory distortions, see D. L. Schacter, ed., *Memory Distortion: How Minds, Brains, and Societies Reconstruct the Past* (Cambridge, Mass., 1997). On confabulation, see M. Moscovitch, "Confabulation," in ibid., pp. 226–51.

4. See P. Gourvitch, "The Memory Thief," *New Yorker*, June 14, 1999, pp. 48–68. I am grateful to Aleida Assmann for drawing my attention to this article.

5. F. Nietzsche, *On the Genealogy of Morality*, ed. Keith Ansell-Pearson, trans. Carol Diethe (Cambridge, 1996), pp. 39 ff.

6. Part 1, in A. Assmann and U. Frevert, *Geschichtsvergessenheit, Geschichtsversessenheit: Vom Umgang mit deutschen Vergangenheiten nach 1945* (Stuttgart, 1999), pp. 19–147, esp. pp. 41–49.

7. R. Koselleck, "Kriegerdenkmale als Identitätsstiftungen der Überlebenden," in O. Marquard and K. H. Stierle, eds., *Identität* (Munich, 1979), pp. 255–76.

8. On this point, see D. Krochmalnik, "Amalek: Gedenken und Vernichtung in der jüdischen Tradition," in H. Loewy and B. Moltmann, eds., *Erlebnis—*

Gedächtnis—Sinn: Authentische und konstruierte Erinnerung (Frankfurt am Main and New York, 1996), pp. 121–36.

9. A. Assmann, *Zeit und Tradition: Kulturelle Strategien der Dauer* (Cologne, Weimar, and Vienna, 1999), p. 64.

10. This refers in particular to the critique directed by H. Cancik and H. Mohr at the "extension of the metaphorical use of memory to 'society' and 'culture,'" in "Erinnerung/Gedächtnis," in *Handbuch religionswissenschaftlicher Grundbegriffe* (Stuttgart, 1990), vol. 2, pp. 299–323.

11. Cited according to E. Otto, *Das Deuteronomium* (Berlin, 1999), p. 82, in the translation into German by S. Maul, both of whom I would like to thank for their assistance on this and many other questions. [All translations from secondary texts are by the translator of the current volume unless otherwise stated. All text in square brackets is the translator's interpolation.—Trans.]

12. C. Lévi-Strauss, *La Penséee sauvage* (Paris, 1962), p. 309. See C. Lévi-Strauss, *Strukturale Anthropologie* (Frankfurt am Main, 1960), p. 39.

13. W. Müller, "Die Nonhongschinga und die strukturale Anthropologie," in H. P. Duerr, ed., *Sehnsucht nach dem Ursprung: Zu Mircea Eliade* (Frankfurt am Main, 1983), pp. 264–82, esp. p. 270.

14. Ibid., p. 274.

15. M. Granet, *Das chinesische Denken* (Frankfurt am Main, 1985), p. 67; see also ibid., pp. 69 ff. Quoted in G. Dux, *Die Zeit in der Geschichte* (Frankfurt am Main, 1989), p. 225.

16. J. Piaget, *Die Entwicklung des Erkennens* (Stuttgart, 1975), vol. 2, p. 77; quoted in Dux, *Die Zeit in der Geschichte*, p. 224.

17. H. Beinlich, *Die "Osirisreliquien": Zum Motiv der Körperzergliederung in der altägyptischen Religion* (Wiesbaden, 1984).

18. Bible quotations are from the Revised Version.—Trans.

19. The Hebrew text does not speak of writing ("shall be upon thy heart"), but it does in Jeremiah 31:33 ["and in their heart I will write it"—Trans.].

20. "Conversational Remembering"; see the discussion from a psychological viewpoint in D. Middleton and D. Edwards, eds., *Collective Remembering* (London, 1990), pp. 23–45. The contribution of J. Shotter in the same volume is also of importance for the role of speaking in the construction of a shared memory. See pp. 120–38.

21. The fulfillment of this injunction is described in Joshua 8:30–35.

22. Originally, all three festivals were harvest festivals (Matsah: barley harvest; Shavuot: wheat harvest, alternatively, at the end of the grain harvest; Sukkot: fruit harvest). It is assumed that it was only with the loss of the land in the Diaspora that the close tie between the feast dates and the agrarian cycle was broken and the festivals were converted into festivals of remembrance. I am concerned here to show the role played by memory even in the founding texts.

23. On the Matsah festival as Zikharon, festival of remembrance, see Exodus 12:14; Leviticus 23:24. See the literature given in Cancik and Mohr, "Erinnerung/Gedächtnis," in *Handbuch religionswissenschaftlicher Grundbegriffe* (Stuttgart, 1990), vol. 2, notes 73–77.

24. In the post-biblical era Shavuot has acquired the additional meaning of a feast to commemorate the revelation on Mount Sinai and the "giving of the Torah." See M. Dienemann, "Schavuot," in F. Thieberger, *Jüdisches Fest und jüdischer Brauch* (1937; reprint, 1967; Königstein im Taunus, 1979), 280–87. See C. Hardmeier, "Die Erinnerung an die Knechtschaft in Ägypten," in F. Crüsemann, C. Hardmeier, and R. Kessler, eds., *Was ist der Mensch . . . ? Beiträge zur Anthropologie des Alten Testaments* (Munich, 1992), pp. 133–52.

25. "And Moses wrote this law . . . and commanded" that it be read out in a regular cycle before all Israel, every seven years during the Feast of Tabernacles; 31:9–13. This chimes with the customary arrangement in Hittite treaties of reading the text out at regular intervals. See V. Korosec, *Hethitische Staatsverträge: Ein Beitrag zu ihrer juristischen Wertung* (Leipzig, 1931), pp. 101 ff. Ezra reads the law out to the people day after day during Sukkot, from the first day to the last (Neh. 8:1–18). See also the ruling at the end of the "Testament" of the Hittite King Hatusilis I (sixteenth century B.C.): " . . . and this tablet should always be read out every month (to the successor to the throne); in this way you will always remember my words and my wisdom." (Laroche, "Catalogue des textes hittites," no. 6, in Cancik and Mohr, *Handbuch religionswissenschaftlicher Grundbegriffe*, p. 314.)

26. The book of Deuteronomy closes with a great song that recapitulates the warning against the terrible consequences of disloyalty and forgetfulness in a condensed poetic form. This song is supposed to remain alive in the oral tradition of the people and so constantly remind it of its commitments.

27. The obligation to adhere strictly to the law is expressed in the frequently reiterated demand "not to add unto the word . . . neither shall ye diminish from it" (4:2; 12:32). On "canonic formulas" and their various forms, see J. Assmann, *Das kulturelle Gedächtnis: Schrift, Erinnerung und politische Identität in frühen Hochkulturen* (Munich, 1992), pp. 103–7.

28. See A. and J. Assmann, eds., *Kanon und Zensur* (Munich, 1987). On the origins of the Hebrew canon and the significance of the Book of Deuteronomy as a kind of crystallized nucleus of the biblical process of canonization, see the contribution in this volume by F. Crüsemann. See also F. Crüsemann, *Die Tora: Theologie und Sozialgeschichte des alttestamentlichen Gesetzes* (Munich, 1992), esp. pp. 310–23. For the wider importance of the principle of "canon," see the contributions by C. Colpe and A. and J. Assmann.

29. *Ve-'atem tihju-li mamlechet kohanim vegoj kadosh*, Exodus 19:6.

30. On this point, see G. Braulik, "Das Deuteronomium und die Gedächtniskultur Israels: Redaktionsgeschichtliche Beobachtungen zur Verwendung von

lamed," in G. Braulik, W. Gross, and S. McEvenue, eds., *Biblische Theologie und gesellschaftlicher Wandel* (Fs. N. Lohfink SJ) (Freiburg, 1993), pp. 9–31; following on from N. Lohfink, "Der Glaube und die nächste Generation: Das Gottesvolk der Bibel als Lerngemeinschaft," in N. Lohfink, *Das Jüdische am Christentum* (Freiburg, 1987), pp. 144–66; and J. Assmann, "Religion als Erinnerung: Das Deuteronomium als Paradigma kultureller Mnemotechnik," in *Das kulturelle Gedächtnis,* pp. 212–28. A similar point could be made, according to H. J. Gehrke, about the laws in ancient Crete, which, according to a note in Aelian, were learned by heart together with melodies. The subject matter of what was to be learned consisted in the first place of the laws, and after that came hymns to the gods and, finally, songs of praise in honor of worthy forbears. The double meaning of the Greek word *nomos,* "law" and "song" (hence *noimen* for musical notation), derives from this memory technique.

31. A. Oz, "Israelis und Araber: Der Heilungsprozess," in *Trialog der Kulturen im Zeitalter der Globalisierung, Sinclair House Gespräche,* 11th dialogue (December 5–8, 1998), Herbert-Quandt-Stiftung (Bad Homburg von der Höhe), pp. 82–89, quotation, p. 83.

32. The speech was published in M. Walser, *Erfahrungen beim Verfassen einer Sonntagsrede* (Frankfurt am Main, 1998). The subsequent debate was documented in F. Schirrmacher, ed., *Die Walser-Bubis-Debatte* (Frankfurt am Main, 2002), and analyzed in G. Wiegel and J. Klotz, eds., *Geistige Brandstiftung? Die Walser-Bubis-Debatte* (Cologne, 1999); J. Rohloff, *Ich bin das Volk,* vol. 21 (Hamburg, 1999). See also A. Assmann and U. Frevert, *Geschichtsvergessenheit, Geschichtsversessenheit: Vom Umgang mit deutschen Vergangenheiten nach 1945* (Stuttgart, 1999), pp. 53–96.

33. A. Assmann, *Erinnerungsräume: Formen und Wandlungen des kulturellen Gedächtnisses* (Munich, 1999), pp. 130–45.

34. Ibid., p. 136.

35. Y. H. Yerushalmi, *Freud's Moses: Judaism Terminable and Interminable* (New Haven, Conn., 1991).

36. J. Derrida, *Mal d'archive* (Paris, 1995).

37. R. J. Bernstein, *Freud and the Legacy of Moses* (Cambridge, 1998).

38. J. W. von Goethe, *Werke* (Hamburger Ausgabe, 1952), ed. Erich Trunz, vol. 2, *West-östlicher Divan, Rendsch Nameh: Buch des Unmuts* (Munich, 1998), p. 49. [*Poems of the West and the East,* trans. J. Whaley (Bern and New York, 1998), p. 189.]

39. G. Jonker, *The Topography of Remembrance: The Dead, Tradition, and Collective Memory in Mesopotamia* (Leiden, 1995).

40. M. Halbwachs, *La Topographie légendaire des évangiles en Terre Sainte* (Paris, 1941).

41. On this point, see J. Assmann, *Das kulturelle Gedächtnis,* chap. 7.

CHAPTER 1: INVISIBLE RELIGION AND CULTURAL MEMORY

1. On the concept of "tradition," see A. Assmann, *Zeit und Tradition: Kulturelle Strategien der Dauer* (Cologne, Vienna, and Weimar, 1999).

2. T. Luckmann, *The Invisible Religion* (New York and London, 1967).

3. A. Assmann and D. Harth, eds., *Mnemosyne: Formen und Funktionen der kulturellen Erinnerung* (Frankfurt am Main, 1991). See also J. Assmann and T. Hölscher, eds., *Kultur und Gedächtnis* (Frankfurt am Main, 1988); A. and J. Assmann, "Schrift, Tradition, Kultur," in W. Raible, ed., *Zwischen Festtag und Alltag* (Tübingen, 1988), pp. 25–50; J. Assmann, *Das kulturelle Gedächtnis: Schrift, Erinnerung und politische Identität in frühen Hochkulturen* (Munich, 1992), and now especially, A. Assmann, *Erinnerungsräume: Formen und Funktionen des kulturellen Gedächtnisses* (Munich, 1999).

4. Luckmann, *The Invisible Religion*, p. 41.

5. On this point, see J. Assmann, *Maʾat: Gerechtigkeit und Unsterblichkeit im Alten Ägypten* (Munich, 1995).

6. J. Assmann, *Der König als Sonnenpriester: Ein kosmographischer Begleittext zur kultischen Sonnenhymnik in thebanischen Tempeln und Gräbern* (Abh. des Deutschen Archäologischen Instituts VII, Glückstadt, 1970); *Sonnenhymnen in Thebanischen Gräbern* (Mainz, 1983), pp. 48 ff.; *Maʾat*, pp. 205–12; M. C. Betrò, *I testi solari del portale di Pascerientaisu* (Pisa, 1989).

7. See also J. Assmann, *Ägypten: Theologie und Frömmigkeit einer frühen Hochkultur* (Stuttgart, 1992), pp. 11–14.

8. P. L. Berger and T. Luckmann, *The Social Construction of Reality* (Harmondsworth, U.K., 1967), p. 49.

9. On the distinction between primary and secondary religions, see T. Sundermeier, "Religion, Religionen," in K. Müller and T. Sundermeier, eds., *Lexikon missionstheologischer Grundbegriffe* (Berlin, 1987), pp. 411–23; J. Assmann, *Maʾat*, pp. 279–83.

10. Luckmann, *The Invisible Religion*, p. 43.

11. Ibid., p. 45.

12. See *The Social Construction of Reality*, pp. 77 ff.

13. Luckmann, *The Invisible Religion*, p. 45.

14. For one example among many, see M. Mauss, *Essai sur le don*, German translation, *Die Gabe* (Frankfurt am Main, 1968); M. Sahlins, *Stone Age Economics* (London, 1972); C. Lévi-Strauss, *Les Structures élémentaires de la parenté* (Paris, 1947).

15. On this concept, see Chapter 5.

16. On the basis of the narrative character of formative texts, particularly in their early and original forms, one is tempted to juxtapose them to the other principle of Jewish text-interpretation, the Aggadah that is concerned with storytelling.

17. Karl Jaspers, *Vom Ursprung und Ziel der Geschichte* (Munich, 1949); see S. N. Eisenstadt, ed., *Kulturen der Achsenzeit, ihre Ursprünge, und ihre Vielfalt* (Frankfurt am Main, 1987). Here we must mention above all the name of E. A. Havelock, who devoted his entire life's work to the study of this transition in the context of ancient Greek culture. See on this point A. and J. Assmann, "Einleitung: Schrift—Kognition—Evolution: Eric A. Havelock und die Technologie kultureller Kommunikation," in E. A. Havelock, ed., *Die Schriftrevolution im antiken Griechenland* (Weinheim, 1990), pp. 1–36 (with further literature on this subject), as well as Chapter 6, below.

18. On this point, too, see above all, E. A. Havelock, *Preface to Plato* (Cambridge, 1963), where he speaks of "preserved communication."

19. See, for example, P. Zumthor, *Introduction à la poésie orale* (Paris, 1983).

20. For greater detail on this point, see J. Assmann, "Der zweidimensionale Mensch: Das Fest als Medium des kollektiven Gedächtnisses," in J. Assmann and T. Sundermeier, eds., *Das Fest und das Heilige: Kontrapunkte des Alltags, Studium zum Verstehen fremder Religionen* 1 (Gütersloh, 1991), pp. 13–30.

21. For a fuller account of what follows, see J. Assmann, *Das kulturelle Gedächtnis*, pp. 88–97.

22. L. Oppenheim, *Ancient Mesopotamia: Portrait of a Dead Civilization* (Chicago and London, 1964).

23. See J. van Seters, *In Search of History* (New Haven, Conn., 1983).

24. See J. Assmann, "Die Entdeckung der Vergangenheit," in H. U. Gumbrecht and U. Link-Heer, eds., *Epochenschwellen und Epochenstrukturen im Diskurs der Literatur- und Sprachhistorie* (Frankfurt am Main, 1985), pp. 484–99; D. B. Redford, *Pharaonic King-Lists, Annals, and Day Books: A Contribution to the Study of the Egyptian Sense of History* (Mississauga, Ont., 1986).

25. C. Colpe, "Sakralisierung von Texten und Filiationen von Kanons," in A. Assmann and J. Assmann, eds., *Kanon und Zensur* (Munich, 1987), pp. 80–92.

26. See C. Meier, "Die Entstehung einer autonomen Intelligenz bei den Griechen," in S. N. Eisenstadt, ed., *Kulturen der Achsenzeit: Ihre Ursprünge und ihre Vielfalt* (Frankfurt am Main, 1987), vol. 1.1, pp. 89–127.

27. The verses at the end of Hölderlin's poem *Patmos* (first version) sum up the essence of the matter astonishingly accurately:

> Wir haben gedienet der Mutter Erd'
> Und haben jüngst dem Sonnenlicht gedient,
> Unwissend, der Vater aber liebt,
> Der über allen waltet,
> Am meisten, dass gepfleget werde
> Der feste Buchstab, und bestehendes gut
> Gedeutet. Dem folgt deutscher Gesang.

We have served Mother Earth
And lately have served the sunlight,
Unknowingly, but the Father
Who reigns over all loves most that
The solid letter be cared for and the existing be well construed.
By this German song abides.

Sämtliche Werke und Briefe, ed. Michael Kaupp (Darmstadt, 1998), vol. 1, p. 453;
Poems of Hölderlin, trans. Michael Hamburger (London, 1943), p. 223.

CHAPTER 2: MONOTHEISM, MEMORY, AND TRAUMA

1. S. Freud, *Moses and Monotheism*, in *The Pelican Freud Library*, vol. 13, *The Origins of Religion*, ed. A. Dickson (Harmondsworth, U.K., 1985), pp. 237–386.

2. S. Freud, "The Aetiology of Hysteria," in *The Complete Psychological Works of Sigmund Freud*, trans. and ed. J. Strachey (London, 1962), vol. 3, p. 192. On Freud's use of archaeological metaphors for psychoanalytical memory work, see also K. Stockreiter, "Am Rand der Aufklärungsmetapher: Korrespondenzen zwischen Archäologie und Psychoanalyse," in L. Marinelli, ed., *Meine . . . alten und dreckigen Götter*, from Sigmund Freud's collection, catalogue of the exhibition in the Sigmund Freud Museum, Vienna, from November 18, 1998, to February 17, 1999 (Basel, 1998), pp. 81–93.

3. For Freud's reading of the Bible in general, see T. Pfrimmer, *Freud, lecteur de la Bible* (Paris, 1982). This tracks down not only all of Freud's biblical allusions and reminiscences, but also the syllabus of the religious studies course that Freud attended in Vienna.

4. See, for example, E. Rice, *Freud and Moses: The Long Journey Home* (New York, 1990); I. Grubrich-Simitis, *Freuds Moses-Studie als Tagtraum* (Weinheim, 1991); B. Goldstein, *Reinscribing Moses, Heine, Kafka, Freud, and Schoenberg in a European Wilderness* (Cambridge, Mass., 1992); Y. H. Yerushalmi, *Freud's Moses: Judaism Terminable and Interminable* (New Haven, Conn., 1991); J. Derrida, *Mal d'archive* (Paris, 1995); J. Assmann, *Moses the Egyptian: The Memory of Egypt in Western Monotheism* (Cambridge, Mass., 1997) [*Moses der Ägypter: Entzifferung einer Gedächtnisspur* (Munich, 1998)]; R. J. Bernstein, *Freud and the Legacy of Moses* (Cambridge, 1998); "Sechzig Jahre 'Der Mann Moses': Zur Religionskritik von Sigmund Freud, Wege zum Menschen," *Monatsschrift für Seelsorge und Beratung* 51, no. 4 (May–June 1999).

5. Freud, *Moses and Monotheism*, p. 329.

6. Ibid., p. 378.

7. Ibid., p. 347.

8. Bernstein, *Freud and the Legacy of Moses*, pp. 27–74.

9. C. Caruth, ed., *Trauma: Explorations in Memory* (Baltimore, 1995).

10. Ibid., pp. 7–8; Bernstein, *Freud and the Legacy of Moses*, p. 42.

11. Freud, *Moses and Monotheism*, p. 383.

12. O. H. Steck, *Israel und das gewaltsame Geschick der Propheten* (Neukirchen-Vluen, 1967).

13. On this point see, S. L. Gilman, *Sigmund Freud: Medicine and Identity at the Fin de Siècle* (Baltimore, 1993).

CHAPTER 3: FIVE STAGES ON THE ROAD TO THE CANON

1. See M. Halbwachs, *La Mémoire collective* (Paris, 1950).

2. On the process of habitualization, see P. Bourdieu, *Zur Soziologie der symbolischen Formen* (Frankfurt am Main, 1974), pp. 125–58. On the process of becoming unconscious, see the contributions of M. Erdheim, *Die gesellschaftliche Produktion von Unbewusstheit* (Frankfurt am Main, 1984), and *Die Psychoanalyse und das Unbewusste in der Kultur* (Frankfurt am Main, 1988).

3. In other words the layer of text marked *R* which Martin Buber and Franz Rosenzweig interpreted as *Rabbenu* (our teacher), that is, the binding authority in the sense of the "implicit author."

4. One of the principal representatives of this "hermeneutics of the canon" is J. A. Sanders; see his books *Torah and Canon* (Philadelphia, 1972), *Canon and Community* (Philadelphia, 1984), and *From Sacred Story to Sacred Text* (Philadelphia, 1987). On the concept of inspired interpretation, see P. Schäfer, "Text, Auslegung und Kommentar im rabbinischen Judentum," in J. Assmann and B. Gladigow, eds., *Text und Kommentar* (Munich, 1995), pp. 163–86.

5. H. G. Kippenberg, *Die vorderasiatischen Erlösungsreligionen in ihrem Zusammenhang mit der antiken Stadtherrschaft* (Frankfurt am Main, 1991), pp. 157 ff., with references to the relevant literature.

6. On this question, see the contributions of B. Kienast, "Die altorientalischen Codices zwischen Mündlichkeit und Schriftlichkeit," in H. J. Gehrke, ed., *Rechtskodifizierung und soziale Normen im interkulturellen Vergleich* (Tübingen, 1994), pp. 13–26; J. Renger, "Noch einmal: Was war der 'Kodex' Hammurapi—ein erlassenes Gesetz oder ein Rechtsbuch," in Gehrke, *Rechtskodifizierung*, pp. 27–59. See also E. Cancik-Kirschbaum, "'König der Gerechtigkeit'—ein altorientalisches Paradigma zu Recht und Herrschaft," in G. Palmer et al., eds., *Torah-Nomos-Jus. Abendländischer Antinomismus und der Traum vom herrschaftsfreien Raum* (Berlin, 1999), pp. 52–68.

7. On the general significance of writing for legal culture, see J. Weitzel, "Schriftlichkeit und Recht," in H. Günther and O. Ludwig, eds., *Schrift und Schriftlichkeit—Writing and Its Use* (Berlin and New York, 1994), pp. 610–19.

8. On this point, see A. Leroi-Gourhan, *Le Geste et la parole*, vol. 2, *La Mémoire et les rythmes* (Paris, 1965).

9. A. Assmann, "Exkarnation: Über die Grenze zwischen Körper und Schrift,"

in A. M. Müller and J. Huber, eds., *Raum und Verfahren: Interventionen 2* (Basel, 1993), pp. 159–81; see also, J. Assmann, *Herrschaft und Heil: Politische Theologie in Altägypten, Israel und Europa* (Munich, 2000), pp. 178–84, n. 112; E. Otto, "Exkarnation ins Recht und Kanonbildung in der Hebräischen Bibel," in *Zeitschrift für Altorientalische und Biblische Rechtsgeschichte* 5 (1999): 99–110.

10. On the phenomenon of performative writing, see J. Assmann, "Inscriptional Violence and the Art of Cursing: A Study of Performative Writing," in *Stanford Literature Review* 9 (1992): 43–65.

11. For the theory of the "living nomos," see A. A. T. Ehrhardt, *Politische Metaphysik von Solon bis Augustin I* (Tübingen, 1959), pp. 168 ff.; E. R. Goodenough, "Die politische Philosophie des hellenistischen Königtums," in H. Kloft, ed., *Ideologie und Herrschaft in der Antike* (Darmstadt, 1979), pp. 27–89.

12. On this point, see K. J. Hülkeskamp, "Written Law in Archaic Greece," in *Proceedings of the Cambridge Philological Society* 38 (1992): 87–117.

13. See F. Crüsemann, *Die Tora: Theologie und Sozialgeschichte des alttestamentlichen Gesetzes* (Munich, 1992).

14. Ibid., pp. 232–322.

15. See note 9, above.

16. H. Lethen, *Verhaltenslehren der Kälte. Lebensversuche zwischen den Kriegen* (Frankfurt am Main, 1994), p. 7.

17. See my contribution in Gehrke, ed., *Rechtskodifizierung und soziale Normen.*

18. Joshua 1:8; Deuteronomy 6:66; Deuteronomy 6:7 (cf. 11:19); Deuteronomy 6:7.

19. H. G. Kippenberg regards this as a general principle of imperialist policy: "If colonizers wish to turn the territories they have conquered into an Empire, they must transform themselves into the protectors or even inventors of the traditions of the subject peoples." H. G. Kippenberg, "Die jüdischen Überlieferungen als patrioi nomoi," in R. Faber and R. Schlesier, eds., *Die Restauration der Götter: Antike Religion und Neo-Paganismus* (Würzburg, 1986), pp. 45–60, here, p. 51, with a reference to J. H. Grevemeyer, ed., *Traditionale Gesellschaften und europäischer Kolonialismus* (Frankfurt am Main, 1981), pp. 16–46; G. Leclerc, *Anthropologie und Kolonialismus* (Munich, 1973). See also P. Frei and K. Koch, *Reichsidee und Reichsorganization im Perserreich* (Fribourg, 1984); R. G. Kratz, *Translatio imperii: Untersuchungen zu den aramäischen Daniel-Erzählungen und ihrem theologie-geschichtlichen Umfeld*, in *Wissenschaftliche Monographien zum Alten und Neuen Testament* 63 (1991): 161 ff., 225 ff.

20. W. Spiegelberg, *Die sogenannte Demotische Chronik*, Demotische Studien 7 (Leipzig, 1914), pp. 30–32; E. Meyer, "Ägyptische Dokumente aus der Perserzeit," in SPAW [Sitzungsberichte der preussischen Akademie der Wissenschaften Berlin (Verlag der Königl. Akademie der Wissenschaften)] (1915): 304 ff.

21. A. B. Lloyd, "The Inscription of Udjahorresnet: A Collaborator's Testament," in *Journal of Egyptian Archaeology* 68 (1982): 166–80.

22. On this point, see "Der Spätzeittempel als Kanon," in J. Assmann, *Das kulturelle Gedächtnis: Schrift, Erinnerung und politische Identität in frühen Hochkulturen* (Munich, 1992), pp. 177–95.

23. Ezra 7:14. On Ezra's mission, see H. Donner, *Geschichte des Volkes Israel und seiner Nachbarn in Grundzügen,* vol. 2, *Grundrisse zum Alten Testament,* ATD Ergänzungsreihe 4/2 (Göttingen, 1986), pp. 416 ff.; F. Crüsemann, "Der Pentateuch als Tora," in *Evangelische Theologie* 49 (1989): 250–67; O. H. Steck, *Der Abschluss der Prophetie im Alten Testament: Ein Versuch zur Vorgeschichte des Kanons* (Neukirchen-Vluyn, 1991), pp. 13–21.

24. The Persian title of the Book of Ezra means "Scribe of the Law of the God of Heaven"; H. H. Schaeder, *Ezra der Schreiber* (Tübingen, 1930), saw Ezra as a Persian secretary of state and special commissioner concerned with Jewish affairs.

25. Y. H. Yerushalmi, "Reflexions sur l'oubli," in *Usages de l'oubli,* Colloques de Royaumont (Paris, 1988), pp. 7–21, here p. 15.

26. J. Blenkinsopp, *Prophecy and Canon: A Contribution to the Study of Jewish Origins* (Notre Dame, Ind., 1977); B. Lang, "Vom Propheten zum Schriftgelehrten: Charismatische Autorität im Frühjudentum," in H. von Stietencron, ed., *Theologen und Theologien in verschiedenen Kulturkreisen* (Düsseldorf, 1986), pp. 89–114; see also S. Z. Leiman, *The Canonization of Hebrew Scripture: The Talmudic and Mishnaic Evidence* (Hamden, Conn., 1976); O. H. Steck, *Der Abschluss der Prophetie im Alten Testament: Ein Versuch zur Vorgeschichte des Kanons* (Neukirchen-Vluyn, 1991). On the end of prophecy, see Flavius Josephus, *Contra Apionem* 1, § 8, *The Works of Flavius Josephus,* trans. W. Whiston, revised by the Rev. A. R. Shilleto (London, 1890), vol. 5, p. 181.

> The prophets who succeeded Moses wrote down what happened in their times in thirteen volumes. The remaining four volumes contain hymns to God and precepts for the conduct of human life. Our history has also been written in detail from Artaxerxes to our own times, but is not esteemed equally authoritative as the before-mentioned books, because there was not an exact succession of prophets. We revere as Scripture only what they bequeathed to us.

27. N. Lohfink, "Der Begriff des Gottesreichs vom Alten Testament her gesehen," in J. Schreiner, ed., *Unterwegs zur Kirche: Alttestamentliche Konzeptionen* (Freiburg, 1987), pp. 33–86; J. Assmann, *Herrschaft und Heil,* pp. 46 ff.

28. *Separate itself from the outside world:* not through territorial frontiers but through the *limiting symbolism* of their way of life and mode of conduct, and above all, by virtue of the laws that made contact difficult with nonmembers (keeping the Sabbath, the ban on exogamous marriage, the ban on shared eating, etc.). *Create an internal community:* through emphasis on membership, as can be seen from the numerous new self-descriptions, such as "the children of exile" (*bene*

haggolah), "the remains," "the men of the Covenant," "the assembly" (*qahal*), "the congregation" (*jahad*), *synagogé*, and so on. See E. P. Sanders, ed., *Jewish and Christian Self-Definition*, vol. 2 (Philadelphia, 1981).

29. B. Stock, "Textual Communities," in *The Implications of Literacy: Written Language and Models of Interpretation in the Eleventh and Twelfth Centuries* (Princeton, N.J., 1983), pp. 88–240.

30. On this point, see Sanders, ed., *Jewish and Christian Self-Definition*, vols. 1–3 (Philadelphia, 1980, 1981, and 1984).

31. Libraries (*pr mdȝt* "house of scrolls," specialized sacred libraries, *hierá bibliothéke*, according to Diodorus Siculus, 1.49.3) were attached to temples and contained the writings necessary for carrying out the relevant tasks. See G. Burkhard, "Bibliotheken im alten Ägypten," in *Bibliothek, Forschung und Praxis* 4, no. 2 (1980): 79–115.

32. B. Lang, ed., *Das tanzende Wort: Intellektuelle Rituale im Religionsvergleich* (Munich, 1984).

33. Clement of Alexandria, *The Miscellanies*, bk. 6, chap. 4, §§ 35.1-37, in *Writings*, vol. 2, trans. Rev. William Wilson (Edinburgh, 1869), pp. 323–24; see G. Fowden, *The Egyptian Hermes: A Historical Approach to the Later Pagan Mind* (Cambridge, 1986), pp. 58 ff.

34. Clement of Alexandria, in *Writings*, vol. 2, pp. 323–24.

35. The Greek title *prophetes* translates the Egyptian title *hm-ntr*, "servants of god" = high priests, and has no connection, therefore, with the Hebrew concept of a prophet. The highest-ranking priest carries the books that have the greatest authority, presumably because he is the only one authorized to interpret them.

36. On the book catalogues, see A. Grimm, "Altägyptische Tempelliteratur: Zur Gliederung und Funktion der Bücherkataloge von Edfu und et-Tod," in *Studien zur Altägyptischen Kultur*, suppl. 3 (1988): 168 ff.; D. B. Redford, *Pharaonic Kinglists, Annals, and Daybooks: A Contribution to the Egyptian Sense of History* (Mississauga, Ont., 1986), pp. 214 ff. From Tebtunis we have, for example, rituals, hymns to the gods, cosmographical and geographical books, astronomy, magic, wisdom books, dream books, medicine, books on temple administration, onomastics, and so on; see W. J. Tait, *Papyri from Tebtunis in Egyptian and Greek* (London, 1977); E. Reymond, *From the Contents of the Libraries of the Suchos Temples in the Fayyum 2: From Ancient Egyptian Hermetic Writings* (Vienna, 1977); Fowden, *The Egyptian Hermes*; J. Osing, "La Science sacerdotale," in D. Valbelle et al., eds., *Le Décret de Memphis*, Colloque de la Fondation Singer-Polignac (Paris, 1999), pp. 127–40.

37. On the organization of the books in the Hebrew Bible, see B. Lang, "The 'Writings': A Hellenistic Literary Canon in the Hebrew Bible," in A. van der Kooij and K. van der Toorn, eds., *Canonization and Decanonization* (Leiden, 1998), pp. 41–65.

38. On this point, see A. I. Baumgarten, *The Flourishing of Jewish Sects in the Maccabean Era: An Interpretation* (Leiden, 1997), esp. chap. 3, "Literacy and Its Implications," pp. 114–36.

39. H. Stegemann, *Die Essener, Qumran, Johannes der Täufer und Jesus* (Freiburg, 1994), p. 121.

40. See H. G. Kippenberg, "Die jüdischen Überlieferungen als *patrioi nomoi*," in Faber and Schlesier, *Restauration der Götter*, pp. 45–60, and also Baumgarten, *Flourishing of Jewish Sects*.

41. See C. Colpe, "Die Ausbildung des Heidenbegriffs von Israel zur Apologetik und das Zweideutigwerden des Christentums," in Faber and Schlesier, *Restauration der Götter*, pp. 61–87.

42. On this point, see O. Loretz, *Des Gottes Einzigkeit: Ein altorientalisches Argumentationsmodell zum "Schma Jisrael"* (Darmstadt, 1997).

43. On this point, see my book *Moses the Egyptian: The Memory of Egypt in Western Monotheism* (Cambridge, Mass., 1999).

44. See M. Halbertal and A. Margalit, *Idolatry*, trans. Naomi Goldblum (Cambridge, Mass., 1992), pp. 37–66.

45. M. Halbertal has elaborated this aspect of the canon as a comprehensive grounding of a life form and a collective identity in his book *People of the Book: Canon, Meaning, and Authority* (Cambridge, Mass., 1997).

46. M. Bakhtin, *The Dialogic Imagination*, trans. and ed. C. Emerson and M. Holquist (Austin, 1981), p. 84.

47. *Menahot* 29b, in *The Babylonian Talmud*, trans. E. Cashdan (London, 1948), p. 190.

CHAPTER 4: REMEMBERING IN ORDER TO BELONG

1. I base these remarks on a talk by W. Müller-Funk, "Remembering and Forgetting," that was broadcast on Austrian radio.

2. G. Kubler, *The Shape of Time: Remarks on the History of Things* (New Haven, Conn., 1962).

3. Tablet BM 5645 rto. 2–7, ed. A. H. Gardiner, *The Admonitions of an Egyptian Sage* (Leipzig, 1909), pp. 97–101; M. Lichtheim, *Ancient Egyptian Literature*, vol. 1, *The Old and Middle Kingdoms* (Berkeley, Calif., 1975), pp. 146 ff.; B. G. Ockinga, "The Burden of Kha^ckheperre^csonbu," in *Journal of Egyptian Archaeology* 69 (1983): 88–95.

4. S. H. Innis, *Empire and Communications* (Oxford, 1950).

5. H. Asselberghs, *Chaos en beheersing: Documenten uit aenolithisch Egypte* (Leiden, 1961); W. Davis, *Masking the Blow: The Scene of Representation in Late Prehistoric Art* (Berkeley, Calif., 1992).

6. On this point see J. Assmann, "Sepulkrale Selbstthematisierungen im Alten

Ägypten," in A. Hahn and V. Kapp, eds., *Selbstthematisierung und Selbstzeugnis: Bekenntnis und Geständnis* (Frankfurt am Main, 1987), pp. 208–32.

7. On this point, see J. Assmann, *Das kulturelle Gedächtnis: Schrift, Erinnerung und politische Identität in frühen Hochkulturen* (Munich, 1992), pp. 29–86.

8. See especially the second essay in *The Genealogy of Morality*, ed. K. Ansell-Pearson, trans. C. Diethe (Cambridge, 1994).

9. Ibid., p. 39.

10. See Part 1, in A. Assmann and U. Frevert, *Geschichtsvergessenheit, Geschichtsversessenheit: Vom Umgang mit deutschen Vergangenheiten nach 1945* (Stuttgart, 1999), pp. 19–147, esp. pp. 41–49.

11. *The Genealogy of Morality*, p. 41. On the relationship between pain and memory in the context of medical research on pain, see N. Birnbaumer and R. F. Schmidt, "Schmerz und erinnerte Empfindung," in *Akademie-Journal: Magazin der Union der deutschen Akademien der Wissenschaften* 1 (1999): 6–10. The authors preface their study with a different quotation from Nietzsche: "Memory is a suppurating wound."

12. H. Weinrich, *Lethe: Kunst und Kritik des Vergessens* (Munich, 1997), p. 167.

13. On this point, see the relevant Egyptian passages in my book *Herrschaft und Heil: Politische Theologie in Altägypten, Israel und Europa* (Munich, 2000), pp. 136 ff.

14. J. Assmann, *Maʾat: Gerechtigkeit und Unsterblichkeit im Alten Ägypten* (Munich, 1995), p. 110.

15. Circumcision is perhaps the last remnant of primitive initiation tortures, but it is carried out by expert doctors and in Egypt it seems for the most part to have lost its original meaning of an initiation. At least, the sources contain nothing to suggest that the procedure was accompanied by any special ceremonial. Circumcision has evidently ceased to have any connection with the use of cruelty to "make memories." Among the Egyptians making memories had long since assumed the civilized forms of school instruction.

16. A. Assmann, "Exkarnation: Über die Grenze zwischen Körper und Schrift," in A. M. Miller and J. Huber, eds., *Interventionen* (Basel, 1993), pp. 159–81.

17. See J. Assmann, *Maʾat*, pp. 122–59.

18. However, this memory is not accompanied by any history, any normative past. Time only assumes a linear shape and is only viewed retrospectively as far as the individual is concerned and his need to account for himself. This past never transcends the horizon of an individual life. Looked at on a larger scale, this culture lives within a completely different notion of time: instead of the linear time of accountability and responsibility, there was the cyclical time of rhythmic renewal.

19. M. Halbwachs, *La Topographie légendaire des évangiles en Terre Sainte* (Paris,

1941); on Halbwachs's theory of memory, see G. Namer, *Mémoire et société* (Paris, 1978). See also Introduction, note 1.

20. Erving Goffmann, *Frame-Analysis: An Essay on the Organization of Experience* (Harmondsworth, U.K., 1975).

21. T. Luckmann, *The Invisible Religion* (New York and London, 1967).

22. For Warburg's theory of memory, see R. Kany, *Mnemosyne als Programm: Geschichte, Erinnerung und die Andacht zum Unbedeutenden im Werk von Usener, Warburg und Benjamin* (Tübingen, 1987); C. Ginzburg, "Kunst und soziales Gedächtnis: Die Warburg-Tradition," in Ginzburg, *Spurensicherungen, Über verborgene Geschichte, Kunst und soziales Gedächtnis* (Berlin, 1983), pp. 115–72.

23. See J. Assmann, *Das kulturelle Gedächtnis*, pp. 48–66.

24. See, in particular, S. J. Schmidt, ed., *Gedächtnis: Probleme und Perspektiven der interdisziplinären Gedächtnisforschung* (Frankfurt am Main, 1991).

25. On this point, see A. Leroi-Gourhan, *Le Geste et la parole*, vol. 2, *La Mémoire et les rhythmes* (Paris, 1965), as well as A. Assmann, *Erinnerungsräume: Formen und Wandlungen des kulturellen Gedächtnisses* (Munich, 1999).

26. Freud, *Moses and Monotheism*, in *The Pelican Freud Library*, vol. 13, *The Origins of Religion*, ed. A. Dickson (Harmondsworth, U.K., 1985), p. 347; Y. H. Yerushalmi, *Freud's Moses: Terminable and Interminable* (New Haven, Conn., 1991), p. 30.

27. B. Goldstein, *Reinscribing Moses, Heine, Kafka, Freud, and Schoenberg in a European Wilderness* (Cambridge, Mass., 1992), p. 118.

28. Freud, *Moses and Monotheism*, p. 384.

29. See also Isaiah 8:1: "Take thee a great tablet, and write upon it with the pen of a man." And Isaiah promises, "Bind thou up the testimony, seal the law among my disciples. And I will wait for the LORD, that hideth his face from the house of Jacob" (Isa. 8:16).

CHAPTER 5: CULTURAL TEXTS SUSPENDED
BETWEEN WRITING AND SPEECH

1. On this point, see J. Assmann, "Der Eigen-Kommentar als Mittel literarischer Traditionsstiftung," in J. Assmann and B. Gladikow, eds., *Text und Kommentar* (Munich, 1995), pp. 355–73.

2. P. Hartmann, "Zum Begriff des sprachlichen Zeichens," in *Zeitschrift für Phonetik, Sprachwissenschaft und Kommunikationsforschung* 21 (1968): 205–22; the quotation is on p. 212.

3. K. Ehlich, "Text und sprachliches Handeln: Die Entstehung von Texten aud dem Bedürfnis nach Überlieferung," in A. Assmann, J. Assmann, and C. Hardmeier, eds., *Schrift und Gedächtnis* (Munich, 1983), pp. 24–43.

4. See A. Assmann, "Was sind kulturelle Texte?" in A. Poltermann, ed., *Literaturkanon—Medienereignis—Kultureller Text* (Berlin, 1995), pp. 232–44, which

shows that one and the same ensemble of linguistic signs can be constituted either as a "literary text" or a "cultural text," depending on the different frames in which it is retrieved.

5. The term *Knigge* is used in German to refer to an authoritative manual of etiquette and social conduct. It derives from Adolf Freiherr von Knigge (1752–96), whose book on this subject, *Über den Umgang mit Menschen*, appeared in 1788.— Trans.

6. Ehlich, "Text und sprachliches," pp. 24–43 and 30 ff., which cites the Jewish institution of messengers: *hassalah kassolah 'oto*, "the messenger is like the man who sends him."

7. B. Fabian, *Frankfurter Allgemeine Zeitung* (April 22, 1987), p. 33; see A. Assmann and J. Assmann, "Schrift, Tradition und Kultur," in W. Raible, ed., *Zwischen Festtag und Alltag: Zehn Beiträge zum Thema "Mündlichkeit und Schriftlichkeit"* (Tübingen, 1988), pp. 25–50, esp. p. 30.

8. P. Zumthor, *Introduction à la poésie orale* (Paris, 1983), pp. 245–61.

9. On this point, see A. Assmann, "Schriftliche Folklore: Zur Entstehung eines Überlieferungstyps," in Assmann, Assmann, and Hardmeier, *Schrift und Gedächtnis*, pp. 173–93.

10. P. Smith, "La Lance d'une jeune fille: Mythe et poésie au Rwanda," in J. Poullion and P. Maranda, eds., *Échanges et communications: Mélanges offerts à C. Lévi-Strauss* (The Hague and Paris, 1970), vol. 2, pp. 1381–1408.

11. See P. Borgeaud, "Pour une approche anthropologique de la mémoire religieuse," in *La Mémoire des religions* (Geneva, 1988), pp. 7–20.

12. K. Ehlich, "Text und sprachliches Handeln." See note 3, above, with the reference to D. Schmandt Besserat, "The Earliest Precursor of Writing," in *Scientific American*, no. 6 (1978), pp. 38–47.

13. On this point, see W. Schenkel, "Wozu man in Ägypten eine Schrift brauchte," in Assmann, Assmann, and Hardmeier, *Schrift und Gedächtnis*, pp. 45–63; A. Schlott, *Schrift und Schreiber im Alten Ägypten* (Munich, 1989), pp. 95–118.

14. In Egypt, the emphasis lies in the realm of political representation and immortalization. These two realms were kept apart so strictly that two distinct writing systems were used: hieroglyphics for representative, cursive script for archival purposes. See J. Assmann, *Stein und Zeit: Mensch und Gesellschaft im Alten Ägypten* (Munich, 1991), pp. 24–27; 79–81. In Mesopotamia, in contrast, the emphasis lies on the archival function.

15. L. Oppenheim, *Ancient Mesopotamia: Portrait of a Dead Civilization* (Chicago and London, 1964). W. W. Hallo distinguishes between three categories within the Mesopotamian tradition: *canonical, monumental,* and *archival*. See for example, "Sumerian Historiography," in H. Tadmor and M. Weinfeld, eds., *History, Historiography, and Interpretation* (Jerusalem and Leiden, 1986), pp. 10 ff. Oppenheim's *stream of tradition* would correspond to his *canonical* realm. However,

since we are using the term *canon* in its strict sense here, namely for texts not considered as such, but as parts of a coherent, sanctified corpus of tradition, we prefer concepts like *stream of tradition* or *great tradition* (in R. Redfield's sense).

16. On the relationship of written and oral traditions in Mesopotamia, see F. Stolz, "Tradition orale et tradition écrite dans les religions de la Mésopotamie antique," in Borgeaud, *La Mémoire des religions*, pp. 21–35.

17. J. Assmann, "Der literarische Text im alten Ägypten: Versuch einer Begriffsbestimmung," *Orientalistische Literaturzeitung* 69 (1974): 117–26. See A. Loprieno, *Topos und Mimesis: Zum Ausländer in der ägyptischen Literatur* (Wiesbaden, 1988); A. Loprieno, "The Sign of Literature in the Shipwrecked Sailor," in U. Verhoeven and E. Graefe, eds., *Religion und Philosophie im Alten Ägypten* (Leuven, 1991), pp. 209–18; "Defining Egyptian Literature: Ancient Texts and Modern Literary Theory," in A. Loprieno, ed., *Ancient Egyptian Literature: History and Forms* (Leiden, 1996), pp. 39–58; J. Assmann, "Kulturelle und literarische Texte," in ibid., pp. 59–82.

18. On the equivalence of the Egyptian term *sbōjet* and the Hebrew *musar*, see R. N. Whybray, *Wisdom in Proverbs* (London, 1965), p. 62.

19. The development into the more specialized and comparatively unburdened space of a written tradition only takes place much later. Here the texts seem to serve the purpose of pure pleasure, idle entertainment, and pleasure. I presume, without being able to discuss it further here, that this more specialized space goes along with, and indeed cannot be separated from, the emergence of a kind of classicism and hence a form of canonization.

20. For Israel, see R. N. Whybray, *The Intellectual Tradition in the Old Testament* (Berlin, 1974); F. W. Golka, "Die israelitische Weisheitsschule," *Vetus Testamentum* 33 (1983): 257–70; B. Lang, "Klugheit als Ethos und Weisheit als Beruf: Die Lebenslehre im Alten Testament," in A. Assmann, ed., *Weisheit* (Munich, 1991), pp. 177–92; G. Theissen, "Weisheit als Mittel sozialer Abrgrenzung und Öffnung: Beobachtung zur sozialen Funktion frühjüdischer und urchristlicher Weisheit," in Assmann, *Weisheit*, pp. 193–204. For Egypt, see H. Brunner, *Altägyptischer Erziehung* (Wiesbaden, 1957); "Die 'Weisen,' ihre 'Lehren' und 'Prophezeiungen' in altägyptischer Sicht," in *Zeitschrift für ägyptische Sprache und Altertumskunde* 93 (1966), pp. 29–35, reprinted in *Das Hörende Herz: Kleine Schriften zur Religions- und Geistesgeschichte Ägyptens, Orbis Biblicus et Orientalis* 80 (Fribourg, 1988): 59–65. On Mesopotamia, see A. Sjöberg, "The Old Babylonian Eduba," in *Assyriological Studies* 20 (1975): 159–79.

21. We might ask why variation should exist in the first place, and why human beings are not satisfied with repetition. As we have recently learned, there are neurological reasons for this. The organization of the brain ensures that everything that is constant and repetitive is always blanked out as background noise. In this way, what is novel and different can emerge as a signal and can be processed

in the form of information. This basic polarity of redundancy and information, repetition and deviation, takes place in the brain in processes that lie beneath the threshold of consciousness. Even so, we can trace its effects on the plane of consciousness through various levels of complexity right up to that of cultural processes. Meaning always constitutes itself like a relief in the shape of figures against a background of redundant noise. On this point, see S. J. Schmidt, ed., *Gedächtnis: Probleme und Perspektiven der interdisziplinären Gedächtnisforschung* (Frankfurt am Main, 1991), particularly the contributions of Schmidt himself, Roth, Singer, and Hejl.

22. See on this point, A. Assmann, "Die bessere Muse: Zur Ästhetik des Inneren bei Sir Philip Sidney," in W. Haug and B. Wachinger, eds., *Innovation und Originalität* (Tübingen, 1993), pp. 175–95. [See also, "The Complaints of Khakheperre-sonb," in M. Lichtheim, *Ancient Egyptian Literature*, vol. 1, *The Old and Middle Kingdoms* (Berkeley, Calif., 1975), p. 146.—Trans.]

23. Papyrus Chester Beatty, IV, verso 6, pp. 11 ff., trans. H. Brunner, *Die Weisheitsbücher der Ägypter* (Zurich, 1991), p. 230. [Translation here from M. Lichtheim, *Ancient Egyptian Literature*, vol. 2, *The New Kingdom* (Berkeley, Calif., 1976), p. 177.]

24. Ibid., III, pp. 5 ff. Brunner, *Die Weisheitsbücher der Ägypter* (Zurich, 1991), p. 225. See on this point, Brunner, "Die 'Weisen,' ihre 'Lehren' und 'Prophezeiungen,'" in J. Assmann, *Stein und Zeit*, pp. 173 ff., 306 ff. The fact that these "sages" are named points to a written tradition. We are concerned with authors, not bards. But their status as authors, although culturally established, is still semifictional in a twilight world halfway between pseudepigrapha and authorhood.

25. On this question, see J. Assmann, "Gibt es eine Klassik in der ägyptischen Literaturgeschichte? Ein Beitrag zur Geistesgeschichte der Ramessidenzeit," in *Der XXII. Deutsche Orientalistentag, Suppl. Zeitschrift der Deutschen Morgenländischen Gesellschaft* 6 (Wiesbaden, 1985), pp. 35–52; J. Assmann, *Stein und Zeit*, pp. 303–13.

26. For *The Dispute Between a Man and His Ba* [*ba* = soul—Trans.], see Papyrus Berlin, 3024; trans. Lichtheim, *Ancient Egyptian Literature*, vol. 1, pp. 163–69. On the interpretation of the text, see J. Assmann, *Ägypten: Eine Sinngeschichte* (Munich, 1996), pp. 199–210. For *Great Hymn to the Sun*, see E. Hornung, *Gesänge vom Nil* (Zurich, 1990), pp. 137 ff.

27. We may add that the reception of Khakheperre-sonb is not much better. But at least it is based on two extant texts that prove that it was part of the school tradition and hence belonged among the "classics." Both Ipuwer and Khakheperre-sonb are mentioned among the "classics" on inscriptions on a Ramessid tomb in Saqqara. See J. Assmann, *Stein und Zeit*, p. 307. Khakheperre-sonb is also listed among the eight classics in Papyrus Chester Beatty.

28. All these texts can be found in English translation in Lichtheim, *Ancient Egyptian Literature*, vol. 1, pp. 211–15, 215–22, and 149–63.

29. On the typology of the "canonic formula," see J. Assmann, "Fiktion als Differenz," in *Poetica* 21 (1989): 239–60, and esp. 242–45; J. Assmann, *Das kulturelle Gedächtnis: Schrift, Erinnerung und politische Identität in frühen Hochkulturen* (Munich, 1992), pp. 103 ff.

30. M. Fishbane, "Varia Deuteronomica," in *Zeitschrift für alttestamentliche Wissenschaft* 84 (1972): 349–52.

CHAPTER 6: TEXT AND RITUAL

1. Moses Mendelssohn, *Jerusalem*, in *Schriften über Religion und Aufklärung*, ed. M. Thom (Berlin, 1989), pp. 422 ff.

2. J. Assmann, *Das kulturelle Gedächtnis: Schrift, Erinnerung und Identität in frühen Hochkulturen* (Munich, 1992). See also my essay "Schrift und Kult," in M. Fassler and W. Halbach, eds., *Geschichte der Medien* (Munich, 1998), pp. 55–81. It has not been possible to avoid some textual overlap with this last article.

3. T. Sundermeier, "Religion, Religionen," in K. Müller and T. Sundermeier, eds., *Lexikon missionstheologischer Grundbegriffe* (Berlin, 1987), pp. 411–23.

4. See C. Colpe, "Sakralisierung von Texten und Filiation von Kanons," in A. Assmann and J. Assmann, eds., *Kanon und Zensur* (Munich, 1987), pp. 80–92.

5. On the concept of the "cultural text," see A. Poltermann, ed., *Literatur-kanon—Medienereignis—kultureller Text: Formen interkultureller Kommunikation und Übersetzung* (Berlin, 1995).

6. On this question, see Chapter 5, Section 3b.

7. Quoted from W. Warburton, *The Divine Legation of Moses Demonstrated on the Principles of a Religious Deist, from the Omission of the Doctrine of a Future State of Reward and Punishment in the Jewish Dispensation* (London, 1738–41), vol. 1, pp. 192–93. Warburton emphasizes the terminology of the mysteries through his use of italics and capitals.

8. A. Dihle, the article "Heilig" (Holy), in E. Dassmann et al., eds., *Reallexikon für Antike und Christentum: Sachwörterbuch zur Auseinandersetzung des Christentums mit der antiken Welt* (Stuttgart, 1988), vol. 14, pp. 1–63.

9. A. Dihle, "Buch und Kult," unpublished MS. I am very grateful to A. Dihle for allowing me to consult this text.

10. Mendelssohn, *Jerusalem*, p. 422.

11. On this point, see J. Assmann, "Ägyptische Geheimnisse: Arcanum und Mysterium in der ägyptischen Religion," in A. Assmann and J. Assmann, eds., *Schleier und Schwelle*, vol. 2, *Geheimnis und Offenbarung* (Munich, 1998), pp. 15–41.

12. M. Lichtheim, *Ancient Egyptian Literature*, vol. 1, *The Old and Middle Kingdoms* (Berkeley, Calif., 1975), p. 155.

13. Ibid., p. 156.

14. Das Todtenbuch, chapter 148 (Papyrus of Nu), LL, 19 ff.

15. M. Lichtheim, *Ancient Egyptian Literature*, vol. 3, *The Late Period* (Berkeley, Calif., 1980), p. 120.

16. After R. Givéon, *Les Bédouins Shosu des documents égyptiens* (Leiden, 1971), pp. 168 ff.

17. Ibid., pp. 170 ff.

18. Papyrus Salt, 825, V.10–VI.3, ed. P. Derchain, *Le Papyrus Salt 825: Rituel pour la conservation de la vie en Egypte* (Brussels, 1965), vol. 1, p. 139, 2,7*.

19. Papyrus Salt, 825, VII.1, VII.5.

20. Iamblichus, *De mysteriis*, VI.5.

21. S. Sauneron, in *Bulletin de la Société Française d'Egyptologie* 8 (1951): 11–21.

22. Iamblichus, *Über die Geheimlehren*, trans. Theodor Hopfner (Leipzig, 1922), 6.6.

23. Ibid., 7.4.

24. Ibid., pp. 121 ff.

25. Ibid., pp. 159 ff.

26. On this point, see the apposite observations of H. te Velde, "Some Remarks on the Mysterious Language of the Baboons," in J. H. Kamstra, ed., *Funerary Symbols and Religion* (Kampen, 1988), pp. 129–136, esp. pp. 134 ff.

27. Giordano Bruno, *De magia*, quoted from F. Yates, *Giordano Bruno and the Hermetic Tradition* (Chicago, 1964), p. 263.

28. B. Lang, ed., *Das tanzende Wort: Intellektuelle Rituale im Religionsvergleich* (Munich, 1984). See also Lang, *Heiliges Spiel: Eine Geschichte des christlichen Gottesdiensts* (Munich, 1998), pp. 161–71.

29. A. Lorenzer, *Das Konzil der Buchhalter: Die Zerstörung der Sinnlichkeit. Eine Religionskritik* (Frankfurt am Main, 1984).

30. On this question, see especially, M. Halbertal, *People of the Book: Canon, Meaning, and Authority* (Cambridge, Mass., 1997).

31. F. Kittler, "Die Heilige Schrift," in D. Kamper and C. Wulf, eds., *Das Heilige: Seine Spur in der Moderne* (Frankfurt am Main, 1997), pp. 154–62, quoted on p. 154.

32. Ibid., p. 159. Kittler believes that the procedure of *onomata asema* goes back as far as the Egyptian texts of the late Ramessid period (around 1150 B.C.), and refers in this context to F. Dornseiff, *Das Alphabet in Mystik und Magie* (Leipzig and Berlin, 1925), pp. 52 ff., which is itself based on E. Meyer, *Geschichte des alten Ägypten* (Berlin, 1887). But there seems to be a confusion here. Without wishing to dispute the occasional occurrence of barbaric-sounding proper names and expressions in syllabic scripts, I regard this as an entirely marginal phenomenon that has nothing in common with Iamblichus's theory of sacred language and its asemanticity. By its very nature hieroglyphic script is unable to reproduce asemantic sound patterns (which classical linguistic theory referred to as *voces inarticulatae*).

CHAPTER 7: 'OFFICIUM MEMORIAE': RITUAL AS THE
MEDIUM OF THOUGHT

1. Papyrus Jumilhac XVII.19–XVIII.11; these are no more than a few lines from a considerably longer account of the connection between rituals and both the cosmic and political orders. J. Vandier, *Le Papyrus Jumilhac* (Paris, 1960), pp. 129 ff.

2. E. Hornung, *Ägyptische Unterweltsbücher* (Zurich, 1984), p. 18. This A-B-A structure is common to all pictures of the sun. The sun god is normally placed in the center between worshippers who stand to the right and left of him. Here the image has been turned round horizontally by ninety degrees so as to expand it at will and to be able to absorb all the information that is important to know pertaining to the sun god's journey through the night.

3. This pessimistic world picture is based on the idea that the world as it is does not correspond to the pristine condition of "the first time," but has undergone a number of phases of dramatic deterioration which the Egyptians thought of not as a "fall" (*lapsus*), but as a "splitting" and "separation." The myth that is central to this idea ascribes this splitting to an uprising of human beings against the hegemony of the god of the sun and creation. This uprising put an end to the golden age of an undivided world. It was because of this that evil came into the world in the shape of death, conflict, lack, and disorder, and the world can only be sustained by keeping evil constantly in check. But sustaining the world is the chief task. This is what distinguishes this world picture from that of the religions that radically negate the world.

4. On this point see A. Schlott-Schwab, *Die Ausmaße Ägyptens nach altägyptischen Texten* (Wiesbaden, 1981). The Egyptians reckoned that the overall length of Egypt amounted to 106 *jtrw*. The calculation of the circumference of the earth by Eratosthenes was not only carried out in Egypt, but was also based on ancient Egyptian geodesics. It is well known that Eratosthenes determined the circumference of the earth by measuring shadows and arrived at the figure of fifty times the distance between Syene and Alexandria, namely 5,300 jtrw.

5. H. Beinlich, *Die "Osirisreliquien": Zum Motiv der Körperzergliederung in der altägyptischen Religion* (Wiesbaden, 1984), pp. 208 ff.

6. Herodotus, *The Histories*, trans. Aubrey de Sélincourt (Harmondsworth, U.K., 1971), bk. 2, p. 109.

7. Ibid., p. 112. On this question, see H. Beinlich, "Die Nilquellen nach Herodot," *Zeitschrift für ägyptische Sprache und Altertumskunde* 106 (1979): 11–14; and H. J. Thissen, " . . . αιγυπτιαζων τη οωνη . . . Zum Umgang mit der ägyptischen Sprache in der griechisch-römischen Antike," in *Zeitschrift für Papyrologie und Epigraphik* 97 (1993): 239–52, esp. 243 ff.

8. Strabo, *The Geography*, 17.1, 5, trans. H. C. Hamilton and W. Falconer (London, 1889), vol. 3, pp. 224 ff.

9. Asclepius, 24–26, ed. Nock and Festugière, Collection Budé (Paris, 1960),

pp. 326–29; the Coptic version: Nag Hammadi Codex, vi, 8.65.15–78.43, ed. M. Krause and P. Labib (Glückstadt, 1971), pp. 194–200. The Latin *inrationabilitas bonorum omnium* corresponds to "the absence of good words" in Coptic. The demise of linguistic understanding and the growth of violence belongs among the central motifs of Egyptian descriptions of chaos; see J. Assmann, "Königsdogma und Heilserwartung," in *Stein und Zeit: Mensch und Gesellschaft im Alten Ägypten* (Munich, 1991), pp. 259–87.

CHAPTER 8: A LIFE IN QUOTATION

1. K. Hübner, *Die Wahrheit des Mythos* (Munich, 1985); C. Jamme, *Einführung in die Philosophie des Mythos*, vol. 2, *Neuzeit und Gegenwart* (Darmstadt, 1991). In K. Hübner's book, *Gott hat an ein Gewand: Grenzen und Perspektiven philosophischer Mythos-Theorien der Gegenwart* (Frankfurt am Main, 1991), Thomas Mann's project of the "humanization of myth" is briefly mentioned on pp. 285 ff.

2. On p. 219, however, there is a reference in a footnote to Mann's essay "Freud and the Future." See "Freud and the Future," trans. H. T. Lowe-Porter, in *Essays of Three Decades* (London, 1947).

3. J. Burckhardt, *Weltgeschichtliche Betrachtungen*, ed. J. Oeri (Berlin and Stuttgart, 1905), p. 23.

4. I am indebted to my brother, M. Assmann, for telling me about this letter.

5. *Betrachtungen eines Unpolitischen*, in *Gesammelte Werke* (henceforth *GW*) (Frankfurt am Main, 1960–74), vol. 12, p. 145. See W. Lepenies, *Die drei Kulturen* (Reinbek, 1988; 1st ed., Munich, 1985), p. 358. In contrast, it is unlikely that Mann would have taken offense if a specialist in Old Testament studies had pointed out, without acknowledging Thomas Mann as the source of the idea, that when Benjamin met his brother Joseph again, he was no longer a boy but must have been forty-five years old. That is an example of a position that he adopted in a spirit of playfulness.

6. First published in *Imago* 22 (1936): 257–74. Freud wrote to Arnold Zweig on June 17, 1936, "Thomas Mann who gave his lecture on my work five or six times in different places was kind enough to repeat it for me personally on Sunday, the 14th of this month in my room here in Grinzing" (*Briefwechsel* [Frankfurt am Main, 1968], p. 141).

7. "Freud and the Future," p. 421.

8. *GW*, vol. 9, p. 493 ["Freud and the Future," p. 422].

9. I owe the interpretation of the descent into hell as a "Nekyia" as the equivalent of an invocation of the Muses to a conversation with A. Assmann. [The Nekyia is a reference to Odysseus's descent to the underworld in book 11 of *The Odyssey*.—Trans.]

10. On the distinction between track [*Spur*] and path [*Bahn*], see A. Assmann, "Schrift und Gedächtnis—Rivalität oder Allianz," in M. Fassler and W. Halbach,

eds., *Inszenierungen von Information: Motive elektronischer Ordnung* (Giessen, 1992), pp. 93–102, esp. pp. 93 ff.

11. "There is no beginning in the rolling sphere." Thomas Mann, *GW,* vol. 4, p. 190 [*Joseph and His Brothers,* trans. H. T. Lowe Porter (London, 1999), p. 125].

12. W. R. Berger, *Die mythologischen Motive in T. Manns Roman "Joseph und seine Brüder"* (Cologne and Vienna, 1971).

13. *GW,* vol. 9, p. 493 ["Freud and the Future," p. 422]. See "Primeval norm and primeval form of life, the timeless schema and the formula that has existed since time immemorial and into which life flows when it reproduces its traits from the unconscious" (*GW,* vol. 11, p. 656).

14. *Joseph and His Brothers,* p. 131.

15. " . . . the extent to which his life is but formula and repetition and his path marked out for him by those who trod it before him." *GW,* vol. 9, p. 494 ["Freud and the Future," p. 422]. "For we move in the footsteps of others, and all life is but the pouring of the present into the forms of the myth." *Joseph and His Brothers,* p. 551.

16. In *Die Einheit des Menschengeistes* [The Unity of the Human Spirit], Thomas Mann briefly sketches "the history of the Magna Mater and the Queen of Heaven." *GW,* vol. 11, pp. 751–56.

17. *GW,* vol. 11, p. 665.

18. It can only be made permanent in what Nicolaus Luhmann calls the "secured form of repetition" (quoted in A. Assmann, *Schrift und Gedächtnis,* pp. 93 ff.). It does not exist, or persist in written form, for writing is a medium of displacement and archiving; it is not a medium of mythic communication and circulation. On the contrary, myth must always be recalled into the realm of communication from that of writing.

19. *Joseph and His Brothers,* p. 303 [Assmann's italics].

20. M. Eliade, *Le Mythe de l'éternel retour* (Paris, 1949).

21. *Joseph and His Brothers,* p. 601.

22. Ibid., p. 389.

23. On this point, see K. Hamburger, *Thomas Manns biblisches Werk* (Frankfurt am Main, 1984), pp. 39 ff., and especially, this quotation: "You create timelessness for the senses of the people, and invoke the myth to unfold in the precise present."

24. *GW,* vol. 11, p. 656.

25. The fact that we are dealing here with Schopenhauer's "veil of Maya" and, in the case of the mythic images, with Nietzsche's "powerful delusions," the "healthy fictions" that men need in order to act at all, belongs to the external analytical perspective which is only hinted at in the novel.

26. In Thomas Mann's view, this polarity of the vertical time axis—the conjunction of myth and messianism, or memory and hope—is the specific feature

that characterizes the myth of the Israelites. Israel is the people which is vertically anchored in *both* directions, whereas Mesopotamia and Egypt live entirely in memory and the past. Thomas Mann borrows this idea from Merezhkovsky. Formulated in this way, it undoubtedly goes too far. The opposite of a religion of redemption is not a cult of the dead or a religion of memory and the past. Memory and hope always go together. The distinction is whether the hoped-for new order is a matter of preserving the world or changing it.

27. Weber claimed that he himself was quite unmusical as far as religion was concerned, that is to say, he had no talent for religion.—Trans.

28. Berger, *Die mythologischen Motive*, p. 58.

29. *Joseph and His Brothers*, p. 825.

30. Cited by H. Lehnert, "Thomas Manns Vorstudien zur Josephstetralogie," in *Jahrbuch der deutschen Schillergesellschaft* 7 (1963): 501.

31. *Joseph and His Brothers*, p. 469.

32. See J. Assmann, "Der zweidimensionale Mensch: Das Fest als Medium des kollektiven Gedächtnisses," in J. Assmann, ed., *Das Fest und das Heilige: Religiöse Kontrapunkte zur Alltagswelt* (Gütersloh, 1991), pp. 13–30.

33. *Joseph and His Brothers*, p. 888. See also "Not without roots was the occurrence—it happened, it recurred" (*GW*, vol. 5, p. 445); "It was a recurrent something that was taking place" (p. 594).

34. *Joseph and His Brothers*, p. 265: Joseph learns Akkadian.

35. These texts can be found in English translation in M. Lichtheim, *Ancient Egyptian Literature*, vol. 1, *The Old and Middle Kingdoms* (Berkeley, Calif., 1975). [The Literary Controversy can be found in *The Ancient Egyptians*, ed. Adolf Erman (New York, 1966), pp. 214–34.—Trans.]

36. Apart from the tale of "The Two Brothers," texts occasionally referred to include "the proverbs of *The Book of the Dead*" (what is meant is chapter 125), in *Joseph and His Brothers*, p. 864; the "Instruction of Ptahhotep," p. 866; "The Eloquent Peasant" [The Peasant's Complaints], *GW*, vol. 4, pp. 884 ff.; "The Guile of Isis," *Joseph and His Brothers*, pp. 888 ff. For a full account of this question, see E. Blumenthal, "Thomas Manns Joseph und die ägyptische Literatur," in E. Staehlin and B. Jäger, eds., *Ägypten-Bilder*, Orbis Biblicus et Orientalis 150 (Fribourg and Göttingen, 1997), pp. 313–32.

37. See, from a psychological point of view, D. Middleton and D. Edwards, eds., *Collective Remembering* (London, 1990), pp. 23–45. Shotter's essay in the same volume is a further important contribution to our understanding of the role of speech in the construction of a common memory (pp. 120–38).

38. *Joseph and His Brothers*, p. 72.

39. Ibid., p. 73.

40. I have not succeeded in discovering the source of Thomas Mann's phrase. I assume that it is either an ad hoc formulation or a private reminiscence.

41. "And thou shalt teach them diligently unto thy children, and shalt talk of them when thou sittest in thine house, and when thou walkest by the way, and when thou liest down, and when thou risest up" (Deut. 6:7; see 11:20). The Haggadah or Aggadah of Jewish tradition exemplifies this process of making something present through the act of narration. What is understood by the Haggadah is the exegetical or homiletic interpretation of biblical events and stories. The classical form of such a hermeneutic actualization of a narrative is the Pesach Haggadah, the liturgy of the Seder night. It creates the framework for that delightful conversation in which people entertain each other by retelling the story of the exodus from Egypt as if they had been present. The point of this conversation is to induct the children present into the "we" with which people reach an agreement about their common history: "We came forth from the land of Egypt."

42. S. Freud, *Moses and Monotheism,* in *The Pelican Freud Library,* vol. 13, *The Origins of Religion,* ed. A. Dickson (Harmondsworth, U.K., 1985), p. 381; see Y. H. Yerushalmi, *Freud's Moses: Terminable and Interminable* (New Haven, Conn., 1991), p. 33.

43. *Moses and Monotheism,* p. 345.

44. *GW,* vol. 10, p. 755 = *GW,* vol. 9, pp. 495 ff., where it is enlarged upon; see also *GW,* vol. 11, pp. 659 ff. Karl Kerényi cites *GW,* vol. 9, pp. 495 ff., in extenso in "Der mythologische Zug der griechischen Religion," in *Antike Religion* (Munich and Vienna, 1971), pp. 40 ff. He notes critically, "This mythical identification did not go as far as Thomas Mann suggests and as frequently really was the case in late antiquity. Even where this identification was at its strongest, it was more of an *imitatio per ludum,* a playful imitation. This precise description can be found in Juvenal, who used these words to rebuke the opposite practice in a secret women's cult (Satire VI, 324); *nil ibi per ludum simulabitur, omnia fient ad verum* [no make-believe here, no pretence, and each act is performed in earnest]. As in a game, myth could be cited in real life: this maintained the proper relationship of life to myth, among the Romans as well as the Greeks" (pp. 41 ff.).

45. Marcel Proust, *In Search of Lost Time,* vol. 1, *Swann's Way,* trans. C. K. Scott Moncrieff and Terence Kilmartin, revised by D. J. Enright (London, 1992), p. 94. See M. Fortes, "The Concept of the Person," in *Religion, Morality, and the Person: Essays on Tallensi Religion* (Cambridge, 1987), p. 252.

46. *Joseph and His Brothers,* p. 131. This is identical with *GW,* vol. 11, pp. 659 ff.

47. *Joseph and His Brothers,* p. 1139.

48. Ibid., p. 123. See also "the deeper the roots of our being go down into the layers that lie below and beyond the fleshly confines of our ego, yet at the same time feed and condition it—so that in our moments of less precision we may speak of them in the first person and as though they were part of our flesh-and-blood experience—the heavier is our life with thought, the weightier is the soul of our flesh" (ibid., p. 121).

49. Gergen, in S. J. Schmidt, ed., *Gedächtnis: Probleme und Perspektiven der interdisziplinären Gedächtnisforschung* (Frankfurt am Main, 1991), p. 45.

50. "Freud and the Future," p. 423.

51. *Joseph and His Brothers*, p. 551.

52. See: "He [Reuben] was not the man to be unique in misconstruing the significance of the question as to who one was, in whose footsteps one walked, to what past one's present had reference, in order to give it reality" (*Joseph and His Brothers*, p. 335). Reality is making the past present.

53. See Arthur Schopenhauer, "Transzendente Spekulation über die anscheinende Absichtlichkeit im Schicksale des Einzelnen," in *Parerga und Paralipomena* (Leipzig, 1895), vol. 1, pp. 229–55. For Mann's comments, see "Freud and the Future," pp. 415 ff. Life and destiny are explained here as the product and organization of psychic forces whose activities are largely or entirely removed from the sphere of conscious volition.

54. "Freud and the Future," p. 422.

55. *Joseph and His Brothers*, p. 389. Karl Marx was probably the first to discover that present action can be legitimated by quotations from the past. He regards it as the typical strategy of periods of revolutionary crisis that suffer from a corresponding absence of legitimation. "Precisely in such epochs of revolutionary crisis they timidly conjure up the spirits of the past to help them; they borrow their names, slogans and costumes so as to stage the new world-historical scene in this venerable disguise and borrowed language." Thus the French Revolution made use of "Roman costumes and Roman slogans" (Karl Marx, *The Eighteenth Brumaire of Louis Bonaparte*, in *Political Writings*, vol. 2, *Surveys from Exile* [Harmondsworth, U.K., 1973], pp. 146–47). Here Marx unmasks the French Revolution with the gaze of the critic of ideology. The gaze with which Thomas Mann observes early mankind is quite different. And yet, despite what seem to be utterly different approaches, the two meet in what Thomas Mann calls a "life in quotation," and they agree further that what is at stake is legitimation.

56. "Freud and the Future," p. 424; see *GW*, vol. 10, p. 755.

57. *Joseph and His Brothers*, p. 748.

58. Ibid., p. 854. On the history of the reception of the Ishtar episode in the Gilgamesh epic, see H. Petriconi, "Die gescholtene Astarte," in *Metamorphosen der Träume: Fünf Beispiele zu einer Literaturgeschichte als Themengeschichte* (Frankfurt am Main, 1971), pp. 53–98.

59. Ibid., p. 750.

60. Ibid., p. 389. The text is in the singular, but refers to both men.

61. Ibid., p. 853.

62. In "*Joseph and His Brothers*: A Lecture," Thomas Mann explicitly endorses this definition. "If I were to state what I personally understand by religiosity I would say that it is *attentiveness* and *obedience*" (*GW*, vol. 11, p. 667).

63. "For while in the life of the human race the mythical is an early and primi-

tive stage, in the life of the individual it is a late and mature one. What is gained is an insight into the higher truth depicted in the actual, a smiling knowledge of the eternal, the ever-being and authentic; a knowledge of the schema in which and according to which the supposed individual lives, unaware, in his naive belief in himself as unique in space and time, of the extent to which his life is but formula and repetition and his path marked out for him by those who trod it before him" ("Freud and the Future," p. 422, and reused in *GW*, vol. ii, p. 656). Karl Kerényi quotes this passage on the very first page of the introduction to his book on Greek mythology, and the English philologist W. C. K. Guthrie supports it further in a review in which he quotes the old Aristotle as saying that the preoccupation with myths became dearer to him the lonelier and the more secluded his life became.

64. "Freud and the Future," pp. 423 and 425.

65. Ibid., p. 425. "I am he," this "primordial dramatic expression in which an actor announces himself," plays the part of a leitmotif in the novel (*Joseph and His Brothers*, p. 875; p. 878; p. 863). "Isis am I, the Great Mother" (p. 776); *Joseph and His Brothers*, pp. 1108 ff.).

66. A. Assmann, *Erinnerungsräume: Formen und Wandlungen des kulturellen Gedächtnisses* (Munich, 1999); A. Haverkamp and R. Lachmann, eds., *Memoria: Vergessen und Erinnern* (Munich, 1993).

67. Thomas Mann seems not to have known of either man. As we have said, we are not concerned here with reconstructing influences, but with establishing a community of problems, such as the one he found himself in without his knowledge with Max Weber and Werner Sombart during his work on *Buddenbrooks*. The question of how such communities can be formed even though the participants are unknown to one another is easily answered. We are talking about a generation of scholars, researchers, thinkers, and writers all of whom have been influenced by Nietzsche and by the forms in which Nietzsche introduced these problems. Thomas Mann's own mapping of the frame of reference for the *Joseph* novels mentions other names, for instance, L. Woolley, *Ur und die Sintflut*; E. Daqué, *Urwelt, Sage und Menschheit*; A. S. Yahuda, *Die Sprache des Pentateuch*; O. Goldberg, *Die Wirklichkeit der Hebräer*; S. Freud, *Totem and Taboo*; M. Scheler, *Die Stellung des Menschen im Kosmos*; G. Benn, *Fazit der Perspektiven* (so given in L. Woolley's review); A. Jeremias, *Handbuch der altorientalischen Geisteskultur* (*GW*, vol. 10, pp. 751–56).

68. *Mnemosyne*—a picture series with which to explore preexisting values in the representation of life in movement in the age of the European Renaissance. See Fritz Saxl on the organization of the complete edition of Warburg's writings, in vol. 1 (Leipzig and Berlin, 1932). On Warburg as a theoretician of cultural memory, see R. Kany, *Mnemosyne als Programm: Geschichte, Erinnerung und die Andacht zum Unbedeutenden im Werk von Usener, Warburg und Benjamin* (Tübingen, 1987).

69. The relevant works of Maurice Halbwachs to have appeared in English

include *The Collective Memory*, trans. Francis J. Ditter, Jr., and Vida Yazdi Ditter (New York, 1980), and *On Collective Memory*, trans. and intro. by Lewis M. Coser (Chicago, 1992). The latter includes a partial translation of *La Topographie légendaire des évangiles en Saint Terre*. In this book Halbwachs goes a step further and includes cultural objectifications in his conception of collective memory.

70. See Joseph's conversation with Khamat in the boat that transports him as a prisoner to the feast of Zawi-Re. What matters is that "a human being entertains himself, he does not pass his life like the dumb brutes" (*Joseph and His Brothers*, p. 859), though we should note that what is meant by entertainment is Joseph's ability "to be in harmony with higher things" and "to mirror himself in the highest."

71. B. Strauss, *Paare, Passanten* (Munich, 1984), p. 26.

72. Recent anthroposophy asserts in all seriousness that the Egyptian kings existed on a different plane of consciousness from that of ordinary people; see F. Teichmann, *Die Kultur der Empindungsseele—Ägypten -Texte und Bilder: Ein Beitrag zur historischen Menschenkunde* (Stuttgart, 1990), p. 26.

73. E. Brunner-Traut, "Mythos im Alltag: Zum Loskalender im Alten Ägypten," in *Gelebte Mythen: Beiträge zum Altägyptischen Mythos* (Darmstadt, 1988), pp. 16–30. [Following the Egyptian astrologers, the Egyptian days were the last Monday in April, the second Monday in August, and the third Monday of December.—Trans.]

74. See C. Leitz, *Tagewählerei: Das Buch "ḥꜣt nḥḥ ph.wj dt" und verwandte Texte, Altägyptische Abhandlungen* 55 (Wiesbaden, 1994).

75. M. Fishbane, *Biblical Interpretation in Ancient Israel* (Oxford, 1985). As early as the first page of his monumental work, Fishbane adopts the expression "a life in quotation" and applies it to the Jewish world of a life within the horizon of a revealed scripture.

76. A. Assmann, "Das Gedächtnis der Moderne am Beispiel von T. S. Eliots 'The Waste Land,'" in H. G. Kippenberg and B. Luchesi, eds., *Religionswissenschaft und Kulturkritik* (Marburg, 1991), pp. 373–92; A. Assmann, *Zeit und Tradition: Kulturelle Strategien der Dauer* (Cologne, Weimar, and Vienna, 1999), pp. 150–56. See also Petriconi, *Metamorphosen der Träume*.

77. E. Goffmann, *The Presentation of Self in Everyday Life* (New York, 1959).

78. "For as a historian of religion I cannot allow myself to throw the Greek god into the same pot as the Egyptian one" (letter of April 1, 1934). Thomas Mann's view was: "Incidentally, in this last volume the mythologies, Jewish, Egyptian, and Greek go together so readily that one liberty more or less makes no difference" (letter of September 7, 1941, quoted according to *GW*, vol. 11, p. 664).

79. *GW*, vol. 11, p. 664.

80. *GW*, vol. 10, pp. 751–56, a review of A. Jeremias, *Handbuch der Altorientalischen Geisteskultur* (1913).

81. T. Mann, *Briefwechsel mit Autoren*, ed. H. Wysling (Frankfurt am Main, 1988), p. 231.

82. O. Goldberg, *Die Wirklichkeit der Hebräer: Einleitung in das System des Pentateuch* (Berlin, 1925). See, recently, M. Voigts, *Oskar Goldberg, der mythische Experimentalwissenschaftler: Ein verdrängtes Kapitel jüdischer Geschichte* (Berlin, 1992).

83. C. Colpe, "Die wissenschaftliche Beschäftigung mit 'dem Heiligen' und 'das Heilige' heute," in D. Kamper and C. Wulf, eds., *Das Heilige: Seine Spur in der Moderne* (Frankfurt am Main, 1987), pp. 33–61, and note 5 on p. 58.

84. A. Assmann, "Jaspers' Achsenzeit, oder Schwierigkeiten mit der Zentralperspektive in der Geschichte," in D. Harth, ed., *Karl Jaspers. Denken zwischen Wissenschaft, Politik und Philosophie* (Stuttgart, 1989), pp. 187–205. This makes use of the term of a "humanist credo," which also proves surprisingly accurate as a description of Thomas Mann.

85. E. Lévinas, *Humanisme de l'autre homme* (Paris, 1972).

CHAPTER 9: EGYPT IN WESTERN MEMORY

1. O. Paz, *Sor Juana Inés de la Cruz oder Die Fallstricke des Glaubens* (Frankfurt am Main, 1994; Spanish original, 1982), p. 23 [translation here from the German edition].

2. See Chapter 1, note 32.

3. J. W. von Goethe, *Werke* (Hamburger Ausgabe, 1952), ed. Erich Trunz, vol. 2, *West-östlicher Divan, Rendsch Nameh: Buch des Unmuts* (Munich, 1998), p. 49. [*Poems of the West and the East*, trans. J. Whaley (Bern and New York, 1998), p. 189.]

4. This speech was given on the occasion of the award of the History Prize to Jan Assmann on November 20, 1998.—Trans.

5. R. Herzog, *Staaten der Frühzeit: Ursprünge und Herrschaftsformen* (Munich, 1998). [Roman Herzog was president of the German Federal Republic from 1994 to 1999.—Trans.]

6. See D. P. Walker, *The Ancient Theology: Studies in Christian Platonism from the Fifteenth to the Eighteenth Century* (London, 1972), for the idea of *theologia* or *philosophia prisca* as a primeval universal knowledge that began with Hermes Trismegistus and Zoroaster and came to the West via Orpheus and Pythagoras. For a more recent study, see M. Stausberg, *Faszination Zarathustra, Zoroaster und die europäische Religionsgeschichte der frühen Neuzeit*, 2 vols. (Berlin, 1999).

7. The term *cosmotheism* was coined by Lamoignon de Malesherbes with reference to the ancient, and in particular the Stoic, worship of the cosmos or *mundus* as the supreme being. In his edition of the *Naturalis historia* of Pliny the Elder of 1782, he cited a characteristic sentence of this religion: "mundum, et hoc quodcumque nomine alio coelum appellare libuit, cujus circumflexu teguntur cuncta, numen esse credi par est" ["The world and this expanse—or whatever other name

men are pleased to call the sky that covers the universe with its vault—are proper-
ly held to be a deity"; Pliny the Elder, *Natural History*, trans. John F. Healy (Harmondsworth, U.K., 1991), p. 10]. He also suggested that Pliny "should be called a
cosmotheist rather than an atheist, i.e. someone who believes that the universe is
God." See E. J. Bauer, *Das Denken Spinozas und seine Interpretation durch Jacobi*
(Frankfurt am Main, 1989), pp. 234 ff.

8. See A. Grafton, *Cardano's Cosmos: The Worlds and Work of a Renaissance Astrologer* (Cambridge, Mass., 1999). Cardano, the inventor of the "cardan shaft"
that was named after him, was a mathematician, medical doctor, astrologer, philosopher, and encyclopedist.

9. On the study of hieroglyphics in modern times, see especially, L. Dieck-
mann, *Hieroglyphics: The History of Literary Symbol* (St. Louis, 1970); M. V. David,
Le Débat sur les écritures et l'hiéroglyphic aux XVIIe et XVIIIe siècle (Paris, 1965); E.
Iversen, *The Myth of Egypt and Its Hieroglyphs in European Tradition* (Copenhagen,
1961; reprint, Princeton, N.J., 1993).

10. I. Casaubon, *De rebus sacris et ecclesiasticis exercitationes XVI: Ad Cardina-
lis Baronii Prolegomena in Annales* (London, 1614), pp. 70 ff.; see F. Yates, *Giordano Bruno and the Hermetic Tradition* (Chicago, 1964), pp. 398–403; A. Grafton,
"Protestant Versus Prophet: Isaac Casaubon on Hermes Trismegistos," in *Journal
of the Warburg and Courtauld Institutes* 46 (1983): 78–93, reprinted in A. Grafton,
Defenders of the Text: The Tradition of Scholarship in an Age of Science, 1450–1800
(Cambridge, Mass., 1991), pp. 145–61.

11. On the history of the Christian Hebraists, especially in the seventeenth
century, see F. E. Manuel, *The Broken Staff: Judaism Through Christian Eyes* (Cambridge, Mass., 1992), and A. L. Katchen, *Christian Hebraists and Dutch Rabbis:
Seventeenth Century Apologetics and the Study of Maimonides' Mishneh Torah* (Cambridge, Mass., 1984).

12. In 1670 Spencer published his dissertation on *Urim* and *Thummim*, and
in 1685 his monumental magnum opus, *De Legibus Hebraeorum Ritualibus et
Earum Rationibus Libri Tres* (Cambridge, 1685), and frequently reprinted (e.g.,
The Hague, 1686; Leipzig, 1705; Cambridge, 1727; and Tübingen 1732). My quo-
tations come from the edition of 1686. On Spencer, see J. Assmann, *Moses der
Ägypter: Entzifferung einer Gedächtnisspur* (Munich, 1998), chap. 3, pp. 83 ff.

13. I base this account on the translation by S. Pines, *The Guide of the Perplexed*
(*Dalalat al-ha'irin*), by Moses Maimonides (Chicago, 1963). Maimonides wrote in
Arabic (in Hebrew script). The translation into Hebrew [*More Nevukhim*] by Ibn
Tibbon was completed in 1204.

14. There is no recent literature on the Sabeans (in Arabic, '*ummat Sa'aba*, in
Latin, *zabii*). The work that is still standard comes from the middle of the nineteenth century, D. Chwolsohn, *Die Ssabier und der Ssabismus*, 2 vols. (St. Peters-
burg, 1856). On the Sabeans or Zabii, see also T. Gale, *Philosophia generalis in duas*

partes determinata (London, 1676), pp. 139–40. Th. Hyde, *Historia religionis veterum Persarum, eorumque Magorum* (Oxford, 1760), pp. 122–38, turns the chronology back to front and treats Sabeanism as a degenerate form of Zoroasterism. Thomas Stanley devoted the last volume of his monumental *History of Philosophy*, 3 vols. (London, 1665–72; London, 1687 = New York and London, 1978), to the "History of the Chaldaick Philosophy," in which the Sabeans are discussed on pp. 1062–67. See Stausberg, *Faszination Zarathustra*, index, p. 1058, on Sabeans, Sabeanism.

15. *The True Intellectual System of the Universe: The First Part, wherein All the Reason and Philosophy of Atheism is Confuted and its Impossibility Demonstrated* (London, 1678; London, 1743). R. Cudworth had written this book as early as 1671, but postponed its publication until 1678, and even then only published the first part. The second part never appeared, and nor was it to be found among his unpublished manuscripts. (R. H. Popkin, "Polytheism, Deism and Newton," in J. E. Force and R. H. Popkin, *Essays on the Context, Nature, and Influence of Isaac Newton's Theology* [Dordrecht, 1990], p. 31). See also Stausberg, *Faszination Zarathustra*, pp. 426–32.

16. The inscription is mentioned by Plutarch, *De Iside*, cap. 9, 354c, and Proclus, *In Platonis Timaeum*, 1.30d-e. Marsilio Ficino, who discusses this passage in his *Timaeus* commentary (*Op. Omnia*, 2.1439), makes no mention of Sais, and links this *aureum epigramma* only with Minerva, not with Isis. But he already translates *chiton* or *peplus* with "velum," and interprets the passage as pointing to the unknowability of the divine.

17. In Proclus, the text has *chiton* (a fine linen undergarment) instead of *peplos* (cloak), *no one* (which includes the immortals) instead of *no mortal man*, and this sentence is followed by, "however, the fruit of my body is the sun."

18. On this topic, and as an introduction to the immensely complicated literature on the subject, see M. Neugebauer-Wölk, *Esoterische Bünde und bürgerliche Gesellschaft: Entwicklungslinien zur modernen Welt im Geheimbundwesen des 18. Jahrhunderts* (Wolfenbüttel and Göttingen, 1995); M. Neugebauer-Wölk, ed., *Aufklärung und Esoterik* (Tübingen, 1999).

19. W. Warburton, *The Divine Legation of Moses Demonstrated on the Principles of a Religious Deist, from the Omission of the Doctrine of a Future State of Reward and Punishment in the Jewish Dispensation* (London, 1738–41). See especially, "Moses the Egyptian," chap. 4.

20. Clement of Alexandria, *The Miscellanies*, bk. 5, chap. 11, p. 263; Warburton, *Divine Legation*, vol. 1, p. 191.

21. C. Riedweg, *Jüdisch-hellenistische Imitation eines orphischen hieros logos— Beobachtungen zu OF 245 und 247* (the so-called *Testament of Orpheus*) (Tübingen, 1993); see Orphicorum Fragmenta. 245 und 247, ed. O. Kern. They are to be found in their shortest form in Pseudo-Justinian, *Ad Graecos cohortatio*, 15.1,

and *De monarchia dei*, 2; and in a longer version, in Clement of Alexandria, *Protreptikos*, 74.4 ff. (this is the passage cited by Warburton), and *Miscellanies*, bk. 5, 78.4 ff., as well as Eusebius, *Praeparatio Evangelica* 13, 12.5, ed. K. Mras, vol. 2, pp. 191 ff. H. Erbse, *Fragmente griechischer Theosophien* (Hamburg, 1941), pp. 15 ff. and 180 ff. See also C. Riedweg, *Pseudo-Justinian, Ad Graecos de vera religione* (previously "Cohortatio ad Graecos"), introduction and commentary (*Schweizer Beiträge zur Altertumswissenschaft* 25, no. 1 (1994) (index "Orphicorum Fragmenta," p. 245). The hymn was first quoted by Aristobulos, a Jewish author of the second century B.C., in a version that diverged sharply from that of later sources. See also E. Bickerman, *The Jews in the Greek Age* (Cambridge, Mass., 1988), pp. 225–31.

22. On this book, see J. Assmann, *Moses the Egyptian: The Memory of Egypt in Western Monotheism* (Cambridge, Mass., 1997), chap. 5, as well as M. Meumann, "Zur Rezeption antiker Mysterien im Geheimbund der Illuminaten: Ignaz von Born, Karl Leonhard Reinhold und die Wiener Freimaurerloge 'Zur Wahren Eintracht,'" in M. Neugebauer-Wölk, ed., *Aufklärung und Esoterik* (Tübingen, 1999), pp. 288–304. There is much biographical information about Reinhold and the order of Illuminati to which Reinhold belonged in H.-J. Schings, *Die Brüder des Marquis Posa* (Tübingen, 1996).

23. F. Schiller, "Die Sendung Moses," in *Sämtliche Werke*, ed. H. G. Göpfert and G. Fricke, vol. 4, *Historische Schriften* (Munich, 1958), pp. 783–804. For the influence of Reinhold on Schiller, see Christine Harrauer, "'Ich bin, was da ist . . .': Die Göttin von Sais und ihre Deutung von Plutarch bis in die Goethzeit," in *Sphairos: Wiener Studien. Zeitschrift für Klassische Philologie und Patristik* 107–8 (1994–95): 337–55; W. D. Hartwich, *Die Sendung Moses: Von der Aufklärung bis Thomas Mann* (Munich, 1997), pp. 29–47; J. Assmann, "Das verschleierte Bild zu Sais: Schillers Ballade und ihre ägyptischen und griechischen Hintergründe," *Lectio Teubneriana* 8 (Leipzig, 1999).

24. See Voltaire, "Les Rites egyptiens," in *Essai sur les moeurs et l'esprit des nation, Oeuvres complètes* (Paris, 1819), vol. 13, p. 103: "Il se serait fondé sur l'ancienne inscription de la statue d'Isis, 'Je suis ce qui est'; et cette autre, 'Je suis tout ce qui a été et qui sera; nul mortel ne pourra lever mon voile' [It must have been based on the ancient inscription on the statue of Isis, 'I am that I am'; and that other one, 'I am all that ever has been and that will be; no mortal will be able to lift my veil']." Was Voltaire the originator of this strange duplication of the inscription of Sais?

25. See E. Graefe, "Beethoven und die ägyptische Weisheit," *Göttinger Miszellen* 2 (1972): 19–21. Graefe refers here to A. F. Schindler, *Biographie von Ludwig van Beethoven* (Münster, 1860), p. 161. The English edition of Schindler, *The Life of Beethoven*, translated and published in 1841 by I. Moscheles (London, 1966), vol. 2, p. 163, contains the following remarks on this point and on Beethoven's religious convictions in general: "If my observation entitles me to form an opinion on the subject, I should say he (i.e., Beethoven) inclined to Deism; in so far as that

term might be understood to imply natural religion. He had written with his own hand two inscriptions, said to be taken from a temple of Isis." Beethoven's text, which Schindler reproduces in facsimile, runs:

"I am what is"//
//"I am everything that was, that is and that will be; no mortal man has ever lifted my veil//
//He is unique and of himself, and all things owe their existence to this unique being//."

The sentences are separated from each other by double oblique strokes. The third may have been added later; the handwriting seems smaller and hastier. Beethoven was no Freemason, but had close friends among both Freemasons and Illuminati, including his teacher, Neefe. Solomon rightly points out that these sentences were familiar to most educated people at the time, and that they had even found their way into the masonic rituals.

26. On this point, see H. Kippenberg, *Die Entdeckung der Religionsgeschichte: Religionswissenschaft und Moderne* (Munich, 1997), pp. 45–79; M. Olender, *Les Langages du paradis* (Paris, 1988). [English trans.: *The Languages of Paradise: Race, Religion, and Philology in the Nineteenth Century*, trans. Arthur Goldhammer (Cambridge, Mass., and London, 1992).]

27. On the discovery of the Amarna-religion, see E. Hornung, "The Rediscovery of Akhenaten and His Place in Religion," *Journal of the American Research Center in Egypt* 29 (1992): 43–49, as well as E. Hornung, *Echnaton: Die Religion des Lichtes* (Zurich, 1995), pp. 9–27.

Cultural Memory | *in the Present*

Jacques Derrida and Elisabeth Roudinesco, *For What Tomorrow . . . : A Dialogue*

Elisabeth Weber, *Questioning Judaism: Interviews by Elisabeth Weber*

Jacques Derrida and Catherine Malabou, *Counterpath: Traveling with Jacques Derrida*

Martin Seel, *Aesthetics of Appearing*

Nanette Salomon, *Shifting Priorities: Gender and Genre in Seventeenth-Century Dutch Painting*

Jacob Taubes, *The Political Theology of Paul*

Jean-Luc Marion, *The Crossing of the Visible*

Eric Michaud, *The Cult of Art in Nazi Germany*

Anne Freadman, *The Machinery of Talk: Charles Peirce and the Sign Hypothesis*

Stanley Cavell, *Emerson's Transcendental Etudes*

Stuart McLean, *The Event and its Terrors: Ireland, Famine, Modernity*

Beate Rössler, ed., *Privacies: Philosophical Evaluations*

Bernard Faure, *Double Exposure: Cutting Across Buddhist and Western Discourses*

Alessia Ricciardi, *The Ends Of Mourning: Psychoanalysis, Literature, Film*

Alain Badiou, *Saint Paul: The Foundation of Universalism*

Gil Anidjar, *The Jew, the Arab: A History of the Enemy*

Jonathan Culler and Kevin Lamb, eds., *Just Being Difficult? Academic Writing in the Public Arena*

Jean-Luc Nancy, *A Finite Thinking*, edited by Simon Sparks

Theodor W. Adorno, *Can One Live after Auschwitz? A Philosophical Reader*, edited by Rolf Tiedemann

Patricia Pisters, *The Matrix of Visual Culture: Working with Deleuze in Film Theory*

Andreas Huyssen, *Present Pasts: Urban Palimpsests and the Politics of Memory*

Talal Asad, *Formations of the Secular: Christianity, Islam, Modernity*

Dorothea von Mücke, *The Rise of the Fantastic Tale*

Marc Redfield, *The Politics of Aesthetics: Nationalism, Gender, Romanticism*

Emmanuel Levinas, *On Escape*

Dan Zahavi, *Husserl's Phenomenology*

Rodolphe Gasché, *The Idea of Form: Rethinking Kant's Aesthetics*

Michael Naas, *Taking on the Tradition: Jacques Derrida and the Legacies of Deconstruction*

Herlinde Pauer-Studer, ed., *Constructions of Practical Reason: Interviews on Moral and Political Philosophy*

Jean-Luc Marion, *Being Given That: Toward a Phenomenology of Givenness*

Theodor W. Adorno and Max Horkheimer, *Dialectic of Enlightenment*

Ian Balfour, *The Rhetoric of Romantic Prophecy*

Martin Stokhof, *World and Life as One: Ethics and Ontology in Wittgenstein's Early Thought*

Gianni Vattimo, *Nietzsche: An Introduction*

Jacques Derrida, *Negotiations: Interventions and Interviews, 1971–1998*, edited by Elizabeth Rottenberg

Brett Levinson, *The Ends of Literature: The Latin American "Boom" in the Neoliberal Marketplace*

Timothy J. Reiss, *Against Autonomy: Cultural Instruments, Mutualities, and the Fictive Imagination*

Hent de Vries and Samuel Weber, editors, *Religion and Media*

Niklas Luhmann, *Theories of Distinction: Re-Describing the Descriptions of Modernity*, edited and Introduction by William Rasch

Johannes Fabian, *Anthropology with an Attitude: Critical Essays*

Michel Henry, *I am the Truth: Toward a Philosophy of Christianity*

Gil Anidjar, *"Our Place in Al-Andalus": Kabbalah, Philosophy, Literature in Arab-Jewish Letters*

Hélène Cixous and Jacques Derrida, *Veils*

F. R. Ankersmit, *Historical Representation*

F. R. Ankersmit, *Political Representation*

Elissa Marder, *Dead Time: Temporal Disorders in the Wake of Modernity (Baudelaire and Flaubert)*

Reinhart Koselleck, *The Practice of Conceptual History: Timing History, Spacing Concepts*

Niklas Luhmann, *The Reality of the Mass Media*

Hubert Damisch, *A Childhood Memory by Piero della Francesca*

Hubert Damisch, *A Theory of /Cloud/: Toward a History of Painting*

Jean-Luc Nancy, *The Speculative Remark: (One of Hegel's bon mots)*

Jean-François Lyotard, *Soundproof Room: Malraux's Anti-Aesthetics*

Jan Patočka, *Plato and Europe*

Hubert Damisch, *Skyline: The Narcissistic City*

Isabel Hoving, *In Praise of New Travelers: Reading Caribbean Migrant Women Writers*

Richard Rand, ed., *Futures: Of Jacques Derrida*